A Struggle Through The Twentieth Century

JIM HOLDING

To Irene

CONTENTS

FOREWORD

Those who read this book are in for a treat. They will find it entertaining and at times amusing to the point of being hilarious. In this aspect, it is reminiscent of "No Time for Sergeants" where the reading of certain passages evokes healthy laughing out loud.

From his humble beginnings before WWI in the Bible Belt of East Texas, Dr. Eugene V. (Jim) Holding has become a highly educated man. Happily, this erudition has not affected Jim's "down home" talent for storytelling. In a sense, of course, the book is autobiographical. However, it is not in the mold of most life stories; instead, it is a vivid account of Jim's everyday life experiences, at times uproariously funny, at times poignant, as seen through the eyes of a close observer and oft-times participant.

Jim's early years were lived in the throes of the Great Depression. He actually signed on with the old CCC, the Civilian Conservation Corps, one of the New Deal efforts to respond to the plight of the jobless, if not homeless, young men during the '30s. Then came WWII. Jim was of an age that called for military service. He saw action in France as a GI and suffered the bizarre tragedy of being run over by a tank on the front line.

The military doctors, after noting that Jim was lucky to be alive, gave it as their opinion that he would never walk again. He fooled them, he not only walks, but in recent years has even won ballroom dance contests. As a part of his self-prescribed convalescence regimen, Jim opted to consult a chiropractor. The results of this treatment were so encouraging and finally successful, that he decided to become a chiropractor himself. He has practiced his profession as such for 51 years.

His insatiable intellectual curiosity has led Jim into other studies. He has earned his Ph.D. in clinical psychology and after that, a law degree by attending evening classes.

Otherwise, Jim is an inveterate world traveler. There are few places in Europe, Asia, and Australia where he has not been. He will tell you that the most significant consequence of his world travels is reinforcement of his belief that the USA, for all of its shortcomings, is still the best place on the planet to live.

It is important for the reader to know something of Jim Holding's life as above recounted. With this insight, the reader will better understand and better appreciate the perspective from which Jim writes. His love of life and of the folks he writes about reflects, at times, the moods and the feelings of Mark Twain and Will Rogers.

"Why" presents a fascinating and delightful slice of what life was about before America became homogenized following WWII. We are indebted to Jim for preserving these bygone vignettes for the millions of our younger countrymen who are not old enough to have experienced them first hand.

F. DOUGLAS MCDANIEL

Associate Justice
California Court of Appeals

PROLOGUE

Why were people hugging each other? Why were they shooting guns into the air and slamming bridge planks against the frozen ground to make a loud noise? Why were all the dogs howling?

Why? Because the war was over on November 11, 1918. The armistice was signed by the U.S.A. and Germany.

I was only three years old, but I remember World War I well, hearing all the bad things about it day after day. Whatever we wanted but couldn't buy, my parents blamed on the war. We couldn't get flour, only one package of Aunt Jemima Pancake Mix a week. That meant we had to eat cornbread, which I did not like at all. We couldn't get pinto beans and had to put up with soy beans. The longer soy beans cook, the harder they get, and they sounded like dropping pebbles when Mama scooped them onto my plate.

I got fed up with the war and decided to strike back. We had a huge picture of Uncle Sam on the wall. He wore a top hat and pointed his finger straight at me. No matter how I moved—in front of him or to the side—he still pointed that finger. I couldn't read, but I memorized the caption the first time Mama read it to me. "Uncle Sam Wants You." Well, even if he wanted me, I didn't want him because I knew he had something to do with the bad war everybody talked about.

I decided I'd do my part to get rid of him. I had a pair of scissors I used to cut out pictures in magazines. I pulled a chair up under the big picture, raised my scissors and cut Uncle Sam to ribbons. And that's what my dad did to my rear end when he got home.

I sure didn't understand why I'd got a whipping for wanting to help with the war. Then all of a sudden "Why?" was the big question again. WHY? WHY?

I asked so many questions, my dad said he was going to change my name to WHY. They explained to me that my Uncle Jess would be coming home, but Floyd Cato wouldn't be coming home, he was killed in combat.

"WHY did they kill him?" I asked.

That's what war is all about....people kill each other.

A Struggle Through
The Twentieth Century

1

First Shoes

My folks had promised me that "when the war is over" I could get my own shoes, brand new, not handed down by my older brother, Wilburn.

However, after the war was over, something else happened to hold up the new shoes plan. It was the flu epidemic. The news I got was that the whole world was dying. The grownups talked about it all the time. More people died of the flu than were killed in the war. Pneumonia was also killing us off. The only remedy was to keep turning the patient from one side to the other to prevent fluid from settling in the lungs. Just to be safe, I practiced my own prevention, turning my body from side to side whenever I thought of it through the day.

This was long before antibiotics. The well people stayed busy sitting up at night to turn the sick people or walking behind the hearses, attending funerals of the dead. The same people who complained about the war now complained that they couldn't get a shovel into the frozen ground to bury the dead. With nobody to embalm the bodies, prompt burial was essential.

I constantly asked questions: "Why do you whisper and spell words when you are talking about me? or Why is the rooster chasing that hen?" Most often the answer was, "Why do you ask so many questions?"

Earl, an older neighbor, was the only one who'd give me an honest answer. I'd say, "Earl, what time is it?"

His reply was, "Dam'f I know."

I'd say, "Why do you smoke that stinkin' pipe?"

"Dam'f I know. Go ask your Ma."

It didn't take me too long to figure out that most of the time they didn't know the answers to my questions. They knew I couldn't spell. By the time I'd had some schooling, I discovered they couldn't spell either.

But my big question, after I'd been promised the shoes, was "Why can't I get those shoes now?"

They'd been promised for so long, and money was so short, I really didn't expect I'd ever get them. But the day finally came when my father went to town and shopped around for a bargain that would be the right size. He didn't take me and my feet along to try them on. Instead, he had me stand on a piece of cardboard and he drew an outline of my foot with a pencil. He folded the cardboard and put it in his overalls' pocket and went off to town.

The story of his shopping came home with him. He told it before he let me open the box. The salesperson brought out several boxes at one time, different styles and different sizes. Dad finally selected a pair of black high-button shoes.

When the lid came off the box, the new-shoe smell was as wonderful as the fact that each shoe was wrapped in its own piece of tissue paper. In the box also was a celluloid button hook.

I could hardly wait to try them on.

But Dad took one look and moaned. "Something's wrong here," he said, holding up the shoes. "We'll have to take them back. Both shoes are for the same foot." He touched the soles together. "Hell! They ain't even the same size."

I begged to try them on anyway. I wanted to see my feet in those new, good-smelling shoes.

"All right, try them on," said Mama. "But you can't keep them."

Both shoes were for the left foot, but they were big enough so that I could slip into them and I quickly buttoned them up, using the new hook. My older brother and sister admired them as I strutted around the room, but they joined with my parents insisting that I take them off so they could be exchanged.

I refused. As the family huddled in consultation, Mama said to Papa, "You won't get a chance to go to town again for quite a while. Why don't you just let him keep the shoes. He likes them so much."

My brother added, "If he scuffs the soles or stretches the leather, the store won't exchange them."

That was my clue. I bolted out the door and circled the yard, scuffing the shoes into the dirt as I ran. Then, remembering the button hook, I figured that if it was required to put the shoes on, it was probably needed to take them off. I sneaked back into the house, grabbed the button hook and threw it into the fireplace. The celluloid flashed and burned quickly.

I won that round. The family decided to let me keep my two left shoes and I slept in them that night.

2

A "Jim" By Any Other Name . . .

"Jim" is a nickname. I got it from Jim Ferguson who was the governor of Texas in the early part of the century. He was a liberal governor who was always trying to help someone out—help criminals out of prison, for instance.

The governor was the only one with authority to pardon a prisoner. Jim used that authority frequently. He had a special arrangement through an elite committee whereby a person up for parole could get a pardon for fifty dollars. To qualify, he had only to slip Jim a fifty-dollar bill. The money collected for these "pardons" went into a special fund. The fund was held in Jim's pocket.

Although Jim was the first and only governor of Texas who was ever impeached, he enjoyed an important position during his reign. After his impeachment, his wife took over as governor of Texas. Her name was Miriam A. Ferguson. She was known as MA Ferguson. When Jim joined the President of the United States, Woodrow Wilson (1913-1921), on a safari to Africa, they got a lot of publicity. Jim and the President had their pictures taken with the game they bagged and these photos were published in all the newspapers, tabloids, and magazines. There was our Texas governor smiling into the camera. His foot was on the head of an elephant or tiger and the butt of his rifle was on the animal's stomach.

These "great white hunters" inspired a couple of Texas boys. My brother Wilburn, who was about six years older than me, decided we should also go on a safari. So we pretended. Wilburn was Woodrow Wilson and I got to be Jim Ferguson.

We didn't have guns and there wasn't any game bigger than a coyote or wild pig in our corner of Texas. But we sharpened long sticks and pretended they were rifles. The big leaves from the oak and cotton-wood trees were our game. The largest were elephants, the smaller were jackals and tigers.

Wilburn taught me how to spell my name by using the barrel of his "rifle" to spell "Jim" in the sand whenever I was able to stab a particular large-leaf "elephant." We divided our "leaf animals" when we arrived home.

Our "safari" was so informal I didn't call my brother Mr. President, and he didn't call me "Governor." But he did call me "Jim," and the name stuck. My real name is Eugene Victor Holding. But ever since our adventure, I've been called "Jim."

The big difference between me and my nickname-sake is that I've never been impeached. But I've also been smart enough to stay out of politics.

3

New Baby Sister

Until I was four years old, I got all the attention whenever company came. In fact, I was the main attraction.

We had a friend, Lee Pinegar, who could actually throw his voice like a ventriloquist. He would go to the door and talk to his horse tied to a tree in the front. It sounded like the horse talked back to him.

I thought if he could make his horse talk, I could do it too. I called out. "You, Mr. Pinegar's horse. What you doin' eatin' our grass?" I changed my voice and said (from the horse), "Just chompin' a little while I wait for Lee."

Everybody laughed and told me how wonderful I was. "How do you do that?" they asked. They actually paid me for my entertainment. Each visitor gave me a penny.

I also did impressions. I was the "Rich Little" of our neck of the woods. I listened to several characters when they came to our house to visit or loaf, and got their voices and mannerisms down pat. When other neighbors came over, they always wanted me to sit on their knees and do my impressions. They paid me a penny for each impression.

This was during the recession after World War I. Everybody was broke and out of a job and at one time, I was making more money from my ventriloquist acts and impressions than some of the grownups. But the attention was worth more than the money to me.

That's why it was so disastrous when my sister was born. It put me out of a job. All the attention was centered on the new baby.

My parents told me "This is YOUR baby sister." I thought if she was MINE, I could do anything I wanted with her. I had some good ideas, too.

Everyone who visited went straight to the baby instead of asking me for impressions. They thought she was beautiful. I didn't think she was so hot. She had no hair. I had long, red, curly hair, down to my shoulders. She cried when she was left in the crib, and somebody always picked her up. Her diapers always had to be changed and nobody seemed to mind. They just made more fuss over her.

That gave me an idea. I started to wet my pants. It got my family's attention right away. It also got me a spanking. I tried to tell them I didn't wet my pants. My brother did it. They didn't believe me. Before my sister arrived, they had believed everything I told them.

Finally, my mother sat me down and explained that I wasn't the baby of the house any more. I was a Big Boy. They needed my help to take care of the baby.

All babies were born at home at that time, and you could take your time picking out a suitable name. My folks asked me to help pick out a name for her.

When the visitors liked my impressions, they called me "Precocious" and "Hyperactive." I was willing to share those names with my sister because they were too big a mouthful for me. But my folks named her Vestal Dean, after Doctor Dean, who delivered her. That suited me fine.

4

The Wheelchair Grandma

Immediately after World War I money was scarce, but neighbors and family looked after each other, especially the elderly and disabled.

One day when I was about five years old, I visited our neighbors, an old man Lamb and his wife, who lived with their son. She was partially paralyzed and in a wheelchair. When I arrived, she and her chair were out in the yard between the storm cellar and the wagon shed.

I'd never seen anything like this. Her tongue hung out the side of her mouth and she couldn't talk. Her husband sat next to her reading the newspaper to her.

"Allie," he said. "I see where Harding had another little spell of sickness."

Allie didn't seem to understand. He showed her a picture of President Harding in the paper. She nodded her head and stared straight ahead.

Being an inquisitive child, I approached her. All older women, I thought, were grandmas who held children in their laps. I tried to crawl up into hers, and she tried to help me onto her lap. She seemed to want to answer my question, "How did you get hurt?" But she couldn't speak.

At first her own grandchildren gathered around to see what was happening. I doubt that any of them ever sat in her lap, but they soon lost interest and ran away to play. I couldn't understand why they left without talking to their grandmother or giving her some attention.

I was concerned about her injury, one I knew nothing about. My parents always warned me about climbing trees or the dangers of riding a calf. They would say, "You will fall out of that tree and kill yourself." Or, "If you try to ride that yearling, he will throw you off and break your arm."

They gave these warning so often, I thought there were only two ways to be injured.

I asked Grandma Lamb, "Did you fall out of a tree and hurt your arm?"

For the first time, she smiled and shook her head no.

Then I asked, "Have you been riding a calf?"

Both Mr. and Mrs. Lamb laughed, but I didn't understand why.

Then Mr. Lamb said, "She had a stroke."

I had no idea what that was. Her arm was flaccid and I took hold of her elbow. Gently I held her wrist and moved her arm up and down, like you would a pump handle.

Grandpa Lamb smiled at her. "Does that feel better, Allie?"

She nodded her head yes, and smiled broadly.

I'd been sitting in one place long enough and asked if I could go play jump the well rope with the other kids.

Grandpa waved me away saying, "I bet you will be a doctor when you grow up." It was an accurate prediction.

5

It's an "Aeroplane"

In the summer of 1919, when the neighbors gathered to can peaches, they got the surprise of their lives.

"What's that noise?," someone said. "Must be a big truck."

"No, I think it's an airplane," one of the kids said. (It was spelled "aeroplane" then.)

My mother and the grown folks ran out of the house, all excited—they were looking up the sandy road to see what was causing that roaring noise.

"There it is, it's an airplane," Mother yelled.

I was scared. The noise got louder and louder. Everybody was yelling, "look up." I *was* looking up—up the road.

Then my mother sat me upon a big wooden gate and said, "Look up." She put the heel of her hand under my chin with one hand and grabbed a handful of hair with her other hand and shoved my chin up.

There it was—I saw my first airplane. I was startled and crying.

The plane was flying low enough so that we could see the pilot and another guy. They were wearing helmets.

Someone said it was a bi-plane.

"What's a bi-plane?," I asked. "I thought you said it's an airplane."

"It's a bi-plane airplane," said one of the men. He seemed to know what he was talking about. "Bi-plane means two wings."

"It's a military plane from Kelly Field in San Antonio, Texas," said another.

For the rest of the day, all the conversation was about the airplane. Two of the older people claimed they had seen one before—but for the rest of the bunch—it was a "first."

One man ventured to say, "One day we'll be traveling all over the country in airplanes, just like we travel in wagons and cars now."

"Naw," another man replied. "It will never happen. You'll never get me up in one of those things—too dangerous."

6

Proper Punishment

My parents had left me with our neighbors, the Wilsons, while they went to town on business. Mother gave these "baby-sitters" instructions on what to do with me if I got out of hand.

If they thought it was necessary, they could use the razor strap on my rear end, or they could make me sit in the corner and be quiet. Sitting quiet and motionless for ten minutes was about the worst punishment they could dish out for me. I would rather have the razor strap any day.

After about two hours, I became a little obstreperous. I began turning cartwheels in the living room and doing hand stands. Then it happened. I was sentenced to the chair for ten minutes.

Families in our part of the country then lived in the woods and houses were a mile or more apart. People were neighborly and looked out for each other. Nobody waited for a formal invitation. They just "dropped in."

As I looked up from my position in the corner, a neighbor, George, from the other side of the hill, stopped by to chat a spell with Bill Wilson, my sitter.

"Howdy, George. Y'all come in. Drag up a chair," Bill greeted his friend.

"How's all the family?," George asked.

"Okay, I reckon, except my wife. She still has that toothache."

"Why don't she have that tooth pulled?"

"Can't afford it. You know how much the dentist charges to pull a tooth now? Two dollars!"

"Why don't you go see my dentist? He charges only a dollar and six bits to pull a tooth."

"That's not for a wisdom tooth, though, is it?"

"Hell, I don't know. A tooth is a tooth as far as I know."

"She can't even afford a dollar and six bits now. The hens ain't laying, and when we do save up a little egg money, she has to have her coffee, you know. And I can't do without my snuff. She just puts a bag of hot salt on her jaw every night. How's your garden? Got any ripe tomatoes yet?"

"Naw! Damn worms cutting down all my plants. Onions are doing pretty good. Too much rain. I hope the boll weevils don't ruin the cotton again this year. Is that thunder?"

"Yeah. It's gonna rain again. I just hope we don't have another hail storm like we had last week. Beat down all the cotton and corn crops."

"I read in the paper that they had a twister in Honey Grove Tuesday night. That's what I'm afraid of. We don't have any storm cellar, either."

"Well, how about that one they had in Frost, up near Greenville, last week? It blew the roof off the country store, and whole bunch of houses were damaged. Two barns blowed over. All the chickens blown away, and it just picked up the outhouses and made toothpicks outa'em!"

"Well I'll be damned."

"I think I'm getting out of this part of the country. I don't like storms."

"Where would you go, George?"

"I'd go to California."

"California? With all the earthquakes out there?"

"Nah. No big earthquakes in California since 1906. That was in San Francisco."

"My uncle lived in San Francisco and my ma used to hear from him every month. After the big quake in San Francisco, she never heard from him again."

"I have a cousin who lives out there somewhere close to Los Angeles. We got a letter from him and his wife just the other day. They put some orange blossoms in the letter. They said they were sitting in the shade of an orange tree, writing the letter, and thought they would just send a little bouquet. They said it never rains in California, but when it does, there's no thunder or lightning. Just rains a little and stops. I would like that. They said it never gets very cold either."

"What's your cousin doing in California?"

"I think they're picking prunes, or something."

"You know out there in California, your kids would have to go to school with niggers?"

"So what! The Civil War has been over nigh on to sixty years now. We're gonna have to get used to living with niggers."

"Mark my word, one of these days the niggers are going to take over this country. You know, the Bible says . . ."

"Hold it. Hold it! You remember you said last week, and we agreed on it, we're not getting into an argument about the Bible anymore."

"Yeah, I know you don't know anything about the Bible. That's the reason you don't want to discuss it. If you do move to California, George, what are you going to do with your stuff here? And how are you to get out there? You can't drive that old Model T with four bald tires."

"Can't afford to drive my car anyways. Gasoline is up to thirteen cents a gallon now."

"I hear they have almost four million people in California already. You think you could find a place to live with that many people?"

"Oh well, I probably won't go anyway. I just get disgusted with the way things are going around here. That new president, Harding, is not doing anything to help either."

"It's not Harding. It's the damn Democrats up there not doing anything. That thunder is gettin' closer. Looks like hail in that cloud."

"Reckon I better get out of here."

"Y'all come back. Next time bring the little woman."

My sentence sitting still in the corner ended when George left. But it was my first information about that exciting place, California, with its earthquakes and niggers and orange trees. I eventually moved there to pick a few orange blossom bouquets for myself.

7

The Day Louie Lost an Arm

Louie Vincent and his brother Sam owned a new saw mill. It was a partnership. Several people in the area pooled their money and bought into it.

They cut down trees and sawed lumber for anybody who wanted to build a house or barn. The timber was mostly oak. They made boards for all occasions, including bridge planks.

Working around a sawmill is a very hazardous occupation. One hot summer afternoon, Louie got his arm caught in the buzz saw blade. In a split second the blade ripped his hand off, and mangled his forearm, elbow, and cut the muscles of his left arm all the way to his shoulder. The sawmill was located far from civilization. The nearest doctor was several miles away. His office was in his home but he made house calls and was rarely at home. The nearest hospital was seventeen miles away, in Paris, Texas. The only mode of transportation was a buckboard pulled by a team of mules. It would take about four hours to get to the hospital. Louie didn't think he could make it. He was bleeding profusely. They decided to take Louie to one of the neighbor's houses and get something to stop the bleeding.

A bunch of kids too small to work at the sawmill were at the house when the "wagon ambulance" arrived. The patient was a huge man, about six feet four inches and a very rugged individual. He was in a state of shock. The number one medicine then was whiskey. They used it for emergencies such as snake bites and anything that ailed the patient. Of course, whiskey was the worst thing they could give a patient bleeding to death.

This was in the time of prohibition, when you couldn't get store-bought whiskey. The only thing available was bootleg whiskey, also known as white lightning or rot-gut whiskey. It usually did more harm than good.

Louie took matters into his own hands, one hand now, and as usual he got what he wanted. His orders were, "Clear off the dining room table, it's going to be the operating table. Get me some soot from the fireplace to stop the bleeding. Give me a few shots of that whiskey to knock me out. Then get the hand saw and saw my arm off between my elbow and shoulder."

Everyone else then went into shock. They were coming up with all kinds of reasons why he should not be subjected to an ordeal like this. They could not sterilize the surgical tools, and he could get blood poisoning. No antibiotics were available in 1922. Before instruments could be sterilized, they would have to be boiled in water that had to be carried up the hill from the spring. To bring the water to a boil in the iron tea kettle, a fire must be built in the cook stove. That would take a long time. The only butcher knife was dull, and there wasn't much whiskey left.

"It's my arm, or what's left of it, and I know you guys can do it— and hurry! I'm bleeding," Louie said. Louie won! But who would be the "Chief Surgeon?"

"I've never even cut up a chicken," one of them said. "Charlie, I know how good you are butchering hogs, I think you should be the one to do the surgery." That was my dad they were referring to.

They got a clean white sheet and put it on the dining table. The family didn't own regular towels; they used salt sacks and flour sacks for towels, and there were no clean ones. All the towels and sheets on the table were soaked with blood. They ordered all the kids out of the house and raised some windows to let in fresh air. By now it was getting dark. They had fill up the lamp with kerosene and set the lamp in a chair beside the table to furnish light.

Louie showed them how to cut the skin on his arm and peel it back in four slices, like peeling a banana halfway down, then saw off the arm, take the pieces of skin—there would be four strips, and fold them over the stub of the arm—simple!

When they got the butcher knife, it was dirty. They just wiped it off on their pants leg and proceeded to cut. When the hand saw was presented to the "surgeon," it was a little rusty, but nothing could be done about it. When the sawing started, one of the guys fainted. Louie ordered them to give the man some whiskey.

When the surgical procedure was over, they had no gauze or bandage, but they did have turpentine. They poured the turpentine on the arm, and wrapped it in a bandage made out of an old shirt, put twine around it, then put a sock over the stub of the arm, tied it with a strand of bailing wire and put Louie on a cot out under a tree where it was cool. He finally passed out from losing so much blood, and he was still in shock.

The whiskey numbed his nervous system for a little while. They hovered over him all night. The next morning they wanted to take him to the doctor.

Louie said, "What for? He will just charge me twenty-five dollars for nothing. The arm is already gone."

"You don't have to pay him money, just take him a bushel of sweet potatoes and a watermelon," they told him.

Louie would have no part of that. He insisted he would be all right in a few days—and he was.

If the A.M.A. had found out about that surgical procedure, they would have had them all arrested and sent to prison for practicing medicine without a license.

Louie was back to work at the saw mill in about two weeks.

The Vincents were close friends of our family. When Louie came to visit us, he liked to lean back in his chair and put his feet on the wall. He was very heavy and always broke a chair. The chair would come tumbling down to the floor with Louie in it.

He used to drive a team of high-spirited mules. They got out of hand sometimes, but Louie wrapped the lines around the stub of his arm and got them under control. He said he had as much strength in that stub as he did in the other arm.

When he took out a bag of Bull Durham smoking tobacco to roll a cigarette, he would ask, "Will someone roll me a cigarette? I've got a sore finger on my left hand." Then he would lean back in his chair and laugh.

8

Two Cents Worth

One time when Louie Vincent was visiting at our house, John Boles came looking for him. John couldn't read or write, so he always searched out Louie to read his letters and answer them.

John apologized to us. He said he went to school only one day, got into a fight with the teacher, and never went back.

Louie couldn't read or write very well either.

The letter from John's sister was personal, about things that were happening at her farm. This was an important time for Louie, as well as for John, and Louie asked us all to be quiet while he read the letter to John.

"Dear brother John," it began, and went on to say she had been to town and bought a new dress and shoes. They had got the corn planted and the potatoes in just last week.

John hung on every word, sitting forward on the chair and leaning close to Louie. Except for the loudness of Louie's voice, the room was quiet. He sounded like he was addressing a crowd in a large auditorium. "Our sow had five little pigs yesterday," he continued, "and we have fifteen little children and they are all doing well."

"Wait, wait!" John said. Go back and read that last line again. Did she say they have fifteen little children, and they are doing well?"

Louie squinted his eyes and moved a little closer to the light and read the line again. "Oh . . . we have fifteen little *chickens* and they are all doing well."

When Louie finished, John asked if he would write a letter for him. "I always want to answer my sister's letters as soon as I get them," he said.

Louie agreed to write the letter for him. He borrowed a writing tablet and pencil from my sister.

John really poured his soul into that letter, dictating fast and loud.

"Slow down, John. I can't write shorthand. Now what did you want to tell her?"

John wanted Louie to tell his sister how bitchy "Old Lula" was. That was his wife. "She don't want me to go hunting or fishing any more."

Louie wrote down everything. Each time we thought he was finished, John would think of something else to say in the letter.

Finally, Louie asked, "Is that all now?"

"You might tell her to please excuse the bad spelling and handwriting," John said.

Louie bristled. "Why do you want to say that?"

"I thought that's the way all letters are supposed to end," John said and turned to my sister. "Do you have an envelope I can borrow?"

My sister found one for him.

"Do you happen to have a two-cent stamp I can borrow to get this mailed?" John asked.

"No, but you can leave two pennies in the mailbox and the mail carrier will stamp the letter for you," my sister suggested.

"I don't have two pennies," John said, "Could you loan me two cents till I sell something?"

I'd been listening all this time. I had two cents and felt proud to give the pennies to John. He went off through the woods to the nearest rural route box.

It was the last I saw of my two cents.

9

Integration

I was about five years old in 1921. It was peanut harvest time, and all the neighbors turned out to help as was the custom. There was no money exchanged. Each farmer helped the other, swapping labor for labor. The womenfolks' job was to cook for the crew.

On a September morning, about five or six people showed up with a peanut thresher and a separator. One of the crew was black. I had never seen a Negro or heard anyone talk about "colored people." WHY was his face black? I didn't understand. I did find out that he was a son of a slave family, and my grandfather had known him when he was a teenager.

When it was time to eat, we gathered at a makeshift table set up in the yard under a shade tree. Everybody gathered around the table except for the black man, Tom Shear. They had seated him at a separate table, which was a barrel turned upside-down. They served him the same kind of grub the rest of the crew was eating.

I asked WHY he couldn't eat at the table with us?

Tom laughed aloud. He thought it was funny. He was accustomed to this eating arrangement. It didn't bother him.

All through the meal I kept looking over at Tom. I was fascinated by his hair. Mine was red and long and straight. More than anything I wanted to comb Tom's hair. I asked him to let me. When he finished eating, I went into the house and got a comb, and crawled up on Tom's lap and tried to comb his hair. He laughed when I couldn't pull the comb through it.

I gave up on the hair combing, and went back in the house and brought back a book. I asked Tom to read me a story. He gave me that belly laugh, and said, "I can't read."

I asked, "WHY?"

He said, "The white folks wouldn't let the slave children go to school."

"WHY?"

"They might get smarter than the white folks if they went to school," he said. "They didn't want us to learn to read. We could get into trouble if they caught any slaves trying to read."

The next day, we went through the same routine. All the other four or five adults and about six kids crowded around the long table set up for the ranch hands. I really embarrassed the white folks this time. I hid the barrel behind the bushes, and asked my folks in the presence of everybody if Tom could eat with us today. That was a shocker. They didn't say "yes" and they didn't say "no."

In the meantime, I pulled up an orange crate at the corner of the table, next to me—and wanted Tom to eat with the white folks for the first time in his life.

He was thrilled—that was the beginning of integration in that community.

That night, I really caught hell. The old folks agreed that the black people shouldn't eat with the white people. That's just the way it was.

"WHY?" I asked.

"Well, we don't mind, but what will the other people think?"

"Who cares?" was my answer. "I will ask all of them tomorrow if they mind if Tom Shear eats at the same table with all of us." I did ask everybody at once when Tom was present. There were no objections. After all, we did have a lot in common. Tom couldn't read, and neither could I. I liked to give impressions and mimicked the farmers. Tom laughed at my impressions. I told Tom I was five years old, and asked how old he was. He thought he was born in the fall of the year, about cotton pickin' time, but he didn't know what year—maybe 1851 or 1852. He thought he was about 13 when the Civil War ended in 1865.

By the end of the week, the peanut threshing was over. It was a special occasion. My mother was a good cook, and she went all out to celebrate the end of the harvest. She served soul food, such as black-eyed peas, turnip greens, fried chicken, sweet potatoes, fried okra, and peach cobbler.

By then, they'd let me take over the seating arrangement at the makeshift table under a chinaberry tree. I traded the orange crate that Tom had been sitting on after he graduated from his barrel table, for a real chair.

I arranged to have Tom and myself seated at the "head table." This wasn't a black tie event, or a two hundred-dollar-a-plate fund raiser. Instead, all the field hands wore their dusty work clothes. It was made clear by me that if anybody didn't like the seating arrangement, they could leave the table, and go eat off the barrel. Nobody left.

For two people, that was the biggest event that had ever taken place in our lives.

Tom didn't return the next year. He had passed on. I'm sure he died happy, because of our meeting and the integration.

10

Wash Day Blues

Grandpa Coles, my mother's father, lived with us during the early 1920s. He told exciting stories about the Civil War. My older sister and brother ignored Grandpa's stories because they got tired of hearing the same ones over and over. I never tired of hearing them, and I think I was his favorite grandchild, because I liked to listen.

Everybody on our farm near Paris, Texas, had special chores. For us kids, it was doing the weekly laundry. For Grandpa, it was supervising wash day and he had authority to take whatever action was necessary to keep us kids working diligently through the daylong job.

Wash day was hard work. The laundry area was behind our house about a hundred yards down a steep hill beside the spring. Sister and Brother were older, and they got the "best job," that was washing. The wash bench, a lumber platform nailed between two trees, held the wash tub. We also had a three-legged wash pot, held off the ground by brick bats so that a fire could be build under it.

As the youngest, I was in charge of the wash pot. It was my job to scout through the surrounding woods for dead tree limbs, build the fire, and keep it going.

First, using homemade lye soap, Sister doused the clothes in the tub on the bench and she and Brother scrubbed them on the wash board. Then they carried the dripping clothes to the boiling wash pot that was under my care.

Grandpa was fond of telling us how lucky we were to have all the "modern conveniences" for doing the wash.

"Now when I was a kid, growing up in the sixties," he would say—

talking about the 1860s—"we didn't have all this modern stuff to wash our clothes. If we built a fire like you have here the Indians would see the smoke and come and scalp us. We did not have a wash pot or a wash tub or a rub board. We had to wash our clothes in the branch (branch of a stream) and use a rock for a wash board. We couldn't hang any white clothes out to dry on a tree limb. The Indians could spot anything white, like a covered wagon—from many miles away."

Grandpa always brought his newspaper down the hill and chose a "sitting stump" or log where he could keep an eye on us kids. He raised his own pipe tobacco and smoked it through the day as he supervised us from his stump and read the paper, every word, cover to cover. When he fired up that pipe, he was never bothered by black gnats or mosquitoes. They wouldn't come near him.

Besides feeding the fire, I had to keep the clothes submerged with a punching stick. Finally the punching stick was also used to lift the clothes from the hot water and carry them back to the wash bench for rinsing.

Boiling clothes and feeding the fire were boring. As I punched muslin sheets down into the water, I used to hope for a scalping Indian to sneak up on us, just to create a little excitement. Sometimes I was able to prevail upon Grandpa to tell me a story, but he didn't like to be bothered when he was reading.

One day, he was studying his newspaper—probably about that "mess" in Washington—and refused to tell me a story. "Later, boy," he kept saying as he held the paper at arms length and puffed on his pipe.

"Please, Grandpa, the one about how the Indian shot the Yankee that was aiming a musket at you."

"Not now I said, Jimmy."

Brave as he was as a Civil War soldier, I knew Grandpa Coles was not very brave when it came to spiders and snakes. Since he wouldn't tell me a story, I figured a way to get even. I had a rubber spider in my pocket. It had quivering, realistic legs. I fastened it to a long rubber band and the rubber to a thin hickory branch and sneaked up behind him. When the spider appeared before his eyes, dangling between the end of his pipe and his newspaper, he leaped from the log, dropped his pipe and the paper, and came after me. He was amazingly agile considering the arthritis he always complained about.

I outran him, but now I was out in the woods and afraid to go back. Not only had I disrupted Grandpa's reading and terrified him, I had also abandoned my duties at the boiling pot. I knew I was in for punishment of the severest kind—carrying water. A gallon bucket carried in each hand up the steep slope from the spring was considered one unit of punishment. For what I did, I knew I'd get at least ten units.

But I stayed away for the rest of the day, getting back barely in time for supper. Grandpa eyed me when he came in, but he didn't say anything about me or the rubber spider and I guessed he must have finished my chores because my sister and brother didn't say anything either.

Finally, after supper, he took my hand and led me to the front stoop. I was sure I was going to "get it" then, but he motioned for me to sit down on the top step. He settled beside me and took out his pipe.

I waited, my shoulders already aching from the units of water I'd be carrying up from the spring the next day. But Grandpa lit his pipe, took a couple of puffs and turned to me. "Now, Jimmy, which story did you want to hear?"

11

Chicken Peddlers

In the 1920s, ninety percent of the population lived in the rural areas and traveled in their wagons when they had to go to town. They lived off the land, and didn't need much from the city. They were independent. So, the merchants came to us to make their sales.

We were often visited by all kinds of drummers or salesmen—they sold garden seed, Cloverine Salve, Rosebud Salve, farm equipment, clothing and groceries.

The drummers' wagons were department stores on wheels. Cash was practically nonexistent. Barter was the method of exchange. A watermelon was swapped for a straw hat, a bushel and a peck of peanuts for a horse collar, and maybe two fryers for a forty-eight pound sack of flour.

Some drummers had chicken coops mounted on the side of their wagons for the collection of fowl. These were called "chicken peddlers."

The book salesmen were the most despised of all the peddlers. They were high-pressure pitchmen who wouldn't take "no" for an answer.

One day, an encyclopedia salesman came to sell a set of books to Owen Jackson, our neighbor who had four school kids.

Owen had no patience with book people, because he had very little formal education and didn't want his kids to be smarter than their parents.

When the encyclopedia salesman arrived at the house, he sent one of the kids out into the field after their dad. Owen left his plow and rushed home, to be met by the salesman, who said, "Mr. Jackson, you have four kids in school and what you need for them is a good encyclopedia."

"Like hell I do, them kids can walk to school like I did."

12

Grandma's House

We lived in a wooded area in the foothills. My paternal grandmother lived about three miles away, out on the prairie, on a sandy country road where there were houses on either side. It almost seemed like a different world to me, and I learned something new each time I visited. Grandma was left a widow with five small children. Her youngest son, Jess, who had just returned from the war, lived with her.

Grandma's house was set back about one hundred yards from the road. It had a rail fence and a big wooden gate at the road entrance. The latch for the gate was a loop of wire that went over the supporting post and I felt proud when I was tall enough to open it by myself. Sometimes my dad would get out of the wagon and open the gate and let me drive the team of mules through, then he would close the gate and get back into the wagon.

The area in front of the house and on the side next to the hay barn was a meadow. About twice a year, a horse-drawn mower cut the bermuda grass that grew there. A chinaberry tree and a persimmon tree stood in the front yard; in the back were a fig tree and rose bushes.

The house was built right after the Civil War. Grandma was about ten years old when the Civil War started and fifteen when it ended. She had witnessed the horrors of war firsthand. Her relatives fought on both sides of the Mason-Dixon Line—brothers and cousins fighting each other because they happened to have settled on opposite sides of this line.

One time a young soldier from the North stopped by and asked if he could borrow matches. Grandma said the soldier was young and small, but that they were afraid to refuse any request from the enemy. The soldier took the matches and tried to burn down their barn, as ordered by his superior officers. General Sherman had told them to "level" (that is, "burn") everything that would burn.

It had been raining and the barn was too wet to burn. Grandmother told how her mother (my great-grandmother) grabbed the young soldier, one hand snatching the hair of his head, the other the seat of his pants, and threw him face down into the hog wallow, a puddle of dirty water they called the "hog wash."

The other soldiers had a good laugh and apologized to the family. They said the young soldier was only carrying out his orders. They walked off together and did not return to burn anything.

Grandma's house was a "T-Frame" building. Only two kinds of houses were built then, the "T-frame" and the "L-frame." Grandma's house had a big back porch and a front porch that went the full length of the house. The posts that held the porch up had fancy "gingerbread" carvings at the top. The porch was also called a gallery then.

Every room in the house had its own aroma.

In one room was an ironing board where Grandma sprinkled the clothes with water, rolled them tightly and wrapped them until she was ready to iron. The irons were heated on the cook stove or in the fireplace during the winter. Grandma used paraffin or sometimes a branch of green cedar on her iron to make it slick. The hot iron on the cedar made a nice fragrance.

In the kitchen, Grandma baked "light" bread (yeast bread). No one had store-bought bread then.

Grandma often let me sit on the sideboard while she made cherry cobbler from the fruit of a half-dozen cherry trees on the property. It was always a race with the mockingbirds to see who got the cherries first. She showed me how to make pie crust using flour and Mrs. Tucker's shortening.

"When you roll out the dough, you first put flour on the rolling pin to keep it from sticking to the dough. You do not roll the dough from the edge toward the center, as it will roll up and stick to the rolling pin. Always start in the middle and roll toward the edge."

She never used a recipe or measuring spoons—instead, she used a pinch, a tad, a bit, a mite, or a smidgen. She said good cooks never measure their ingredients. From watching her, I learned to make cherry cobbler. I still use the same recipe.

Also, at the back and near the house was a peach orchard where they grew Indian peaches. These sold for a top price. But Grandma saved some for the family. She canned them whole, adding cloves and putting them in Mason fruit jars.

The fruit turned red in the glass jars. The spiced peaches also had their special smells that tickled my nose. She also had dried fruit simmering on the stove with nutmeg and cinnamon.

In the south room of the house, they kept the newly picked cotton from the "back forty" before hauling it to the gin.

In the living room was a big fireplace. It was also a bedroom, with a huge oval picture on the wall of my Uncle Roy, who died of spinal meningitis at the age of four, and Uncle Jess's picture in his army uniform with his wrap-around leggings. Uncle Jess also showed me his new 12-gauge pump gun. It would shoot six times without reloading. He also showed me his fiddle, and let me play it, but my arms were too short to pull the fiddle bow the full length.

They also raised sorghum cane for molasses. The field corn was stored in a slatted crib for the animals. The other barn had hay and stables for the mules.

The garden had cantaloupes and watermelons, sweet potatoes, peanuts, and sunflowers. The crows always got more than their share. They sold all the farm produce they did not use on the farm.

Every farm had chickens—white and brown Leghorns and Rhode

Island Reds. Grandma didn't raise ducks or geese, but her closest neighbor, my cousin, did. Geese talk to each other from one farm to another, and when they migrate north or south, they honk their messages to each other in flight. They and guinea hens are good "watchers." The guineas chatter when strangers come onto the property.

Turkeys were kept by some families, but they are dumb and hard to raise. They literally do not have sense enough to come in out of the rain. They will actually stand in the rain looking toward the sky, and if enough rain gets down their throats they will drown.

In Cuero, Texas, a little town not far from where we lived, they raised a lot of turkeys and drove them to market just like cattle. Thousands of turkeys would march down the main street with turkey herders on either side and behind to keep them moving.

The water supply for Grandma's house came from a dug well, different than a drilled well. The dug well was the closest thing to a refrigerator Grandma had. In the summertime, she kept the milk in a bucket which she let down into the well on a pulley. The bucket would be submerged to within about three inches of its upper edge. This is also how she cooled watermelons.

Grandma shared a lot of wisdom around her kitchen table when I visited. She always had answers for my questions.

"Why is your hand shaking, Grandma?," I asked.

Pushing aside her cup, she said, "Because I drink too much coffee. Don't you ever drink coffee when you grow up."

"I won't." I promised solemnly, knowing I didn't want my hands to shake like that.

"Why is your face so wrinkled, Grandma?"

"That's because I drink coffee. If you drink coffee, your hands will shake and your skin will wrinkle."

I don't know whether it was Grandma's admonition or if it's because I don't particularly like the stuff, but I don't drink coffee, and my hands don't shake and my skin is still smooth.

Remembering her stories about the Civil War, I asked Grandma if I'd have to go if there was another war.

"No, you won't have to go to war. The World War that just ended was the war to end all wars," she told me confidently.

"There's nothing worse than war," she said.

I remembered Grandma's words when I was trying to stay alive in Normandy.

13

By the Good Book

My dad stepped out to the sunny side of the house one cold, windy Sunday morning to shave. He always shaved outside because the light was better there. His razor strap and mirror hung on a nail. I used to watch this operation with great interest, rubbing my own five-year-old chin, trying to feel the whiskers I was assured would eventually grow there.

As Dad began soaping up, our neighbor, George McCoy, came by to chat. He had three dead squirrels by their tails and held them up to show us. As was the custom when visiting, George broke open the gun, pocketed the shells from his shotgun, and sat down on the woodpile.

My dad asked if George didn't think it was sacrilegious to be hunting on Sunday morning.

George said that, for him, it was okay, that it was all right to kill rabbits and squirrels on the Sabbath if you had to put the meat on the table to feed your family. He just happened to have his Bible with him. He opened it and began to read, chapters that to him defended his position. "You aren't gonna argue with the Holy Bible, are you?" he challenged my dad.

Dad said George was taking the verses out of context and went back into the house to get his own Bible. By then, one side of his face was shaved and the other half lathered. He left off shaving and both men thumbed from chapter to chapter through the Good Book, reading aloud, trying to outdo one another in their explanations of the meaning of what the Bible says.

The north wind had dried up the lather on Dad's face, and he went back to lathering and strapping his razor. Each time he raised the razor to his chin, George would find another quote that angered Dad.

Finally, after an hour or more of arguing, George had had enough. He reloaded his gun and marched off, dangling the squirrels in one hand, the Bible clasped under his arm.

After church that morning, as on most Sundays, all the righteous people showed up at our house with their Bibles to discuss religion and have arguments that nobody ever won. I was too young then to read, but I heard enough stories from the Bible to give me a good acquaintance with it. Most of the kids went off to play when these Bible discussions were going on, but I hung around and listened.

My Bible instruction wasn't confined to church and the living room. On one occasion, we were coming from town in the wagon and met another neighbor going to town. The red clay road was narrow and the ruts made by the wagon wheels were deep. There was barely enough room for the wagons to pass without forcing one into the ditch.

Both wagons pulled up and Dad and the friend exchanged salutations, then the subject switched to the new preacher in town.

Nobody knew his denomination, but he was a good speaker. There was only one church and all denominations used it.

One of the parties made reference to the "Campbell Light Preacher." My dad took offense. He said our church was called "Church of Christ." He further argued that the original founders were the Christians of Antioch—that just because Alexander Campbell founded the church, it didn't make them "Campbell Lights."

As the argument continued, I saw the sky darkening in the distance. The cloud had a white edge and that meant hail and wind. We were a long way from home, and our wagon bed was open to the skies. Sometimes we borrowed a "wagon sheet" and "bows." The sheet was a covering that we tied over bent pieces of wood—the bows—to make a shelter. On this trip, I was assigned to protect our groceries packed in a cardboard box beside me. Among these was a forty-eight-pound cloth sack of flour and a gallon of kerosene. My job was to keep the kerosene from getting too close to the flour, which would pick up the odor from the kerosene and make the biscuits taste like coal oil. As bad, if the flour got wet, it turned into paste and was unusable.

I could tell the mules heard the thunder. They were restless, pawing the earth, anxious to get home to be fed. I was hungry, too, but when Dad mentioned the coming storm to the other driver, he said he wasn't afraid of storms. The Lord would take care of him.

This only prolonged the argument about religion. Dad said the Lord would take care of us, too. They discussed the fact that the Bible said the rain falls on the just and the unjust, and if you have faith, no harm can come to you.

Personally, I was praying that a bolt of lightning would strike near enough to stop the argument. I never did find out why it was so important to these grownups to argue about religion.

But, besides giving me a pretty good acquaintance with "Matthew, Mark, Luke, and John," the discussions taught me that nobody ever changed his mind, no matter how many verses his opponent quoted. And rain or shine, wind or weather, talking religion was the best way in the world to get friends into an argument.

14

How's Your Ma?

My birthday, being in May, came during squirrel season, and mother always cooked fried squirrel for the occasion. She fixed other special foods, too.

Wild blackberries and dewberries were ripe then, and it was up to me to gather them in the woods near the house. If the woods were wet with rain, as they often were in May, the snakes would be out to find their share of berries. It was also the season for poison ivy, mosquitoes, and chiggers.

I was really happy to have arrived at my sixth birthday because that meant only one more year and I'd be able to go to school. On that special May morning, I got up early and took a bucket into the woods and picked it full of berries.

When my mother woke up, she was pleased and said she'd make a berry cobbler to go with the squirrel for my birthday treat.

However, checking the cupboard, she discovered she had no sugar. "And we don't have any money to buy sugar," she told me sadly. But she cheered up and added, "Why don't you go over to 'Grandma' Burton's house and borrow a cup of sugar—maybe two cups, for a big cobbler?"

"Oh, no. I don't want to go to that old lady's house. She drives me crazy," I said.

"She's a nice lady who lost all her family and she can't remember some things like she used to, but she likes you very much and always asks about you," my mother said.

"She does?" I didn't believe she remembered well enough to know who I was.

"Yes, indeed. Now you go over there and be nice to her. Get the sugar and hurry back, you hear?"

When I arrived at Mrs. Burton's house, I told her that it was my sixth birthday and I had picked a bucket of wild blackberries for a cobbler, but we had no sugar and my mother had asked me to borrow a couple of cups of sugar.

"Of course, that's what neighbors are for," she replied, grabbing me in a big bear hug.

I was embarrassed, feeling too old for that sort of stuff. I backed away.

Granny Burton said, "You will be starting school next year, won't you?"

"Yes, ma'am."

She went to a dresser drawer and took out two shoeboxes of pictures. "Sit there on the sofa," she directed me and began going through the pictures. "Now, this is my cousin. He lives in Milwaukee. He works on Lake Michigan, doing something. This is my husband's stepdaughter by his first wife, and this is Aubrey—looks just like him . . ."

She held it close to my eyes and I nodded, not knowing what else to do.

Then she continued. "Now this is my oldest brother's niece, and this is their baby. He's only three days old in this picture, and this is Aubrey again."

I saw Aubrey's picture three times, and never knew anything about him. We looked through the two cartons of pictures and she went back to get another box.

I said I'd better be going and rose to my feet.

"What's your hurry?" she asked. "Just sit down and I'll get you a glass of buttermilk. How many baby chickens do you have?"

"Thirty-five," I said, taking a guess.

"How's your Ma?" she asked again.

"Fine."

"I want to get you some big bermuda onions from my garden to take to your Ma." She looked at me as though seeing me for the first time. "You're pretty small for your age. Are you getting plenty to eat? If my son had lived, he would be seventy-two by now."

"What happened to him?" I asked.

"A team of mules ran away with him, dumped the wagon bed on top of him and dragged him about a half mile before they got tangled in a tree and stopped." She seemed to be judging whether I under-stood, then asked again, "How many baby chicks do you have now?"

"Forty-two." I knew she wouldn't remember what I told her the first time.

"I want to pick you some string beans to go with the onions." She started for the garden and then turned back. "Do you have any corn meal at home? I went to the grist mill yesterday and took a peck of corn. I've got plenty of meal. I'll give you some to take home." She nodded as though agreeing with herself. Then added, "I'll put an egg on top of the meal. Tell your Ma to put the egg in her corn bread. Makes it better."

I spent more than an hour with this lady and she still hadn't given me the sugar I came for. She'd asked at least three times how many little chickens we had, and "how's your Ma" about six times.

I was afraid to mention the sugar again. It might keep me there another hour.

"Thank you, Mrs. Burton." I was laden with Bermuda onions, green beans, and a paper sack of cornmeal.

"Why do you have to leave?" she asked.

"Ma told me to hurry back because it's my birthday."

"Oh, by the way, how is your Ma anyway?"

15

Caffeine Trip

My family—and all the neighbors—kept a half-gallon pot of coffee on the kitchen stove at all times. When company dropped in, a cup of coffee was always offered.

Watching people socialize and drink coffee was fascinating to me. I noted the different styles and customs. Some drank it without sugar or cream and sipped it from a spoon. Some held the cup wrapped in both hands and drank from the lip of the cup, often making a sucking sound. I always thought they resembled squirrels eating nuts. Some had a mustache cup to protect their mustache from the coffee. In one custom that required a steady hand, the drinker poured his coffee into a saucer and blew on it until it was cool enough to drink it from the saucer. These claimed that this method was proper etiquette in Russia and that they were carrying on the tradition.

Coffee served much more than social purposes. When my mother ran out of coffee, she always got a headache. She would tie a salt sack or wash cloth around her head to relieve the pain. As soon as the hens laid enough eggs that we could sell the surplus, Mother would send me to the store to get coffee beans. A dozen eggs sold for about eighteen cents, the same price as a pound of coffee.

I was convinced that coffee had to be good medicine.

However, my parents and my grandmother warned me not to drink it.

"Why?" I always asked.

Grandmother's reply was, "It will make your hands shake and your skin get wrinkled, just like mine."

Even though I was not allowed to drink it, one of my jobs was to grind the coffee beans in the hand-cranked mill clamped to the kitchen sink. (The beans were probably handpicked in Columbia by Juan Valdez's great grandfather.)

One evening after supper, when it was my turn to do the dishes, I decided it was about time for me to find out about coffee for myself. I waited until both my parents went out to milk the cows.

The big coffee pot sat on the back of the stove. It held the grounds left over from the last meal. I added three or four tablespoons of fresh-ground coffee and filled the pot about half full of fresh spring water. I knew it had to come to a boil, so I added three sticks of blackjack wood, the kind that made the hottest fire.

I kept looking out the window to make sure my folks weren't on the way in from the barn. The pot boiled fast and sent most of the water up in steam. I added more water, threw in another three spoonfuls of ground coffee and punched the fire.

Deciding it had to be right if I was to sample my brew before I was caught, I poured myself a cup. It tasted horrible, but I drank it down, blowing before each sip to cool it. The second cup was stronger than the first as the pot still boiled on the stove.

My folks always admonished me not to throw any food away. I figured that applied to drink also, and poured the last half cup, so thick it was almost like molasses. It was strong enough to float a pocket knife. I had to dig the last of it out with a spoon.

When mother and dad came in carrying their buckets of milk, I was at the sink singing and cleaning the coffee pot as I finished my wash-up chores. She didn't suspect anything.

By eight o'clock, everybody was in bed and asleep, except me. For the first time, I noticed that eight people could snore in different keys.

My heart pounded and when I pressed my head against my pillow, I could hear my jugular vein pulsating. I was scared, but I knew I wouldn't die. You had to be real old, like maybe sixty, to die, and I was only seven.

At the time, I didn't associate my wakefulness with the coffee I'd drunk. I lay there puzzled and heard the grandfather clock strike twelve. Then the old rooster, who always crowed at midnight, announced the hour. At the one o'clock chime, I still wasn't asleep.

It was a clear, cold night with a full moon. Sounds were crystal clear on such a night. Even though we lived six miles from the railroad track, the trains coming through sounded as if they were in our back yard. The lonesome whistle blasted at Arthur City, Powderly, and Hinkley.

I also heard the wild geese and went to the window to watch them fly in V-formation across the face of the bright moon. They honked and goose-gossiped to each other as they headed south. I counted every hour up until about 5:00 a.m.

The next thing I remember is seeing my mother and the rest of the family gathered around, shaking me. "Why didn't you get up and build a fire like you're supposed to?"

"Do you think he's dead?" my sister said.

My mother had two explanations for sickness. We were either constipated or "coming down with something." She made me stay in bed and gave me a double dose of the one medicine she used: Epsom Salts. It kicked in about midnight. We had no indoor plumbing or outdoor plumbing. Our only toilet facility was a low-lying limb of a big oak about fifty yards from the house.

The night before, lying awake, I wondered what it would be like to die. On the Epsom Salts night, I wished I had died.

Now when someone asks, "Do you want a cup of coffee?" I hear the clock chiming the hours and my heart starts to pound. Vivid in my memory is the train whistle and the geese honking, and I say, "No thanks."

Someone asks, "Why don't you drink coffee?" and I tell the story of my "caffeine trip."

16

School, At Last!

Seven was the age for beginning school when I was a child. There was no such thing as kindergarten. I'd been counting the days for at least a year. My first day was when school began right after Christmas. In farm country, the fall harvest had top priority, and the labor force of school-age children was needed in the fields.

My only brother was about six years older than I and had been in school a few years when I started. I pestered him steadily to tell me about school, and I was very proud of him. He'd told me about a bully, Doc Hensley, who regularly terrorized the rest of the kids—and the teacher. I don't know where he got the name "Doc," but that's what all the kids and teachers called him.

On my first day I arrived with my brother, Wilburn, about ten minutes until eight. The school bell would ring at eight o'clock sharp. Wilburn showed me around and told me that as soon as the bell rang, we would have to line up in front of the steps and march into the school house, one by one.

"Be sure to take your hat off as soon as you get inside that door, and be sure to say 'yes, ma'am' to the teacher when she asks you a question."

I was curious about another matter. "Where is that Doc Hensley guy, the one who's been beating up on you?"

"Don't start anything with him," Wilburn said. "He always tackles the new kids on their first day in school, so stay out of his way."

I had only one thing in mind. I wanted to avenge my brother, and I was confident I was tough enough to do it. "Where is he?" I demanded.

"There, in the blue shirt," Wilburn pointed to him.

Hensley was about thirteen or fourteen and looked as big as Jack Dempsey and as mean as Al Capone. His flat nose had been broken and apparently never set and his face was scarred.

I was half his size. As I started toward him, he came to meet me with a smirk on his face. He looked bigger and meaner with every step.

A Christmas tree, taken from inside the school house after the holidays, lay drying on the ground. I picked it up and threw it with all my strength. To my complete surprise—and I'm sure his—it knocked him down.

He crawled out from under the tree, pine needles clinging to his hair and his shirt, and hit me so hard I bounced off the school wall like a football.

Two girls grabbed and held me. Two or three others grabbed Hensley and held him off. A crowd gathered.

Someone asked, "Who is that skinny redheaded kid? He must be stupid to take on Hensley. Nobody does that, not even the teacher."

While the girls held us apart, I was saved by the bell—or maybe he was. We'll never know, but the bell ordered us to line up and we did, Hensley at the end, mumbling as he pulled the pine needles off his clothes.

Some of the girls told the teacher what happened. I think she was delighted. A few days before, Hensley had locked her out of the schoolhouse. She was a small girl, about twenty, and was required to teach all the grades from first to eighth, an enrollment of about eighty. There should have been at least two teachers for that many but the school budget wouldn't allow it.

After I crowned Hensley with the tree, he never bothered me again. He didn't beat up on my brother, either, and he didn't lock the teacher out of the schoolhouse.

The teacher didn't say so, but I knew she was glad to have me as one of her pupils. Of course, I always said, "yes, ma'am" to her.

After my introduction to school, it wasn't as wonderful as I thought it would be. I received my first primer. Its title was *Playmates, A Primer.*

The words on each page were:

"This is Will. How do you do, Will?"

"This is Tom. How do you do, Tom?"

"This is Nell. How do you do, Nell?"

My reaction to these stories was: Who cares?

The second book was *Simple Simon.* It wasn't very exciting either. "Simple Simon met a pieman going to the fair . . ."

Frankly, I didn't care who Simon met or where. I wanted to get out of my seat and have a little fun. I couldn't wait for recess. That's when the boys teased the girls and pulled their pigtails or shot dice on the playground.

The teacher had a favorite punishment for wrongdoing, especially chewing gum in class. She drew a chalk circle on the blackboard at the front of the room and led the one to be punished to it. The miscreant was required to lift up on his toes and keep his nose pressed to the blackboard in the middle of the circle for five to ten minutes, depending on the offense. Sometimes four or five kids at a time would be lined up at the blackboard.

When one reached over and "goosed" his neighbor and they giggled, another five minutes was added to the original sentence.

For a period of time, I had the longest neck and the flattest nose in school.

17

Spelling Bee

When I was in the third grade, the teacher, Mr. Wilhelm, trained his students as though they were a battalion of soldiers. His military training had made him strict but fair. We certainly learned in his class.

He didn't know it but, behind his back, we called him "Old Baldy."

One of the students was General Boles. "General" was not a military rank, it was the boy's name. He was a slow learner and didn't like school at all. His father, John Boles, couldn't read or write, but didn't want his son to grow up without an education. John Boles made his son go to school every day, even in the pouring rain. He promised General if he would attend school he would buy him a new saddle.

General said, "Pa, why are you buying me a saddle? We ain't got no horse."

"Well, maybe you will get a horse next year, if the boll weevils don't eat all the cotton."

General's sister, Jenny, was about two years younger, but they stuck together in times of crisis.

General couldn't pronounce certain words clearly. At one of our reading sessions, it was his turn to read aloud. The page he read from was about a pony. The line read: "My little gray pony lost his shoe."

General couldn't sound the letter "g." It sounded like "d" instead. He read: "My little *dray* pony lost his shoe."

After making him read the same line over two or three times, Mr. Wilhelm lost his patience. He got down on his knees, peered into General's face, pronounced the word *gray* clearly and made General sound his "g's"

General did it. He said, "G-Gray."

Wilhelm got off his knees, went back to his desk and said, "Read it again."

General read: "My little *dray* pony."

Wilhelm jumped to his feet, grabbed one of his biggest switches, pulled General out of his seat, and began to whip him!

Jenny rose from her seat, tears in her eyes, and tried to come to General's rescue.

Wilhelm ordered, "Get back to your seat."

He continued to beat on General.

I think "Old Baldy" was sadistic. All the parents thought he was just a strict disciplinarian, and they approved of everything he did.

One time we were all lined up against the wall for a spelling bee. When Wilhelm gave one of the students a word to spell, the proper procedure was to first pronounce the word, spell, it, then pronounce it again. Example:

Teacher: "horse"

Student: "horse — H-O-R-S-E, horse

Teacher: "farm"

Student: "farm — F-A-R-M, farm."

Teacher: "frog"

General: "frog — S-N-A-R-P, frog."

All the children laughed. Old Baldy "blew his top." He reached into the corner for his stick, yanked General out of line, and gave him his "medicine."

General wasn't trying to be funny. He was just a lousy speller and was scared to death of Mr. Wilhelm.

18

Cotton "Hoedown"

The Civil War had ended about sixty years before I became acquainted with black people. We called them "Negroes." Even though the slaves were free, they were worse off than when they lived on plantations where the masters gave them food and shelter.

Unlike white folks who were always worrying about money and how to get ahead in life, the Negroes were supposed to be always carefree and happy. It was supposed to be a tradition handed down from many generations. They had fewer ulcers and suicides. If a Negro had a dime in his pocket, he was happy. If he didn't, he was happy anyway.

As soon as kids were ten years old, they began working the cotton fields. Just before my tenth birthday, I was on the cotton-picking crew where blacks and whites worked side by side. Hoeing weeds and thinning cotton plants was called "chopping" cotton. It was hard work. A day's work on the farm was sunup until sundown. In the summer months that was thirteen hours.

I was the "water jack" and I worked every bit as hard as the field hands, carrying my one-gallon syrup bucket back and forth, bringing water to the workers. Everybody drank from the same bucket, passing it from one to another, along the rows.

The bucket emptied before everybody got his sip, and I would rush back to the spring to get another load.

When one of the hands got behind, he would just lift his hoe and hurry to catch up with the others. This practice meant weeds were left in some rows. When the sun got low and their energy waned, all the blacks started to sing. One would begin, solo, then another and another joined in, all *a cappella*. And they didn't sing "rap." They harmonized and made up songs as they went along. They also sang songs from the slave days. Some of these such as "Old Black Joe," "Nellie Gray," and "Old Man River" are still sung today.

As they got the rhythm going, rather than clapping or stomping they hit the ground with their hoes, keeping time. It was similar to dancing without a band. They were able to chop cotton longer when they accompanied themselves with their singing and hoe beats.

As darkness came, lightning bugs flew through the air flashing their "on" and "off" signals. The time to stop and go home was when the first whippoorwill called. At that signal, all hoes stopped chopping. The workers shouldered the hoes and walked off.

"Another day, another dollar," they said.

Not everyone got a dollar though. The teenagers got six bits a day and the younger ones got four bits.

Me, the "water jack"? I got nothing. My family owned the field and I was expected to work without pay.

19

Valentine's Day

The one-room school in East Texas where I began school at age seven had an enrollment of eighty-five boys and girls. The only teacher, a small woman about twenty, taught all the grades from first through eighth and also served as principal.

With so many pupils, most of them bigger than the teacher, the older boys were running the school. Discipline in the school was totally out of hand by the time I was eight, and I can't say that I was a model student in either scholarship or deportment.

Several of the parents complained that their children were not getting a good education because the teacher could not control her students. The school board met and concluded that what they needed was a man teacher, someone who was not afraid of the kids, someone who would not "spare the rod and spoil the child." They found Glen Wilhelm, a World War I Veteran who knew the meaning of discipline. He wore brown leather boots, the kind that were laced all the way to his knees, with his pants tucked inside. He weighed about a hundred and eighty pounds and was six feet tall, with thin blond hair — very thin on top. Some of us boys called him "Baldy," out of his range of hearing, of course.

Mr. Wilhelm drove a 1923 Model-T Ford. On the way to school each day, he stopped to cut several hickory switches. When he arrived at school, he stood the switches in the corner of the room. They were essential tools of his disciplinary regime. By 4:00 p.m. daily, the switches showed lots of wear.

One day, a guy sitting several seats in front of me threw a paper ball permeated with spit (we called them "spit wads") and hit me. I was not about to let him get away with that. I pretended to be reading my book while I chewed a page from my pencil tablet for ammunition. When I threw my wad, my intended target ducked, and the ball hit Mr. Wilhelm's bald head, splattering fragments over his desk.

I knew I was in trouble. I kept my head down, as though I were reading, but a downward, sideways glance revealed the booted legs beside my desk. Mr. Wilhelm grabbed me by the hair and lifted me straight up out of my seat.

"No wonder you can't read," he said. "Your book is upside down!"

He led me to the front of the room and reached for the thickest and longest hickory stick in that day's collection.

We all knew what was coming. I was wearing my "payday" overalls and "longhandle" underwear, with a trap door in the back. At that moment, I couldn't remember whether the trap door was up or down, but it wouldn't have been enough protection either way.

Wilhelm's regular method was to whip his victim until he cried. I had never cried before and didn't intend to start then. I clamped my jaws hard shut and made not a sound nor shed a tear. But my rear end was blistered when he stopped beating and told me to go back to my seat.

As I walked down the aisle, a little girl in my row looked at me with big, tear-filled, blue eyes. Traces of already shed tears were on her cheeks. I had never paid much attention to her before that day, but I knew her name was Buena Woods. I really looked at her then. She was about my age and was the most beautiful girl I had ever seen.

From then on, Buena was already in her seat, watching the door when I walked in at eight o'clock. She would look at me. After a long, wondrous meeting of the eyes, we both looked away.

Early in February that year, another kid had the nerve to throw a spit ball at me. I reacted in my usual way, chewing a wad of my own, ready to get even. First I looked all around to make sure that everybody was busy reading, and that Wilhelm wasn't looking my way. Buena's seat was across the aisle, about two behind me. As I glanced in her direction, she was looking straight at me. She didn't speak or change her expression. She just stared with those beautiful round blue eyes. I took the wad from my mouth and put it in my pocket.

What Baldy Wilhelm couldn't do with his hickory switches, and my parents couldn't accomplish with all their screaming, threats, and whippings, Buena did without saying one word.

She really brought a change in my life. I began to save my pennies, bought my first comb and a bottle of hair oil. My folks thought they had finally succeeded in getting me to scrub-up and comb my hair before I went to school. I never told them differently.

Except for Christmas, Valentine's Day was the biggest holiday of the year for young people. None of the kids could afford a store-bought Valentine, nor could they get to town to buy one, even if they had the money.

But on Valentine's Day, I received a card from Buena. It was cut from a piece of tablet paper, colored with red and blue crayola, and decorated with little hand-drawn hearts and flowers. Written on the front of the card was "Happy Valentine 1924." On the inside was printed: "I love you, Jim." I had never received a Valentine from anyone before, but here, I had it in writing. Somebody loved me.

In April of that same year, Buena died of scarlet fever. Every Valentine's Day for the last 74 years, Buena's Valentine comes out of safekeeping and is displayed in my living room for one week. I own nothing that I value more than that Valentine.

20

Sunday School Lessons

Our church, Wrights Chapel, was built on land across from the school. It was a long building with a podium in front, a potbelly stove in the middle, and long benches on both sides of the aisle. The organ was on the podium also. The front door was never locked, and it served as a town hall for the community and a meeting place for all occasions. Most of the people who hung out at the church for their meetings were responsible and well-behaved. However, some roughnecks made trouble.

One guy, Tommy, about fifteen, on a dare from the other guys, rode his donkey into the church. It was in the daytime, and only a bunch of kids were present, rehearsing a play. Some of the girls went home and told their parents. They were furious. They had a conference and concluded that such antics should never happen again.

The parents went to see the constable to have Tommy arrested. The only problem was, the constable was the boy's father. Another problem was the Justice of the Peace was Tommy's cousin. It turned out to be a *nolo prosequi.*

The minister advised Tommy to keep his ass out of the church house.

One Sunday morning a few days before Christmas, Verna Burton, the lady who was teaching the Sunday School class, asked if any of the members knew of any poor kids who might not get presents for Christmas. I raised my hand.

She asked, "Who?"

"Me," I said. A few people laughed. Of course I was joking, because I probably had a dollar six bits, or maybe even more, in my pocket at the time.

The next Sunday morning, Miss Burton called me up to the front of the church and presented me with a Christmas present. She said it was from the Sunday School class, who felt sorry for me. Everybody laughed. I was embarrassed. That was the idea. The laugh was on me.

In that church, we had all the school kids from across the road. Ozell, about thirteen years old, was a slow learner. She was naturally big for her age and her classmates were younger and much smaller. Chester, also thirteen, took delight in embarrassing her. At school he was afraid to torment her, but in church on Sunday, there was nobody to make him behave. Before we went into the church, Chester was making a nuisance of himself. I wanted to step in and help Ozell, but Chester was much bigger than I. Ozell was big enough to flatten him if she wanted to, but she never did. When we finally went into the church, he sat directly behind Ozell and continued to torment her. I was sitting next to the "pest" and the congregation was singing from their hymn books.

Without anyone seeing me, I affixed a sharp pin in the toe of my shoe. I had my legs crossed and was singing along with the congregation.

The church had long benches with horizontal slats. Ozell was on the fleshy side, and part of her anatomy bulged through the slats of the bench. With song book in front of my face, legs crossed, sharp pin in the toe of my shoe, I stuck Ozell with the pin. She screamed and turned around and slapped Chester, sitting directly behind her, so hard it knocked the song book out of his hand and it flew across the aisle. Chester was stunned. He didn't know what had happened, or what had hit him. When Ozell screamed, everybody looked. The lady on the podium kept pumping the organ and the faithful kept singing "Shall We Gather At The River?"

I didn't tell anyone what happened. I was afraid to. But I didn't feel guilty. I rationalized that Chester needed that slap. He never annoyed Ozell after that day. I always wanted to tell him the truth, but I waited too late. When I was back home many years later, they told me he had passed on.

21

Objection Overruled

Macy was a sixteen-year-old school girl. She lived with her parents and three older brothers. She was overprotected because she was the baby.

Doug was a rugged thirty-year-old ranch hand who lived in the same neighborhood. He was on trial for the alleged rape of Macy.

We just happened to be in town on the final day of the trial in Lamar County Court House in Texas. I was about ten years old, and my dad couldn't leave me by myself in the farmer's market square. He wanted to go to the trial and told me they probably wouldn't let me in the courtroom. If they threw me out, I would have to go to the wagon and wait until the trial was over. It was a cold winter day, and I wanted to keep warm.

It appeared that everybody else in town wanted to attend the trial, too. There was standing room only.

My dad told me to get directly behind him and we would push our way into the crowded courtroom, and I wouldn't be discovered. It worked.

It was difficult for me to understand what was happening. It was the third and final day of the trial, and the lawyers were presenting their final arguments.

The District Attorney got the first and last shot. The defense attorney got to make only one plea. He was almost in tears (he was acting) when he described how "the sixteen-year-old slut" had wrongly accused his client, Doug, of rape. She seduced his client, and she was the one who should be on trial, the attorney said. Some of the ladies in the crowd wiped their eyes, feeling sorry for the poor guy.

The defense lawyer was a huge man, about six feet four inches tall. Macy's older brother John was about the same size as the attorney and he was trying to comfort his baby sister.

When the attorney went over and shook his finger at Macy, and called her a troublemaker, John jumped to his feet and grabbed the defense attorney. The Marshal stopped him and made him sit down. The attorney continued by comparing the girl to a bitch dog in heat, and called her a "little whore." This time the brother jumped to his feet and grabbed the attorney by his neck tie. The bailiff tried to pull him off, but he was too big to handle. He then pulled his gun. Someone else jumped up from the crowd and pulled a gun. I don't know whose side he was on.

The Judge was banging his gavel, but nobody was listening. He ordered the spectators to clear the courtroom.

The District Attorney objected. The Judge then ordered only John, the huge brother of the rape victim, to leave the courtroom. The Judge was unhappy because they had disturbed his nap.

The District Attorney always gets to have the last word. When he finished his rebuttal, he asked the jury to find the defendant guilty.

The trial was over, except that the Judge had to read the charges and instruct the jury to disregard what they had witnessed in the court-room a few minutes earlier.

The defense attorney finished, grabbed his briefcase, and headed for the door.

Standing just outside the door was big brother John. The attorney didn't see him in time to defend himself. John hit the lawyer so hard that he knocked him through a plate glass window.

The crowd dispersed and so did my dad and I. We were expecting those guns to be used and we didn't want to get in the path of the bullets.

We lived out in the country, so I never heard the jury's verdict. I'm sure the sixteen-year-old girl didn't have to stand trial for corrupting the morals of the thirty-year-old man who raped her. I often wondered who had to pay for that big plate glass window.

22

Beating the Odds

The notorious Hensley family was well-known in the neighborhood, and in the school district. The youngest son, "Doc" (that's the only name he ever used), was a thorn in the side of his fellow students as well as the teachers. He was about fourteen years old when Mr.

Wilhelm, the new teacher, took over.

Mr. Wilhelm was a military man and he treated his class like soldiers. The only difference was that in the military the Sergeant could not lay a hand on the soldier.

In school, the teacher was mandated to use corporal punishment on the kids. That made him a good teacher, as far as the parents were concerned.

Doc, being the number one problem in school, was the first to test "Old Baldy," as we called Mr. Wilhelm. The first day, Doc got two whippings. The second was really severe, a little on the brutal side.

Doc went home and told his older brothers, Tom and Roy, both in their twenties, what the teacher had done to him. He showed them the red welts on his rear end. They were outraged. Nobody was allowed to lay a hand on their baby brother.

Next morning, Tom and Roy saddled up their horses and rode out to waylay the teacher on his way to school. They planned to "cut Old Baldy off at the pass." They waited at the bend of the road, at the little culvert. When Mr. Wilhelm came along in his Model-T Ford, the Hensley boys stopped their horses in the middle of the road and demanded the teacher get out of his car. Instead, he put his Model-T in reverse, and backed down the muddy road until he found a wide enough place to turn around. The Hensleys were in hot pursuit on their horses.

Meanwhile at school, Doc told the kids that Baldy had not arrived at eight o'clock, the usual time, because he was probably in the hospital. Doc told the other kids about his brothers' plan to get rid of the teacher. Even if he did make it to school, he would be beaten up too badly to teach.

The kids didn't seem to mind. They were having a "ball." They wrote obscenities on the blackboard, smoked cigarettes, and teased the girls.

At ten o'clock, Mr. Wilhelm drove up, having taken a circuitous route back to school. He was two hours late, but he didn't have a scratch on him.

Doc was a little embarrassed and scared.

Mr. Wilhelm reported to the school trustees. He advised them to do something with the Hensley family, as they were interfering with his teaching and threatening his life.

The trustees answered that the Hensley family was Wilhelm's problem. Dealing with the kids and the families was what they paid Wilhelm one hundred and fifty dollars a month to do.

Mr. Wilhelm finally got the school under control. It took a lot of hickory switches and patience, though. By the end of the first year of Wilhelm's reign, all the kids had a healthy respect for their teacher.

"Old Baldy" didn't back down; he backed up and turned around.

23

Young Detective

Once when times were hard and jobs were scarce, everybody who lived in the city was moving to the country. There were no jobs in the country either, but people could hunt and fish for food. When I was hunting on our land one day, I discovered a tent. It appeared that someone had just moved in and pitched it on our land without permission. I went home and told my parents about my discovery.

They told me not to go over there. They didn't like the idea that people would just move in without first getting permission. They might be dangerous people looking for a hideaway. These squatters might have committed a serious crime. They might be fugitives from justice. They might be . .

I decided to find out for myself why they were trespassing. I realized that I wasn't to go near them, but I couldn't resist. After all, they surely wouldn't harm an innocent kid like me. As I walked up to their tent, a man was lying flat on his back with his hat over his face. He appeared to be asleep. Sitting on a log nearby was a teenage boy playing the "Battle Hymn of the Republic" on his harmonica. On the ground next to the sleeping man was a black and white spotted dog. I didn't want to get too close because I was afraid of dogs. When I got within about ten feet, the dog opened one eye and wagged his tail twice. He wasn't a vicious dog, but he wasn't too happy to see me, either. He just closed his eyes and went back to sleep. He didn't even bother to bark.

I could see inside their tent. Two or three shotguns, and a pallet or blanket on the floor. My shotgun was on my shoulder (I would never leave home without it). When the boy stopped playing his harmonica, he beat the slobber out of his instrument on the palm of his hand.

I coughed to get his attention, but he just looked down the canyon and away from me. During the brief intermission in the concert, I could hear the man on the ground snoring. I knew he was still alive.

Without ever looking up, the boy started to play his harmonica again. I didn't recognize the tune. It was a strange sounding thing—it had no end. He just played and played on. I got tired standing there listening. I got the idea that he wanted me to leave. As I walked away through the woods, I could still hear him playing that strange tune.

The next day, I went back to see what was happening. They had moved out — left nothing behind. I have always wondered what they were up to.

24

Blown Away

In our part of Texas, spring was the time for storms. Lightning raced through the sky, turning the ground and trees as bright as midday. A clap of thunder followed, echoing down the canyons. The way to calculate your distance from a storm is to count the seconds between the lightning flashes and the clap of thunder. When they both happen simultaneously, it's time to head for the storm cellar. But what if you don't have a storm cellar? Better pray—real fast.

Animals cope with storms in different ways. Mules will run in circles and are as free as the wind. Cows, on the hand, will stand with their rear ends toward the wind and hail. Animals seem to know instinctively when to prepare for a storm. Hogs can prognosticate the weather more accurately than the meteorologist. When hogs gather leaves, straw or anything that will make a warm bed, you can bet there will be a snow storm or a "norther" within the next eight or ten hours.

The spring months are the time of the worst hail storms, cyclones, and floods, especially the month of May.

If a cloud is black, with a white border underneath, that means wind and hail. Usually there isn't a leaf moving just before a storm—it's still. It's the lull before the storm.

When a cyclone touches down, it picks up rooftops or anything in its path. This wind carries everything up in the air and drops it two or three miles away. A cyclone usually bounces and hits the ground several times before it finally blows itself out. It leaves a path of destruction.

After such a storm, feather beds and mattresses can be seen lodged in trees. Unbelievable things happen, like broom straws driven into telephone poles.

A girl named Ruby was working in the cotton fields one day when a tornado touched down. Everybody had to lie in a prone position between the cotton rows. The wind ripped all the hair off Ruby's head. She was not injured, nor were any of the other hands, but her head looked like a billiard ball.

It was supper time at the Tillman Smallwood home. All the food was on the table. Mrs. Smallwood had poured milk for the children and all were ready to sit down and eat when they heard a loud noise. It sounded like a freight train coming. They knew what it was, a "twister," a cyclone! The folks grabbed the kids in a hurry and made a dash for the storm cellar. They barely made it. After a few minutes in the storm cellar, the children got restless. They wanted to go back to the kitchen and eat supper. After the noise passed, the opened the door of the storm cellar slowly and looked out to see how much was destroyed in the storm. The roof of the house was completely blown off. Where did it go?

It had "gone with the wind." All the family came out to take a look. The dining room table was sitting in the front yard. It had all the victuals still on the table. The milk was still in the glasses. Not a drop was spilled. How could this happen?

Always somebody is ready to explain what happened. There are authorities on everything.

One neighbor told the family he knew exactly what happened. In scientific terms, he said the tornado was in a funnel shape, and when it dipped down, it acted like a vacuum and just sucked the roof off the house, taking everything in the room with it.

Furthermore, a tornado is different from a cyclone, he said. The cyclone spins counterclockwise in the northern hemisphere and clockwise in the southern hemisphere. Tornadoes happen mostly in the middle United States and they have a rotary action. Maybe the family was just living in the wrong part of the country.

Why did this family lose their property and their neighbors didn't?

There's always someone to give an explanation by reading from the Bible. According to the preacher, evil was in that household. The tornado was the Lord's way of reminding the whole family to change their wicked ways. He laid a guilt trip on the five little girls as well as the adults.

When they asked why he thought this happened to the family, and how a broom straw could be driven into a telephone pole by the wind, Earl, another neighbor, gave his usual honest answer, "Dam'f I know."

In East Texas, the Bible Belt, people are frightened of storms. They even sing about them in church. The words to one song are:

> O they tell me of a place
> Where no storm clouds rise.
> *O they tell me of a non-cloudy day . . .*

The Arnold family had a storm cellar on their farm. They used it frequently. Of course, there were snakes down there looking for a cool place to hang out, some toad frogs, and the marsh gas seeped in. When Mr. Arnold took the kerosene lantern into the cellar, which didn't have good ventilation, breathing was difficult. He didn't like going to the storm cellar. His contention was, if you live a good life, the Lord would take care of you. His minister had told him that. After all, he had lived a good life-maybe made a little home brew or occasional drinking, but he rationalized that the Lord would understand—and there was no reason to run to the storm cellar in the middle of the night every time there was thunder.

His wife had a different point of view. She didn't think he had been that good. They had four small children, and they were all scared to death of storms.

Every spring we had storm warnings and storm alerts almost every night. Someone had to stay awake and be ready to give the alarm to dash to the storm cellar, if necessary.

Mrs. Arnold had to do all the watching. She made her husband sleep in his clothes. She had to see that he and the children got to the cellar on time. Mr. Arnold wanted to get his sleep. He had to plow corn tomorrow, and besides "it never stormed," according to him. Just a little wind and rain. A waste of time and sleep. He wouldn't run to the storm cellar like a prairie dog running in his hole every time it thundered.

One stormy night, about one o'clock, Mrs. Arnold wrapped a quilt around the children, woke her husband, grabbed the lantern and said, "Hurry, it's coming." Mr. Arnold was half asleep.

He muttered, "Nothing ever happens. Why do I have to go?"

About twenty minutes later, they opened the cellar door and looked around. The barn was gone, the house was gone. All was blown away.

Mr. Arnold said, "Now this is more like it."

25

Cotton Pickin' Chicken Plucker

When John Bryant was released from the Texas Penitentiary, he used to visit a neighbor of ours and brag about his days in the "pen."

I was about seven years old. After listening to him for a while, it seemed to me and the other youngsters my age that he was a hero. I remember vividly the things he told us about the treatment and especially the beatings he received at the hands of the prison guards. He'd take off his shirt and show us the scars from the whippings.

According to John, the state operated farms and used the prisoners to work them. Most of these were cotton farms. Every year, when the cotton was ready to pick, the guards, one to every ten prisoners, would take a crew of convicts to the cotton fields. Each guard rode a horse. That gave him more speed in case he had to chase a prisoner. Each also carried a high-powered Winchester rifle and a leather buggy whip. These were tough hombres.

On the first day of picking, each prisoner started at sunrise and didn't stop until sunset. He had to keep his head down and his ass up, and no talking was allowed. His quota was set on that first day, like a golfer establishing a handicap. At sundown, his score was the number of pounds of cotton he had picked that day. If he picked two hundred and fifty pounds on the first day, that was his quota. If he was ten pounds short of that quota on the second day, the guard gave him ten lashes across his back with the leather whip. Whatever the number of pounds below the first day's quota, the picker got that number of lashes. No credit was allowed for more pounds picked than your quota.

Another way prisoners collected extra whippings was if they made any audible protest when being whipped: one lash for every scream or other sound. Some guards were skilled at drawing blood with the whip, and in the fields under the hot sun, these open wounds were very painful, especially when salty perspiration ran into them.

With no insecticides in those days, boll weevils often invaded the fields. The worms prevented the cotton boll from opening completely. It was much harder to get the cotton out of the burl, and a picker's efficiency in meeting his quota was reduced. No consideration of this problem was given by the guards. Each prisoner had to pick his quota or take the consequences.

Picking cotton was only one of the farm chores for the prisoners. They also cared for livestock, including chickens. Some of the men butchered the chickens, others plucked and dressed them.

Only the most trusted prisoners got to kill the chickens. It was done with a small, spring-loaded knife. This was put down into the throat of the bird. When a button was pressed, the knife opened and cut the chicken's throat. Of course, the guards didn't care much if one of the "trusted" convicts used the chicken knife on one of his companions. John told us the guards would have been especially glad to have him killed.

John bragged about his work and he was proud of the fact that he had not got any time off for "good behavior." He had a special title. He was not just a cotton picker, but also a chicken plucker, so that made him a "cotton-pickin' chicken plucker."

To me, John Bryant was the most interesting and colorful character I'd ever met. After listening to him talk about his ten years "in the pen," and seeing the scars that laced his muscled back, I thought of him as kind of a hero.

When I told my mother about John Bryant and his interesting career and that I wanted to be a convict when I grew up, she was shocked.

She explained that John had committed a serious crime and he deserved to spend those years in prison.

I asked my standard question, "WHY?"

"A person has to do something really bad to get into the pen," she said.

"That's no problem, I can do that," I said.

But she wouldn't tell me what he had done.

When I asked some of the older boys what John Bryant did to get into prison, they said they didn't know either. It was something about "carnal knowledge," said one, but nobody knew what that meant.

A number of years later, when I was in law school, and learned what "carnal knowledge" meant, I knew my mother was right again. I understood why she didn't want me to go to the penitentiary like John Bryant.

26

Evolution

It was about the mid-twenties when the first radio broadcasting station was built in Texas. Before long, we could pick up one station locally and three stations in Dallas and Ft. Worth.

In Dallas was W.F.A.A., "your neighbor of the air," in the Baker Hotel. Across the street, it was K.R.L.D., the Dallas Times Station in the Adolphus Hotel. Thirty-two miles to the west was W.B.A.P. in the Blackstone Hotel, Ft. Worth. In Paris, Texas, where we lived, the station was K.P.L.T. (Keep Paris Leading Texas).

If you could play any kind of musical instrument, all you had to do was show up and audition in the lobby of the hotel. You might become a radio star and get your own regular scheduled program.

Most of the radio sets then were small. The console sets were huge and very expensive. Most of the sets were made by RCA Victor. Any store that sold them had a display card with dog with his head cocked, listening to a RCA radio. Later, in the thirties, they were actually installing radios in new cars. Some people were building their own radio sets. They called them crystal sets. With the help of two other guys, I built a crystal set. They furnished the technology and chassis and I furnished the cigar box for the cabinet.

We could get all four stations on our set. We witnessed a little technical difficulty when we got several stations at the same time, on the same channel. It was usually a cattle auction station at the Ft. Worth stock yards, a politician making his pitch, the old fiddlers contest, and sometimes an evangelist preacher named Billy Sunday. There was no way we could separate the stations.

A lady lived close by who didn't understand how the radio worked. Nobody knew exactly how a voice could be transmitted through the air and picked up on a little box at a great distance. We told her that everything she said could be picked up on the radio.

Furthermore, when she gossiped about her neighbors, we told her they heard every word she spoke. Afterwards, she whispered when she talked about them.

The Grand Old Opry started about 1925, in Nashville, Tennessee. Only a few of the more affluent families could afford a radio. All the other families would invite themselves to a neighbor who had a radio and they would walk as much as five miles to listen to the Saturday night country music.

Now, only seventy years later, we hear "Live from New York, it's Saturday Night!"

27

Aunt Frankie

There was a lot of tragedy in the Bryant family. The mother was known as "Aunt Frankie." If she had a husband, she didn't talk about him, and as far as I knew, no one ever asked her if her husband was dead or if she was ever married.

She had two grown sons, John and Ely. John was in prison, and his younger brother Ely was still living at home with his mother.

Like most families in that era the Bryants lived on a farm. They were our neighbors about two miles up the road. One of Aunt Frankie's characteristics was her vituperative language. She used language that would make a sailor blush. She could often be heard by the other neighbors chastising her son. When she came to our house, she would use language that our family didn't tolerate. When she was asked "not to use that kind of language," she would apologize, but in a few minutes she would forget and use the same words again. She didn't use blue language—it was more like deep purple. She was a rugged, outdoor, masculine woman.

One day, Aunt Frankie hitched up her team of mules, loaded the wagon with stove wood, and headed for Paris, Texas, to get her rations, but she never made it.

She got to Hinckley, a small community with two stores, a grist mill, cotton gin, and a railroad station. It was a busy place for the railroad depot. They had the U.P., the T.P., and the Atchinson Topeka and Santa Fe.

The railroad tracks made a sharp bend in the shape of a swastika. There were no crossing guards on the track. Apparently, her wagon crossed one set of tracks when a freight train bore down from the opposite direction.

The mules were scared and ran in front of the long freight train. They were hit from the side. The wagon, mules, and Aunt Frankie were pulverized and scattered a half-mile down the railroad tracks.

For several months after the gruesome accident, whenever the neighbors got together, they all agreed that if Aunt Frankie hadn't been so foulmouthed, she would have been a wonderful person. They remembered she had helped all her friends when they were sick or in need of anything.

"Now what is going to happen to Ely? He has always depended on his mother for everything. He will have no mules to pull the plow or the wagon. And what about John, her older son, who will be coming out of the Texas Penitentiary in another year. It will be a shock to him."

The neighbors all agreed on one thing. When they hear a train whistle, they'll think of Aunt Frankie.

28

Politics as Usual

In my part of Texas in the 1920s, the one-room country schools were overpopulated. Sometimes one teacher faced as many as eighty students on each school day, their ages ranging from seven to seventeen or even older, in grades one through eight.

Parents didn't actually have any say in choosing teachers. They elected three trustees to handle the hiring. A teacher who was educationally qualified, could endure the daily trials and, as important, met the disciplinary standards set by the parents, was hard to find. If parents didn't like the teacher, they voted the trustees out of office. In the whole district there were only thirty-eight votes.

If a teacher didn't discipline the kids, he or she was "no good." If he whipped them, he was in trouble. The parent would confront the teacher. "Nobody beats my kid with a stick." On the other hand, some parents couldn't get along with their kids at home and expected the teacher to discipline them.

One year Raymond Lenoir decided to run for school trustee and oust the incumbent, Jessie Paige. Each of the voters in the district had three or four kids in school. Raymond felt he needed to dig up some "dirt" on his opponent, so he started a rumor. He claimed that Jessie was a bootlegger and set about convincing the voters that such a man should be replaced by the upright citizen Raymond Lenoir.

The voters were farmers or sharecroppers who lived in the hills or in Sanders Creek bottom. The election was held in April when everybody was busy plowing and planting their corn and cotton. For Raymond, who was also a farmer, campaigning in the spring wouldn't be convenient. He decided to do his campaigning in February. He rode his horse from farm to farm to catch farmers at home while they were "in hibernation," waiting for planting time. He talked to all thirty-eight of the potential voters and they said they'd vote for him. After a week of campaigning, Raymond rode home along the muddy roads, congratulating himself on being a shrewd politician.

On election day in April, Raymond thought it would be embarrassing for his opponent to get only his own vote and considered voting for Jessie just so the poor guy would get at least two votes. But at the last minute, he changed his mind, reasoning with himself. "What kind of a candidate would I be not voting for myself?"

When the votes were counted, the other candidate got thirty-seven votes. Raymond got only one—his own.

29

Accident or Murder?

Luke Smithson was a quiet young man in his mid-twenties. He was a "little peculiar," as one lady described him. He never hung out with the girls or the guys. Even his older brother Joe didn't seem to understand him.

There was one thing we could count on. When we went to town in the wagon, Luke was always out by the road in front of his house to bum a ride.

Luke had one guy he thought was his friend, but maybe he wasn't—that was the mystery.

Ely Bryant was about Luke's age and was the opposite in personality. He was a happy-go-lucky guy. However, after his mother was killed by a freight train, his personality changed. He was described by some of his friends as the "Bryant orphan."

Luke and Ely went squirrel hunting one day. It was a heavily wooded area with some native pecan trees, and plenty of wild game. Ely carried his .22 rifle, and Luke carried a 12-gauge single barrel shotgun.

Ely didn't come out of the forest alive. He was shot at close range in the back of his head by Luke's 12-gauge shotgun.

The coroner's report read: "Death by a shotgun blast, point blank to the posterior of the skull." It further stated that the pasteboard wadding that separates the buckshot from the gun powder was lodged in the victim's brain.

How could this happen? That was the question on everyone's mind. Were they really friends? If not, why were they hunting together?

In that era, every kid by the age of ten knew how to handle, shoot, and care for all kinds of weapons—especially rifles and shotguns. They were allowed to go into the woods and hunt wild game for food.

Luke explained it this way. He was carrying the shotgun across his shoulder with the barrel pointing forward. The gun was cocked. The trigger must have gotten caught on a limb and the gun fired, striking Ely in the back of his head.

No rational person would believe that theory. You never carry a gun with the barrel pointing forward, and you never point your gun at a human being unless you mean to kill him.

Ely couldn't tell his side of the story. Dead men don't talk.

One of the mortgage bankers in the community of Caviness held the note on Ely's property and also held the mortgage on Luke Smithson's farm.

Since there was no one left in the Bryant family except John, and he was still in prison and hadn't communicated with his family for several years, the banker was in a position to take over the farm.

But how about Luke? "Is he in trouble, does he need a lawyer? He will have to borrow money on the farm."

The banker, wanting to help both parties, made the decision to hire the law firm of Sturgeon, Sturgeon, and Sturgeon to represent Luke. They had a reputation of being the best in the county.

After the lawyers collected their fee, they cut a deal with the district attorney. Their decision: The shooting was accidental.

Luke was never arrested nor stood trial, but he lost the farm.

The community was in a state of turmoil. What kind of justice is this? It would be impossible for an accident to happen the way it was reported. Was Luke "a hired gun?" If so, it was obvious who hired him and why.

The next time my Dad and I went to town in the wagon, Luke was standing by the side of the road, waiting for a ride into town. My Dad was uneasy about picking him up, but he was afraid not to.

Luke wore a broad-brimmed black hat, pulled down over his eyes. To see out from under his hat, he would raise his chin, as if he were looking at the stars. If and when he talked, he just mumbled. He always sat flat down in the wagon bed holding on to both sides with his hands as if he was afraid of falling out.

My Dad was a pretty good amateur detective, and he almost got a confession out of Luke one time. When he did talk, he would gossip about everyone in the neighborhood. He seemed to know all about their business. But when we passed the farm of the man who "helped him out," he would clam up.

The case is still an unsolved mystery.

30

My Last Cigarette

Before tailor-made cigarettes came on the market, everyone had to roll his own. If he didn't have cigarette paper, he would tear pieces from a brown paper bag to roll the tobacco in.

The first three popular brands of tailor-made cigarettes were Camels, Chesterfields, and Lucky Strikes. Most smokers couldn't afford the ready rolled, so they rolled their own. If you wanted to really splurge or look like a big shot, you would smoke a cigar when out in public.

A slogan in the twenties was, "What this country needs is a good five cent cigar." They were mostly reserved for politicians though.

On the way home from school every day, some of the boys would go across the road to the church house in search of cigarette butts, and maybe, if we got lucky, a cigar butt.

One day Carl and I went over to the church after a big weekend of preaching, looking for butts. Picking was always better on Monday.

Carl was a rowdy kid, always in trouble at home and school. He didn't read very well, and he hated his teacher. He was a year younger than I. The best way to describe him was an "incorrigible, dumb kid." I was in the same category—except I had another year of experience.

Just as we crossed the road, before we got to the church, we saw a nice cigar butt lying in the grass. Carl made a dash for it. He was ecstatic. He had beat me to it.

"You aren't going to smoke that thing, are you?," I asked.

"Of course I'm going to smoke it, why not? What's wrong with smoking a cigar?"

"Do you know what the Bible says in Ecclesiastes, Chapter Eight,

Verse Seventeen, about smoking cigars?," I asked.

"No, what?"

"You better go home and read it for yourself?"

"You know I can't read—especially the Bible," he shouted back.

"Well—get your Ma to read it to you."

Carl was upset and disgusted as he threw the cigar butt down on the ground and stalked off, mumbling obscenities under his breath.

As soon as he turned his back, I picked up the cigar butt and put it in my pocket.

That Bible quotation, I just "pulled it out of a hat." It worked. I had no idea what that chapter and verse said, or if there were such a thing. I just guessed and Carl of course couldn't challenge the Bible quotation.

The next day, Carl and I went out and gathered a bunch of nice cigarette butts. He was already in trouble with his mother for smoking. Carl's mother was a huge woman with long red hair that hung down to her waist. She had a real Southern accent, and when she got mad, she talked loud and fast, and ran her words together.

Carl told me that his mother had served an ultimatum on him for smoking. He had been caught once before and was serving equivalent to a suspended sentence. She vowed she would kill him if he ever smoked again.

Carl and I took turns behind the barn, he would smoke and I would watch for his mother. Then he would watch, and I would smoke. It seemed like a lot of fun at the time, but it ended when his mother smelled smoke. There was a gentle breeze from the southwest, blowing the smoke from the barn toward the house. She had a nose like a blood hound, and she sniffed us out.

All the kids had a middle name. It was never used until their mother got mad at them. When she used his middle name, he knew he was in trouble.

She walked out into the yard and shouted, "Carl Lee, you come in this house ritenow! And I mean ritenow! I'm gonna tan your butt, boy, you heah?"

When she got Carl inside, I could hear the familiar sounds of the razor strap in action.

Some call it a STROP, and some call it a STRAP. Frankly, I could never tell the difference—felt the same, regardless of how they pronounced it. When Carl's mother got through with him, she said, "Now, you get out there and tell that pesky kid to take his cigarette butts and go home, and don't come back!"

And I did— and I didn't. I wanted to get back and apologize to Carl and make a pact with him. I would never smoke again if he would never smoke again. But I was afraid to go back. I knew I was *persona non grata*.

I don't know what happened to Carl. His mother might have killed him. For me—that was my last cigarette.

31

The New Sheriff

Sheriff Joe Smith of Choctaw County, Oklahoma, had been in office a long time—too long. He was involved with bootleggers. This was in the days of prohibition when it was illegal to make or sell whiskey. However, if you knew how to play your cards, and were willing to help the Sheriff a little, you might never get arrested.

The Chief of Police of Hugo, Oklahoma, got in on the racket later and was giving the Sheriff too much competition. The Chief was getting his cut right off the top. This angered the Sheriff, because he didn't like competition. Things got worse. The Chief ran for Sheriff. The Sheriff had run unopposed for several terms, and of course, always won. He could see the "handwriting on the wall," and it was time to take drastic action.

Les Golden was a tall farm boy, age twenty-four, who knew nothing about politics and didn't particularly care. Joe Smith suggested that Les run for Sheriff against him and the Chief of Police. Joe knew full well if he didn't get a third party in the Sheriff's race to split up the votes, he would lose the election.

Nobody but his immediate family and a few friends had ever heard of Les Golden, and Les turned the Sheriff's offer down flat. His reason was he never finished high school and had no money to run for office. If he were elected, he wouldn't know anything about being a Sheriff.

Joe Smith countered, "Don't be silly, you will never be elected Sheriff. Let me lay it out for you again. You don't have to pay for your filing fee, posters, or the announcement in the paper. I will buy you some new clothes and a ten-gallon hat, so you will look like a Sheriff. I will furnish a flatbed truck for you to speak from. I will write your speeches. What you have to do is go to all the little towns and communities and give your speeches. You don't have to say anything about me, but you must tell the voters how crooked the Chief of Police is. You see, we don't want John Jarvis to be elected Sheriff. If they ask you about me, pretend to answer their questions, and go right back to the Chief and give him hell. He's the no-good guy that we don't want to be elected Sheriff."

"I don't know," Les said. "Nobody knows me. You are very well known."

"That's the reason you aren't voting for me anymore, I'm too well known," said Sheriff Joe. "Now, I can have the posters on every telephone pole and tree in the Red River Valley in three days. We'll go down tomorrow and get you a new hat and clothes for the campaign. Remember, you don't have to pay for anything."

Les Golden for Sheriff. It sure had a nice ring to it, Les thought. He decided to go for it. When he got his new duds and ten-gallon hat, he looked like a real Sheriff. He made a big hit in all the hamlets where he made his speeches.

Come election day, Les tallied eighty-four percent of the votes. The two crooks split the other sixteen percent between them. Les got to keep his new hat and new duds and they didn't cost him a penny. He wouldn't even give the old Sheriff a job as a deputy after he took office.

32

The Scent of Harry

Hunting and trapping fur-bearing animals in the winter months was a common practice in our part of Texas.

Harry Smith, one of our neighbors, about eighteen years old, did more than his share of hunting. He frequently got sprayed by skunks, and never changed clothes after a hunting trip.

Harry came to visit us frequently and thought he was making a big hit with my oldest sister, Nelma. He always wore a black sweater and the salt from perspiration turned the sweater white under his armpits. It was the same sweater he wore when he went skunk hunting. He didn't bathe during the cold winter months, because he feared he'd catch pneumonia. No bath from October till April. He used to sing to Nelma. She couldn't stand him, but she didn't want to hurt his feelings.

In order to kill the odor from the skunks and the B.O., Harry sloshed on cologne that cost about 89 cents a quart. This was his everyday cologne. However, when he came courting to see Nelma, he would use the more expensive perfume. It was called *Blue Waltz*, and cost 25 cents for a small bottle. He must have had a whole bottle on his clothes when he headed for our house.

He always sang when he was walking. Two songs, "The Old Spinning Wheel In The Parlor" and "The Isle of Capri," new and popular at that time, were his favorites. The singing, along with his odor, let us know when he was coming. If the wind was right, we could smell him before we heard him.

Sometimes we would hide and pretend not to be at home, but that didn't discourage him. He just waited.

After he caught all the skunks and coons in our neighborhood, he moved further down the river bottom where there were more skunks and coons. We never heard from him again—what a relief!

33

Not So "Sweet" Potatoes

In 1925, Paris, Texas, had a population of fifteen thousand. It was a beautiful town with wide streets and manicured lawns.

I didn't live in town. I lived fifteen miles out in the country, on a farm. About ninety percent of the families lived on farms then.

The main attraction in town was market square. That's the place where all the farmers brought their produce to sell. If they didn't sell anything, they couldn't buy any groceries to take home. Money was scarce and bartering was common.

One year we had plenty of rain and every farmer had a big crop of sweet potatoes. When my dad and I went to town to buy groceries, the only thing we had to sell or barter was two bushels of sweet potatoes.

Practically everything now is sold by the pound or ounce. Then it was sold by the bushel, gallon, or peck. We arrived on market square in the mid-morning, and had a difficult time finding a place to park our wagon. The huge market square had about one hundred wagons, all loaded with commodities, chickens, eggs, and sweet potatoes.

We knew we couldn't hope to sell our sweet potatoes, so we decided to trade them for something else. The first swap we made was for four frying chickens. Someone came along and offered us a dozen ears of corn and a peck of plums for the fryers. We traded. By the end of the day, we had exchanged about five or six times.

It was getting dark and we were stuck with a bushel of yellow squash. We had no refrigerators then and I had gotten botulism (food poisoning) from yellow squash a few days before that was left over from dinner to supper. I got sick just looking at yellow squash.

I told my dad to please swap the squash for something else — anything.

He said, "You go make a deal with someone out there while I get the mules hitched to the wagon." We knew the family would be waiting at home for us to bring store-bought groceries, and would be disappointed if we didn't bring something home that we all liked to eat.

I went looking for someone to make a deal with. Most of the wagons were gone. I saw one man just about to drive off so I asked if I could swap a bushel of yellow squash for anything he had.

"Anything?" he said.

"Anything!" I said.

"I'll give you two bushels of sweet potatoes."

"It's a deal," I said.

It was the only produce left — the same two bushels of sweet potatoes we brought to town that morning.

34

Doctor's Prescriptions

The Volstead Act prohibited the sale, manufacture, and transportation of alcoholic beverages in the U.S.A. But around our parts, the law was pretty much ignored.

During these Prohibition days, liquor could be bought for medicinal purposes with a doctor's prescription. Whiskey was for snake bites, bad colds, flu, and many other ailments. No legitimate doctor would prescribe alcohol for any physical or mental condition. But one doctor would write a prescription if you requested it. He had a card table and a chair set up on the sidewalk on North Main Street, on the corner by the First National Bank.

On Saturday afternoons, a line of people was always waiting to get prescriptions. The "Doc" was supposed to see the patients and ask what kind of health problems they had, but he never looked up at the patients or asked any questions. A man would walk up to the card table and fake a cough. The doctor would then write his name on a blank prescription pad and collect twenty-five cents for his fee. (Twenty-five cents then was equivalent to about five dollars today.)

Carrie Nation was a temperance leader. She hated liquor, and tried to get rid of it by raiding the stills and busting up the barrels of mash with a sledge hammer. She would go into any place that sold liquor or beer and break all the bottles. She was feared and hated by the bootleggers, but applauded by the prohibitionists. Women didn't drink then, except for a few who hung out with the men in the saloons, or the Speakeasy.

In 1933, the 18th Amendment, or the Volstead Act was repealed by the 21st Amendment.

Things didn't get better. They got worse. You could buy "bottled in bond" at the liquor store legally, but nobody could afford to pay the price. People continued to make their own. The law said you could make up to five gallons a year for your own use, but you couldn't sell any.

One man had his still camouflaged up in the hills. A government scout, a "Revenuer," was sniffing out the location. The bootlegger didn't want to get caught, nor did he want to hurt the man. He was a sharp shooter with a rifle, so he took aim at the crown of the Revenuer's hat and shot it right off the man's head. The Revenuer wasn't injured, but he took off down the hill like a turpentined cat, leaving his hat behind.

The bootlegger picked up the hat with the bullet hole in the top, and kept it for a souvenir. He showed it to all his friends. He thought it was funny.

His friends advised him that the government man had spotted his location, and would surely be back with a posse to destroy his still and take him in for whiskey-making, maybe even for attempted murder. The bootlegger was so shook up that he tore the still down himself.

No official even came back. The local people concluded that the Revenuer was a rookie on the force, and was too embarrassed to report to his superiors what had happened. So the bootlegger finally rebuilt his still and went back into business.

35

By the Acre

One of the neighbors, Mark Schultz, owned a farm with several acres under cultivation. He also had several acres of wooded land that he wanted to clear and put into crops. John Cunningham, one of his sharecroppers, needed a job during the winter months, so he was hired to clear the land.

Mark, the landowner, was frugal. He had the reputation of being a real "slave driver." He was also known as "Mark the Miser." He would work his hired hands and pay them nothing if he could get away with it. He offered to give the timber to John for clearing the land. "Just cut the logs into wood, and sell it right on the land," he said.

However, John knew that selling wood to local people who had their own trees was tantamount to selling an icebox to an Eskimo.

Mark the Miser made an offer. He said, "I'll pay you twenty dollars an acre to clear the land, cut all the underbrush, and burn the logs if you don't want to make firewood out of them. The land must have all the debris removed so it will be ready to plow and plant a crop in the Spring. If you don't want the job, there're plenty of people out of work who would be glad to do the clearing."

John thought it over, and said, "I'll clear the land for twenty dollars an acre if you will let me and my son, Leroy, do it one-half acre at a time, so I can get paid at the end of the week. We can clear one-half acre in a week, that's ten dollars a week."

"O.K.," Mark said, "I'll step it off for you." One acre is seventy-two yards square. Since they didn't have a measuring tape, he just took long steps, which is one yard, or three feet, for the average height person.

Since an acre is seventy-two yards square, one-half acre would be thirty-six yards square. Any fool knows that — just basic arithmetic. Wrong! A piece of land thirty-six yards square is one quarter of an acre, not one-half acre.

When Spring came, and it was time to plow the "new ground" and plant corn, Mark caught his mistake. He went back to complain to John and Leroy. He yelled at them. "You cheated me! You cleared only one quarter of an acre and charged me for clearing one-half acre. You will have to refund all the money you cheated me out of."

"Can't do it," John said. "We spent all the money to buy groceries. Furthermore, you stepped off the land yourself, taking extra long strides to get your money's worth. We didn't cheat you. You cheated yourself."

36

Swimming Lesson

When the creek overflowed and then receded, it left ponds of water. They were ideal for swimming, and the other guys about my age enjoyed taking a plunge. Even at fourteen, I couldn't swim. These temporary ponds were far from civilization, no houses within miles. All the guys took off their clothes and jumped in. They were having a ball, yelling at each other and splashing water.

I took off my shirt — only — and hung it on a dogwood tree. I was about ready to take off my pants, and wade in, when I heard giggling.

I looked over my shoulder and there stood three teenage girls. I was embarrassed and reached for my shirt. The girls said, "You don't need a shirt."

The other guys in the pond, naked as Jaybirds, were afraid to come out. They just stuck their heads out of the water and looked around.

One of the girls told me how handsome I was and that she liked the hair on my chest. (I had about three and a half hairs at the time.) All three of the girls wanted me to go with them and pick wild mushrooms and violets. After a few seconds, they convinced me their plan was more fun than going back into that muddy pond with turtles and water moccasins. They said, "You won't need your shirt. You can come back later and get it."

We went through the creek bottoms, and the woods picking all the wild stuff. They showed me how to tell the difference between a good mushroom and a poison one. (You put salt on them. If they turn black, don't eat them.)

It was almost dark when I got home. I had so much fun with the girls, I never went out with the boys again. As far as I know, my shirt is still hanging on that dogwood tree at the old swimming hole.

It's been more than sixty-five years. It's too late to go back now.

37

That's No "Bull"

When I was thirteen, I had a hankering to join the rodeo circuit and ride the broncos and bulls, just like Tom Mix, Will Rogers, and Buck

Jones. They traveled with the Barnum and Bailey Circus, billed as the "Greatest Show On Earth."

Will Rogers was my idol. He did rope tricks and told stories. He had a syndicated column that I read in our local newspaper.

My parents wouldn't let me ride any of our livestock. They were afraid I'd get hurt. I didn't listen to them.

On the day our neighbor, Benton Woods, died of tuberculosis, my family went to the funeral, all except me. I persuaded them, if they let me stay home, I'd cut the stack of logs in the woodpile into fireplace and stove wood.

While splitting the logs, I remembered seeing the sixteen-gallon keg of homemade grape wine my dad kept in the smoke house. He never let the kids drink wine, but when his friends came over, he took them to the smoke house for a shot of grape wine. They smacked their lips and told dad that he made the best wine they ever tasted. I looked on, but nary a drop could I drink.

I happened to know where the key to the Yale lock was hidden behind the clock on the mantel. I unlocked the smoke house door and helped myself to a cup of wine. After a few minutes, I returned for another cup.

After three trips to the smoke house, I noticed that the wood was splitting much easier than before. I got another notion which seemed like a good idea at the time.

We owned a thousand-pound bull with a ring in his nose. He was a mean one. That bull had never been ridden. What better time to ride him than now? I didn't have a rope to use as a circingle or spurs to make him buck harder. At that time I really didn't think I needed them. I put some hay on the ground, and when the bull put his head down to eat the hay, I jumped on his back. I was sure I could stay on for a few seconds.

I stayed on about one second. He threw me end-over-end. I hit the ground on my head and shoulders. When I was walking north my chin was facing southwest. My eyes were looking up and I could see a lot of stars. Not a chiropractor within fifteen miles. Then I remembered: in the big rodeos, the bull always had a bell. Maybe that's the reason I didn't stay on very long.

When the folks returned from the funeral, it was almost dark. They didn't know about the wine or the bull riding. I was sure glad that bull couldn't talk. They did notice my head was sitting a little crooked on my shoulders. They sympathized with me and said I was working too hard by swinging that ax and splitting the firewood. I certainly agreed with them.

Later, in my rodeo career, I discovered that you are not suppose to drink and ride — and that's no BULL.

38

Farmers' Trade Day

It happened every Tuesday. That was the day when all the farmers brought their commodities to Market Square to sell or trade.

In addition to selling and swapping, there was entertainment, contests, and excitement. But before we could take time for fun, we had to get rid of our hay, wood, eggs, or whatever we were selling. This is how I came to meet some of the most interesting characters in the county.

My job was to take the eggs over to the west side of the square to Wayne Nix, the blacksmith. He was the best farrier in town. He swapped his services, including shoeing our mules, for our eggs. He needed six raw eggs a day, because his doctor had told him he might have tuberculosis. When the doctor brought his saddle horse in for Wayne to shoe all four feet, they had cut a deal. It was an even swap.

Four shoes in exchange for the diagnosis, which was fatigue caused by T.B. Nix didn't like the diagnosis. He told his doctor he didn't have T.B., that his problem was from working too hard wrestling horses and mules to get them shod. The front feet were easy, he said, but the hind feet exhausted him. He charged two dollars for the two front feet and three dollars for the hind feet.

Next door to Wayne Nix's blacksmith shop was C.C. Summers's grocery store. It was a small "Mom and Pop" type store, except it was managed just by Pop. Mom had caught Pop taking a girl friend for a ride in his new 1927 Chevy and left him holding the bag. The Rev. Summers was a huge man about forty years old and almost bald. He was a sloppy dresser and never buttoned his shirt or laced up his shoes.

Summers was more than just a grocery man. He was a part-time preacher. He had a speech impediment. His name was C.C. Summers, but he pronounced it T. T. Tummers. When the audience laughed at his pronunciation, he wasn't bothered.

As an evangelist, he preached anywhere he could get an audience. When Summers got an urge to preach, he just got in his car and drove from "Titty to Titty" spreading the gospel. Pecan Gap and Honey Grove were his favorite places.

His biggest problem was money. The farmers wanted to pay him in sweet potatoes or peanuts, but he couldn't use peanuts for his car. He needed gasoline.

He took out his car and showed me his "take" from the night before. He got more peanuts than he could haul, so he just poured them into the car and returned the donors' buckets. When he opened the doors of the car, the peanuts spilled out on the ground. It was enough to make a preacher curse. He told me I should be a preacher when I got older.

By one o'clock, it was time for the medicine show to start on the square. Two guys peddled bottles of patent medicine and played guitars on the flat bed of a truck. After singing a few songs and gathering a crowd around the truck, they began selling. A large bottle of the concoction was one dollar. They claimed it would cure warts, belly aches, kidney disease, ingrown toenails—any ailment you might have.

In one hour, they would come back for another show. Besides guitar music, they also told jokes. I would listen and go home and tell the jokes to my Mother.

The "straight man" with the guitar said his folks were farmers and asked the other guy what his folks did.

"They are in the iron and steal business," he said.

"Iron and steel business?"

"Yeah! Ma irons all day and Pa steals all night."

At three o'clock was the main event of the day. The greased pig chase. According to the rules, the pig must weigh at least fifty pounds. He was greased with one quart of motor oil, and turned loose on Market Square. Everyone could participate. Whoever caught the pig had to bring him back to the wagon in his arms to pick up his prize.

I haven't been back in more than seventy years. I'll bet they are still chasing that greased pig.

39

Mother-in-Law Seat

Now it's 1928. That year the boll weevils ate the cotton crop. All we could do was hope for a better crop next year. A few farmers got out a bale or two. One day when all the hands were busy picking their damaged cotton, one of the farmers, Bill Jones, returned from town. He had just got his first bale and it was pretty good.

He could hardly wait to come into the field to tell us the news he'd just heard about a a new car called a Model-A Ford. Everybody stopped picking cotton, and stood spellbound, listening to all the features of the new Model-A. "It has four-wheel brakes," he said. "You can stop on a dime."

"Well, I'll be damned," one guy said. "What will they think of next?"

Listening to the guy tell about the new car with all the big changes from the old Model-T, you would swear he was a car salesman, not a cotton farmer.

"This car has a self-starter," he said. "You don't have to get out and crank. If the engine dies, just push a little button on the floorboard with your foot and it will start. It also has a gear shift. You can put it in low gear, high gear, or reverse, by just moving the stick around."

"Sure sounds good," another cotton picker spoke up. "But who could afford a car like that?"

"Cost just a little over five hundred dollars," Jones answered.

"That's about ten bales of cotton," Roy said, "and between the boll weevils and the bank, I'm broke and still owe the bank more money."

Jones said, "You know all them Model-A's aren't black? Now you can get 'em in brown, green, blue, and many other colors."

"I hear Chevrolet is coming out next year with a car that's not a touring car or a coupe, but it has a front seat and one behind called a rumble seat. It opens up, and there's no protection from the weather. You sit outside. They also call it 'the mother-in-law seat.'"

"A mother-in-law seat?" some wise guy named Buster spoke up. "Who in the Hell would want to take his mother-in-law on a trip?"

About four rows over, some elderly lady, obviously someone's mother-in-law, stood up, pulled off her bonnet and shouted, "Listen, Buster! I know you don't have a mother-in-law, and probably never will. You will never have enough money to buy a Model-A Ford, so go back to picking cotton."

40

Early Start

The stranger was standing beside the country road, and flagged down a local bus. He told the driver he was transferring from the Greyhound and asked if he had room for one more passenger.

He was dressed in fancy western wear, and was juggling several boxes in his arms when he found an empty seat in the middle of the bus. He took off his ten-gallon hat and laid it in the seat beside him and stacked his boxes in the aisle.

In an elated voice, he told the passengers he had been to Ft. Worth, shopping for his grandson. "Let me show you what I bought," he said. He began opening boxes and showing the duds. He had a big smile on his face as he held up a shirt.

Everyone in the front of the bus turned around to witness the scene. They were standing in the aisle and asking questions about the fashion show.

"How do you like those boots?" he said. "Wait till I show you his hat. When I was a kid, we didn't have any new clothes like these. I was thirteen when I got my first boots. All I ever got before was hand-me-downs. I made up my mind, this grandson is going to have the very best, even if I have to sell every cow I own. Now here are his spurs. I know he's going to be a cowhand just like his grandpa."

A little lady about three seats from the front of the bus asked, "How old is your grandson?"

"Oh! He ain't been born yet."

41

The Coon Hunt

In the 1920s, a major industry in the winter months was harvesting hides and furs. Shoes, leather pants, and jackets were made from animal skins. Mink coats and coonskin caps were in vogue. Many people in the part of Texas where I lived made part of their living by trapping and hunting opossums, skunks, rabbits—any fur-bearing animals. Mink and raccoon were the most expensive furs.

When I was big enough to tote a gun and learned how to shoot it, I persuaded my parents to let me go coon hunting with my brother. It was about time that I made some money, too.

Wilburn and I gathered up everything we needed for the hunt. "I will sharpen the axe. We may have to chop down a tree," I told my brother.

"You fill up the lantern with kerosene while I look for some extra shotgun shells," he said, adding, "We better take the .22 rifle too."

My mother gave her usual words of caution and told us not to stay out too late.

"We'll be home before midnight," I told her, as we stalked off through the woods, followed by our two coon hounds, eager to hunt.

Few stars were out when we started and, an hour later, the fog began to roll in. We knew the terrain well in the daytime, but at night, everything changed. The lantern began to dim. We turned the wick up, but it didn't help.

"Did you fill the lantern with kerosene?" I asked.

"I thought you filled it up." my brother said.

"No, I told you to fill it up!" I said.

"We better head for home before all the kerosene is burned."

"You're going the wrong direction, that's south." I said.

"No, it's north," he said.

The lantern blaze flickered, then went dark. The fog was so dense we couldn't see each other when we were only an arms length apart.

Dogs are nocturnal. They could run through the woods and brush trying to pick up the trail of a coon. They also kept track of us and never got far from us.

"How far away from home are we?" I asked Wilburn.

"Not more than two miles," he said.

The brush was too thick to maneuver through. We needed a machete to cut a path. We didn't have a machete, nor a compass, nor a watch, and no matches to start a fire. We reached the conclusion that we were lost. Furthermore, our coon hounds had deserted us.

We decided that the only thing to do was to sit down and wait till daylight. The ground was wet and cold. We passed the time by yelling and accusing each other of getting us into the mess.

As daylight approached, the fog begin to lift. I heard a rooster crow and smelled smoke from a chimney. I began to search around through the thick brush and felt a chicken wire mesh fence. As it got lighter, we discovered that the rooster was ours, it was our chimney smoking and the wire mesh was our garden fence. We had sat on the wet ground all night about a hundred feet from our house. The dogs hadn't deserted us, they were home in their warm beds.

"Now, what will we tell mother?" I asked.

"She'll never believe the truth. You better think of something that makes a little more sense."

We sneaked in the front door, and was confronted by Mother. "So you ran out of kerosene and your lantern went out!"

"Yeah, how did you know?"

"Because you were on the other side of the garden fence, about a hundred feet from my bedroom window, screaming and calling each other bad names. I think both of you were right. The bad names were exactly what I was thinking of you."

42

Playing the Game

Politics haven't changed much from the 1920s to the 1990s.

When men get together, they like to argue religion and politics — or both. They talk loud and fast and everybody talks at the same time, and nobody listens. None of them knows what he is talking about.

The word "Democrat" was seldom used by itself in the twenties. It was always "Damn Democrat." I kept looking through the dictionary until I found the word Democrat. It had no prefix. I read the definition carefully, then read the definition of "Republican." According to Webster's dictionary, the two were about the same.

I decided to do some more research on my own. We had no political speeches on radio then. There may have been a little campaigning on the airwaves, but very few families owned a set in the twenties so the politicians didn't try to dominate radio.

We subscribed to only one newspaper, a semi-weekly farm news. I gathered all the other papers I could find — the *Dallas Morning News*, the *Fort Worth Star Telegram*, and the *Cappers Weekly* — and read the editorials, the cartoons, and the commentary about our two candidates.

Herbert Hoover was a Republican from Iowa.

Al Smith was a Democrat from New York. He was also a Catholic. That stirred up a lot of controversy.

"But what's a 'Catholic'?" I did more research.

The big newspapers were endorsing the Republican, Herbert Hoover. Texas had never gone Republican. But he was the lesser of two evils, they said. If Al Smith was elected, the Pope of Rome would rule this country. The Catholics took orders from the Vatican. The President of the United States would be no exception.

Everybody was uneasy about the alternative.

I went back to the newspapers, books, and the Bible to try and find out the difference between a Protestant and a Catholic. The main difference I could find was the Catholics played Bingo.

One day I sat in on a hot debate at our house. About five or six adults were screaming at each other and talking at the same time.

I jumped into the discussion and asked, "Why are all of you against Al Smith?" Everybody stopped talking. They got real quiet and just looked at each other. Nobody seemed to have an answer.

After a long pause, one of the men spoke up and said, "You are too young to know anything about politics. Why don't you go out and play or go drive up the cows? It will be a long time before you are old enough to vote. You have plenty of time."

But someone else said, "Listen to the kid."

"How come you know so much?" one of them asked.

I explained that Al Smith was the underdog, just because he happened to be Catholic.

One man asked another man, "Why do you always vote Republican?"

His reply was, "Well, my Pa was a Republican, my Grandpa was a Republican, so I reckon that makes me a Republican."

"Well!" the other guy said, "I suppose if your Pa was a horse thief and your Grandpa was a horse thief, that would make you a horse thief too?"

"No," the other man said, "That would make me a Democrat."

When the rally broke up, three of the voters had jumped on the Al Smith bandwagon.

Herbert Hoover was elected President. We had four years of the worst depression in American history. Was Hoover responsible? He is still being blamed three generations later.

Everybody wondered if things would have been different if Al Smith were President. Maybe with the Pope in charge, we'd have avoided the Depression and everybody would have made money playing bingo.

43

Lighting Up Life

Nobody had electricity in our area. Everyone used kerosene lamps with glass chimneys that broke easily and always had to be cleaned. One winter day, a fast-talking lamp chimney salesman stopped by to visit Will Jetton who lived just across the hill from us.

Will wasn't very old, but he was nearly blind. He had a pipe in his mouth all day, and he smoked it in bed, for all I know. His doctor told him that smoking was constricting the minute blood vessels in his eyes, and if he didn't stop smoking, he would eventually go completely blind. But Will had been smoking too long to quit.

The lamp globe salesman knew of Will's condition, and figured he had a customer. "You need a better globe, one that won't break and will make the light brighter, and is easy to clean," he told Will.

The Jettons had three sons and they were a two-lamp family. With the boys in school and needing good light to study by, Will thought the new globes sounded good.

The salesman demonstrated how tough his lamp globes were. He threw one over the house and hurried Will around to the other side.

"I don't believe it," Will said, even when the salesman held it close to his eyes for a good view. So the salesman threw the globe over the house a second time. It still did not break.

"How much?" Will asked.

He nearly dropped his pipe when the salesman told him the price.

"Can't afford them," Will said. "I don't have that kind of money."

"That's too bad," the salesman said and began packing up to leave. But he paused, "We might make a trade. I take chickens and eggs, and you could give me your smoked-up globes for a trade-in."

Will thought about what he could trade. He had an old barnyard rooster with a bumble foot. The bird was too old to do anything but crow at sunrise, and lately he'd begun to sleep in and forget. Will thought he could "skunk" the salesman by unloading the old rooster in the deal.

"Couldn't let you have any chickens, but I have a pedigree rooster, if you want him along with a couple dozen eggs and my two old globes."

"No deal," the salesman said. "These are expensive globes. Should last you a lifetime. But, I'll tell you what. If you can throw in a peck of peanuts, I'll trade."

They made the deal, and Will could hardly wait until dark to try out the new lamp chimneys. But first, he wanted to show the boys as soon as they got home from school — tell them the wonderful deal he had made, and how he had "put one over" on the salesman.

When the boys came home, he told them about the trade and said he wanted to demonstrate how tough the new lifetime globes were. He said he would do exactly like the salesman had done, and throw one over the house.

The kids were skeptical. "Won't it break?" said the oldest.

"Just watch," said Will, and the kids took off around the house to be there when the unbreakable globe landed.

The chimney had broken into a thousand pieces. The salesman had thrown two of them over the house and neither broke.

"Go bring the other one," Will ordered. "It must have hit a rock or something."

He threw the second globe over. Again they all ran to see how it had fared. This one had broken into two thousand pieces.

"That's all right Pa," one of the boys consoled him. "We'll just use the old globes tonight."

"Can't," Will said. "Done traded the old globes in for the new unbreakable ones."

44

The Surrey "Snow Job"

In the early twenties, most families lived in rural areas. They were farmers and ranchers, and most transportation vehicles were wagons, buckboards, or, for the "well-off," a surrey or a hack.

The merchants in the city sent their salesmen, "drummers," to "drum up" business.

Cotton was the big money crop and most farmers borrowed money in advance of harvest with the promise to pay as soon as the first bale was picked.

When a drummer showed up at the Johnson house with a new model vehicle, pulled by a team of horses decked out in fancy harness, he explained to the Johnson family that he had gone to a lot of trouble to bring them the new "Spaulding Hack" to demonstrate and wanted to take them for a ride. He was a fast-talking salesman, the "Cal Worthington" of the day.

Of course, the family wanted the Spaulding. It was the "top of the line," the "Cadillac" of horse-drawn rigs. But Johnson said he wanted to wait a while until they saved more money.

As the drummer was about to leave, he asked about other farmers in the neighborhood. "How about Smith? Does he have a good crop this year? Does he usually pay his bills? Has the bank ever foreclosed on him?"

Johnson gave him enough answers to satisfy him, and he went on to the Smiths.

There he told the Smith family he had just left the Johnsons, and they had bought a new Spaulding Hack. There was no way to confirm this, as nobody had a telephone, and the ranches were several miles apart.

"Johnson said you can't afford to buy one now, but I wanted to show it to you anyway. Maybe you can afford it later."

"What's that you say?" said Mr. Smith.

"Well, he didn't actually say you couldn't afford to buy one. He just said he was the only one who could afford a beautiful Hack like this one."

"Martha, come out here!" Smith yelled. "You know what that S.O.B. Johnson said? He told this man he was the only one in the neighborhood who could afford to buy a Spaulding Hack."

"When will you be picking your first bale?" the drummer asked.

"In about two weeks," Smith said. "Will you take a bull yearling for the down payment?"

"Well, that's highly unusual, but maybe I can arrange the deal with my boss. Lets go ahead and fill out the contract. You may get your Spaulding Hack before Johnson gets his."

"Hot damn! Wouldn't that be something?"

"I'll tie the bull on behind. He will lead, won't he?"

"Sure, he'll lead. Give me that pen," said Smith. "Which line do I sign on?"

45

I've Been Stung

Man does not live by bread alone. He needs some honey for his bread. Consequently, he must have some bee hives. We had several on our farm. Like all other living creatures, bees need attention.

When I was about twelve years old, I was appointed, by my family, to take care of the bees. That meant I was an Apiarian. A book from the Department of Agriculture gave me all the information I needed about the care of bees. I didn't read that book to the bees, I knew they wouldn't understand it.

To protect my body from getting stung, I tied my pants legs at the ankles, and my shirt sleeves at the wrists. My special hat was made from a flower sack with a mosquito netting screen in front to let me see through.

Bees are like pets. They will not sting their master. They get used to the odor of all the family around them. If a stranger comes too near the hives, he might get stung.

Bees have their own "army," always on guard. The queen is guarded by all the bees. When bees swarm in the springtime, the new queen leaves the hive, and all the other bees follow. To get the swarm settled down, the beekeeper rings a bell, beats on a plow or some kind of metal object to make a noise. When the queen settles, all the other bees cover her for protection. She could light on a tree limb, or on the side of a building, or just about anywhere she wanted to. The average size of a swarm of bees is about the size of a gallon bucket.

This was when I tested my skill as an Apiarian. To control the bees, I used a smoker. They can't tolerate smoke. I had to transfer the swarm to their new home in a bee hive. We always washed the new hive out with salt water, and used green peach tree leaves, rolled up like a rag dipped in salt water to scrub the inside of the bee hives.

Every bee in the hive has his own specialty. The guard, the bee that gathers honey from the flowers, the water bee that carries water, and the drone bee. The drone is the male. He doesn't do anything. He doesn't make honey or carry water. He can't even sting. He is usually bigger and fatter than the working bee. He just loafs around the hive all day, and sponges off the other bees (I know some people like that).

Some farmers move the hives close to the nectar. Crops such as alfalfa, orange blossoms, or wild sage make delicious honey. Some hives, if they have a good year, can be "robbed" twice in one season.

The honey-gathering bees and the water bees will travel several miles to pick up their loads.

We had a neighbor bootlegger who lived nearby. He made whiskey and beer illegally. After the brew had fermented, he drained the liquid off, and dumped the residue out into the bushes outside his still. It consisted of cracked corn, sugar, and hops. The honey bees found the concoction and started to transport it back to the hives. They actually got drunk on the mash, and couldn't find their way back to the hives.

It was just as well that they couldn't find their way back to the hive. If they mixed alcohol with honey, we would have to sell it for medicinal purposes.

The warning label would read:

Holding's old fashion tincture of honey. Just add lemon juice for symptomatic relief of cough. Take as directed.

46

Booze in the Bee Hive

One bootlegger's name was Bennefield, but they called him "Dinglefinger." He used to go to the country dances and take orders for his whiskey. He always wore a loose-fitting jacket with inside pockets, so that he could carry several bottles. After he took orders at the dance, he would go home to get the bottles and return to deliver the whiskey and collect the money. He sold it for four bits (fifty cents) a pint.

My friend Duggan and I were too young to drink, and as minors, shouldn't even have been at the dance. But we decided to follow Dinglefinger, discover his stash, and just "borrow" a pint that we'd pay for when we grew up.

The night was foggy and visibility near zero. Dinglefinger knew the half-mile trail through the woods to his house better than we, but we managed to keep up without his detecting us.

A part of his property was surrounded by a high fence with barbed wire around the top. Inside the enclosure were about a dozen bee hives. We watched him go to a hive in the middle row and guessed that this was where he stashed his liquor. We waited quietly outside. It was so dark we couldn't see exactly which hive he used for storage, but we could see the bulges in his coat pockets when he passed near our hiding place on his way out, locking the "pen" behind him.

Impatient as we were, we didn't wait long enough before crawling over the fence. It took us a while to decide which hive he got the liquor out of. All looked alike, all painted white, and the hives were the only thing visible in the pitch black night.

We were about to raise the lid on a hive when we heard Dinglefinger coming back. We dropped the lid and ran for the far fence.

A patch of my overalls was left behind on the barbed wire as we scaled the fence, and my main souvenir from the adventure is a scar on my knee to remind me that, unless you're of age, you can't extract booze from a bee hive.

47

How's That?

Bob Wells could sell anybody anything. "A mark of a good salesman," he said, "is to be able to sell people something they don't need or don't want."

One day at a sales meeting, Bob was giving the other new salesmen tips. I was in the audience.

He told us, if you are going fishing, you go to a lake or stream that has fish in the water. If you are going to sell a product, you must go to a neighborhood that has money. It's a good idea to canvass the territory before you make a house call. If you are targeting the older or retired generation, go to the affluent section of the city, where the houses are bigger and older. If kids' toys are lying around, diapers on the clothes line, or tricycles in the driveway, this is the wrong house.

An ideal prospect is a widow. Maybe her husband has just passed on and left her with some life insurance money. She seldom leaves the home for anything and is always glad to see whoever will talk to her. Always wear your best suit and a big smile.

For example, he told us, after copying the name Maggie Clark from a mailbox, he went to the front door.

He had a new product that a lot of people needed but never talked about. When eyesight fails, people wear eyeglasses to see better, but when their hearing fails, they are reluctant to wear a hearing aid.

When he rang the doorbell, he heard Maggie remove latches, chains, and locks. He asked if he might come in. His lips were moving, but his voice wasn't audible.

Maggie leaned forward with hand cupped over her ear. "How's that?" she said.

By this time, Bob had slipped into the living room, and took a fancy little box from his pocket and removed two hearing aids. He continued to talk, but only in a whisper. He helped Maggie put both hearing aids into her ears, then he continued to talk but now with a strong clear voice.

Maggie couldn't believe her ears. She could hear every word Bob said. He explained to her that one of her friends wanted him to come demonstrate the hearing aids.

"What friend?" Maggie inquired.

"Oh no, she made me promise not to mention her name. She said you might be embarrassed, like a lot of people who don't know they have a hearing problem. She was just doing you a favor. I really didn't have time to come over, but I wanted to help you."

"How much do these cost?"

"Well, you are lucky. We have a special on this week. If you will give me the names of three of your friends who might need hearing aids, I'll let you have them for half-price. You can't beat that, can you? The factory price is going up first of next month."

"Oh, I don't know," Maggie said.

Bob removed the hearing aids from Maggie's ears and pretended to be disappointed that she did not accept his offer immediately. He went back to his mumbling. "Do you hear that train whistle?" he asked.

"What train whistle?"

"If you can't hear that train whistle, you really do need these hearing aids."

Maggie took the hearing aids from the salesman and put them in her ears. Bob turned up the volume on his own speech and once again it came out loud and clear.

Maggie bought the gadgets.

48

Transportation to Church

When I was about fifteen, all the guys my age had girlfriends. I had none. All the people came to church in wagons or on horseback. Very few owned cars. Some walked to church because they had no transportation of any kind. I was in that category.

Some walked their girlfriends home. It took a little longer, but was more fun. Some of the girls wouldn't walk if they could ride. They were spoiled. It was apparent that guys who had transportation got the girls.

One guy, a little older than I, owned a 1923 Hupmobile. He parked under a tree at home and the chickens used it for their roost. It always had a flat tire, and he could get only seven miles to the gallon on gasoline. When he could afford to buy gas, he would ride to church in his car. Other times he would walk.

A big girl named Tonya — some called her "Two-Ton Tony" — often rode home after church with Roy in his Hupmobile. If he didn't come in his car, he didn't bother to walk her home. It seemed that Tony wasn't too interested in the guys, but was more concerned about what kind of transportation they had.

I got an idea. Since the guy couldn't afford to buy gasoline for his car, it would be ideal for me to take over Tony. But I didn't have transportation either. I got another idea. We had a neighbor named Roy, who owned a mule that was old and rather thin. His ribs showed through his sides, and he was swaybacked.

I approached the neighbor diplomatically, and asked if I could borrow his mule for one night, to take my girlfriend to church, or rather, take her home from church.

"Absolutely not!" was his answer. "Nobody rides that mule except me."

Knowing that he was a little on the lazy side, I made him an offer he couldn't refuse. If he would let me borrow his mule for one night, I would cut him a rick of wood — that's one-third of a cord.

He scratched his head and thought for a minute, and said, "You cut the wood first, and I'll make a deal with you. You'll have to return the mule to the barn by ten o'clock. I'll pick up the wood before you leave."

"Okay," I said, "but that gives me only half a day to cut a rick of wood."

"Take it or leave it," he said. "Do you want the mule or don't you?"

It was a hot steamy July afternoon, not a leaf moving. I had a one-man saw, axe, and a gallon of water. The water lasted about two hours, but I couldn't stop to get more, because the sun was getting low and the thunderheads were gathering. If it rained, and the church services were canceled, would he give me a rain check on the mule?

I was lucky, it didn't rain, but it had been raining the day before, and the roads were muddy. By sundown, I had the rick of wood ready to deliver. I rushed home and took off my clothes. Everything was wet with perspiration. I put on my white pants, white shoes, white shirt, and white cap. That was the "in" thing.

When I went over to rent the mule, Roy was waiting for me. I had to listen to a lecture from him.

"Don't overload the mule. He may have to stop and rest occasionally. He is scared of cars. Be gentle with him and have him home by ten o'clock." (I was glad he couldn't check the mileage like Hertz or Avis.)

I lucked out. The guy with the Hupmobile was still out of gas. He was on foot. When church was over and they took up a collection, it was time to go home. This was my big chance, but how was I going to handle it? I couldn't wait till Tony was by herself to go ask her if she wanted a ride home. If I waited too long, she would be gone with someone else. This was harder to do than cutting the rick of wood. Finally, I just went right up to her and popped the question.

"Sure," was her answer.

What a relief — and it was so easy. I had been agonizing all day about that moment.

"First, I have to ask my Mother," she said. Her mother was very small compared to her daughter.

Actually, Tony was bigger than both of us put together.

Her mother came over with a kerosene lantern in her hand. She didn't look too happy. "How old are you?" she asked.

I lowered my voice way down into my larynx and added one year to my real age.

She looked as if she didn't believe me, but that wasn't too unusual. Next, she told the other kids to go to the wagon, that she would be there in a few minutes. She continued to thoroughly check me out. She didn't ask me to turn around, she just went around me with the lantern in front of her, looking at my feet, then all the way up to my head. "Where is your horse?" she asked.

"Right over there, tied to the tree," I showed her.

"That ain't no horse, that's a mule," she said.

"Well! About the same as a horse," I explained.

She walked around on the other side of the mule with the lantern, and asked, "Where is the saddle?"

"Well, I don't have a real saddle," I told her. "But this tow sack is stuffed with Bermuda grass hay, and it rides softer than any saddle."

"What tow sack?" she demanded.

"Right here on the ground," I said. "It just fell off."

Whoops! I saw that the mule had gotten hungry. He had ripped the tow sack apart with his teeth and had eaten most of the hay. The sack was a little muddy, but I assured Tony's mother that the mule's back was curved in a rocking chair shape, and her daughter wouldn't need a saddle.

"How is she going to get on without a stirrup to put her foot in?" she asked.

"No problem," I assured her. "I'll give her a hand — or a foot — and she can jump right on."

Tony was wearing a nice long skirt with a lot of frills and starched to make it stand out. Girls didn't wear pants then and sidesaddles had gone out of style. She had never been on a horse before, she told me.

I told Tony to jump on the mule and her mother and I would give her a boost by pushing her feet.

We shoved too hard, and she went all the way over the mule and landed on the ground. It was a good thing she was fat — I mean obese — or she might have broken something. We tried again, this time she made it. The mule's knees almost buckled under all that weight.

Her mother asked, "Where are you going to sit?"

"Oh, I'll just walk and lead the mule," I told her. "I need the exercise."

Her mother went to the wagon with the rest of her family. The last words from her were: "You kids go straight home now, you heah?"

As we got out to the road, we saw two or three horsemen coming up behind us. They apparently had been showing their dates around the countryside. They galloped up behind us with their girls riding in the new saddles, and the guys sitting with their arms around the girls' waists. I tried to stoop down behind the mule, so I wouldn't be recognized. But they splattered red clay on my white pants and on Tony's white dress as they loped by.

One smart guy yelled out, "Hey Tony, why don't you get off that mule and carry him a while?"

A little farther down the road, a Model-T Ford was coming up behind us with about ten people hanging out the side and riding on the running board of the car. I remembered what Roy had told me about his mule being scared of cars. He might even buck the rider off. The narrow country road had deep ruts. I had to lead the mule out of the middle of the road to let the car pass. As they went by, all the kids were screaming and laughing. The mule's load was too heavy to buck off, and he could barely stand under the heavy weight.

We reached the forks in the road. Tony lived down one road and the mule lived down the other. The mule wanted to go to his barn, and we wanted to go to Tony's home. I had to be more stubborn than a mule to convince him he couldn't go home yet.

When we got to Tony's house, her mother was waiting on the front porch. "What kept you?" she asked her daughter.

We explained everything, I think. Her mother still gave me a "go to Hell look," as I rode off down the lane. The mule was so happy to be rid of his heavy load, and to be headed toward home, he galloped all the way to the barn.

Who do you think was waiting for me when I returned the mule? That's right. And he was mad, too.

"What kept you? Do you know what time it is? Where is my grass saddle?"

I started to explain, but Roy cut me off.

"Which girl did you have on this mule tonight?" He ran his hand down the mule's flank. "He's wet with sweat!"

"A girl named Tony," I answered.

"Tony! You mean Two-Ton-Tony?" He went into a rage. "Do you know how much she weighs?"

Before I could answer, he yelled. "At least two hundred pounds. And you! At least one hundred pounds. That's too much weight for one mule."

"Oh, I didn't ride, I walked and led him."

"Yeah! Yeah! A likely story," he shouted, as he patted the mule and talked baby talk into his ear.

"Listen boy," he said, turning to me. "You ain't getting this mule no more, you heah? Besides, you are too young to be chasing after the girls."

I only had one mile left to walk home through the woods. When I got there, you know who was waiting for me? Right again. My mother wasn't too happy either.

"Do you know what time it is?" she said.

I looked at my Big Ben watch, quarter past eleven.

I went to bed and thought things over. I wasn't going out with any more girls until I could furnish my own transportation. I thought, when I grow up, if I live that long, I'm going to buy be a brand new Cadillac and get me the most beautiful girl in the whole wide world, and I did.

49

My First Blind Date

When I was much younger, I got a lot of "friendly advice" about which girls I should and shouldn't date. I was never told about the birds and the bees, but my mother had a way of controlling me indirectly by talking to other people in my presence, or "semi-presence." She wanted me to hear the conversation, but pretended she didn't know I was listening. She gave me such a high reputation that I couldn't afford not to live up to it. She even had me believing it.

We had a neighbor named Elsie, who was a few years older than I. She was the type of girl who smoked cigarettes and drank homebrew, the kind of girl the mothers in the neighborhood called "fast." She already had a boyfriend — in fact, she had several boyfriends — and I wasn't one of them.

She thought I was too young to be dating. However, she did have a friend who would like to meet me. When I asked questions about the girl, I never got straight answers.

"How old is she?" I asked.

"Oh, I don't know exactly, she might be a little older than you, but you will like her, I'm sure."

"Well, how tall is she?"

"I really don't know, but you will like her, just wait till you meet her," Elsie assured me.

"Is she slim or heavy?"

"She is sort of full-figured."

"What's her name?"

"Her name is Hattie, and she saw you somewhere, and she really likes you. She is a lot of fun, especially after she's had a few drinks."

That should have raised a red flag. I think Elsie was trying to get rid of me.

"Anyway," Elsie said, "I've already made a date for you for tomorrow night at eight o'clock. She will be expecting you."

She made it sound like a draft notice or a subpoena — an order that you don't ignore.

I was always taught that you are supposed to listen and obey any order that comes down from anyone who is older or superior in any way. Elsie was a few years older than I, and I was inferior to her in the "pecking" order.

I was ambivalent about the "order" from Elsie, but I didn't want to disappoint anyone, so I decided to go. I had only one day to get ready. The first thing I did was take my new suit and have it pressed. Then I had to wash, starch and iron my shirt. I bought a can of shoe polish and shined my shoes until I could have used them for a mirror to shave by. I bought a new bottle of hair oil — the very best. That set me back another twenty-nine cents.

I didn't sleep much the night before the big event. I was anxious and curious. At eight o'clock on that hot steamy August night, I arrived at Hattie's house. It was small with weeds growing all around it. I had to wait a few minutes in the dusk until exactly eight. I took a deep breath and knocked on the door. The first thing I heard was a dog. The whole house shook and I thought the door would break open any minute. I heard the rattle of chains being taken off the door and a voice said, "Now you be quiet, Baby."

I've always been scared to death of dogs. I'd been bitten twice by rabid dogs and had to take the Pasteur shots in the belly one time.

When Hattie finally got the door open, the first thing I saw was the most vicious dog I'd ever seen. He must have been a combination of a Pit Bull and a Doberman. He was black with mean eyes that shone like diamonds, and a mouthful of teeth that he bared when he looked at me.

When I looked up at Hattie, I realized why Elsie was hesitant to give me a description of her. She was obviously much older than I. Elsie did tell me she was full figured, but if I had to describe her, I would have used a three-letter f-word, instead of "full figured." She was heavy enough to play tackle for the Green Bay Packers. Her hair was straight. She was slovenly dressed and a front tooth was missing. Other than that, she looked pretty good to me at the time.

She said, "Elsie told me all about you, but I didn't think you would come." She pointed to the couch and said, "Sit down." Then she went into the kitchen.

I sat down on the end of the short divan or loveseat — WOW — a broken spring. I moved a little to the left and toward the middle of the seat.

Hattie returned from the kitchen, with a six-pack of beer in her hand. Baby followed her. She said, "Elsie told me you don't drink, so I won't offer you a beer." She plopped down on the other end of the loveseat, and the dog jumped up on the couch between us. I was forced to move back to my end of the couch, and sit on that broken spring that gouged my *gluteus maximus*. I asked Hattie if we could possibly get the dog off the couch.

"Baby," she said, "Why don't you get off the couch?" Baby growled, showed his teeth, and stayed on the couch.

A little while later, I tried again to have the dog removed. Every time I said "dog," he growled and stayed put. I don't think he liked being called a "dog."

Hattie said, "Yeah, he's the boss around here." She opened a bottle of beer and began what would become a four-hour monologue. She rambled on and on, not making much sense. After about two hours had passed, I jumped right in with a witty question. "What's your sign?" But the dog growled me out, and she kept talking.

A small light bulb hung from the ceiling on a cord, and in the corner of the room, a double-barreled shotgun leaned against the wall. No other furniture was in the room.

With no fan and the windows closed, it must have been ninety degrees. My hair oil was running down into my ears and the perspiration had soaked through my coat. The dog had his rear end toward Hattie and the saliva dripped off the end of his tongue onto my left knee and thigh. I could feel his hot breath in my left ear. It smelled like something he dug up from the backyard and eaten it. He needed Scope.

I could look to the right at a blank wall, or I could look straight ahead at a blank wall. If I looked to the left, toward Hattie, I looked down the dog's throat. When I looked straight ahead and rolled my eyeballs to the left, if my "eyeballs clicked," the dog growled. When I managed to sneak a peek, I saw Hattie's bare feet flat on the slab floor bordering the six-pack, which was slowly emptying.

Hattie told me, among other things, that she was married once, but her husband was no damn good and she had to get rid of him. I didn't dare ask how she had to get rid of him. She told me the kind of wedding she wanted for her next marriage. I don't know why she was telling me all about her personal life. I tried to keep count of the bottles of beer she had drunk and wondered when she would have to go to the bathroom. She never did.

About midnight, I got up enough courage to say, I think it's time for me to go home.

"Do you have to go now?" she asked.

"I have to get up early tomorrow for Sunday School," I said.

"Tomorrow is Saturday," she told me.

She was right! When I finally managed to get on my feet to leave, I could see why Hattie didn't have to go to the bathroom after drinking six bottles of beer. It had come out through the pores of her skin. Her clothes were wet and her straight hair was dripping.

I hadn't seen her face for four hours, but she belched, and looked down at me. "What did you say your name was?"

I knew I had made a big hit with her — a lasting impression. As I maneuvered toward the door, the dog was still between us, but he must have been happy, because he was wagging his tail. I, too, was happy to be leaving. So, while the dog wagged his tail, I was wagging my tail right out the front door into the dark steamy night. I felt like a bird just released from a cage. I wanted to fly.

The next day, at work, I wanted to tell the other guys about a "hot date" I had last night, but I didn't dare.

A few weeks later, I overheard a conversation about Hattie and learned that she did, indeed, shoot her husband, and spent time in prison and later in a mental institution. Whether she killed him or not, I never found out. I was afraid to ask any questions. And I certainly didn't mention anything about my date to Elsie. I was afraid she'd set me up with another one of her friends.

50

The Hobo Life

During the Great Depression of the thirties, a lot of people were hungry. One day I decided to visit a hobo camp to see how their lifestyle compared with ours.

I was a young teenager and very curious. I met Hobo Joe at the camp. He was very friendly and loquacious. He invited me to sit down on a dead log, but he stood and talked. He told me how they would steal rides on a freight train when they traveled. They even had hobo conventions every year. They swapped ideas and told jokes. He asked me if I wanted to join them on the next trip on a freight train. He made it sound so interesting, I almost joined them.

Joe said he knew he had a mother, but he wasn't too sure about his father. He was sure he didn't have a birth certificate, nor did he have an address or a telephone number. He didn't pay any union dues. As Joe put it, "I don't owe nobody nothin'."

He taught me how to wash clothes in the branch, and how to wrap a garment around a small sapling and twist both ends until most of the water was out, then hang the garment on the limb of the tree in the sun until it dried.

Joe explained the difference between a hobo, tramp, and bum. According to Joe, the hobo was the elite, the most sophisticated and smartest of the transients. They were more independent. The tramp begged for handouts or stole. The bum was at the bottom. He raided garbage cans for food and picked up cigar butts. "They are shiftless. They don't take baths, or wash their clothes, and most are winos."

Joe said it was easy to get all the food they needed off the land.

There was wild game in the woods, fish in the streams, and plenty of native pecan trees, black walnuts, and wild persimmons. He showed me how they cooked their food in an old discarded oil drum. Their cooking utensils consisted of cans and buckets they had scrounged from the town dump. Joe boiled eggs and made coffee in the same bucket, both at the same time.

Joe had no formal education, but he was "woods smart." He kept up on what was happening in the world by retrieving discarded newspapers and magazines from trash cans, reading them before converting them into mattresses and covers.

The best thing I learned from Joe was his recipe for Hobo Rock Stew. He described it in every detail. As I sat in the shade of a red oak tree beside the stream, he stepped to the edge of the water and returned with a white rock.

"First," he said, "you pick up a smooth white rock, about the size of a hen's egg, or maybe as large as a baseball." He held the rock, caressing it with his thumb as he turned it over and over.

"It develops its best flavor on a cold rainy day when farmers are home trying to stay warm and dry. You go out looking for a farm house that has cows, hogs, and maybe a garden. Knock on the door, tip your hat when the lady of the house comes to the door, and ask if she can lend you a pot to boil up a rock stew." He turned and patted my knee. "She might slam the door in your face and leave you standing in the rain. But don't be discouraged. Keep going. Pretty soon, you'll find a family that wants to learn how to make the stew. Show them the rock."

He held the rock toward me, displaying its round shape and smoothness. "It has to be a special rock. You tell them you'll show them how to make your own special Hobo Rock Stew."

Holding the rock in front of him, Joe pantomined dropping the rock into the pot. "The stew can be cooked on the wood cook stove or the fireplace."

Most fireplaces, in the country then, had a pot rack inside. People saved fuel by heating the room and cooking at the same time.

"Once the water starts to boil," Joe says, "ask if they have salt to put in the water. Next ask if there's some meat of any kind, a soup bone, or leftover steak to make it taste better. After the meat boils a while, ask if there are any potatoes or carrots the family can spare. Maybe some onions or a little garlic, or some catsup and chili powder for color."

By now Joe is stirring with an imaginary spoon, and I can almost smell the aroma of that stew. He raises the spoon to his lips. "Needs a little more pepper, you might say," he tells me, winking.

"By this time each of the kids is holding up a bowl, waiting to sample the rock stew. It smells so good. You take the pot from the fireplace and use two long spoons to remove the rock. Everybody tastes the stew and says it's delicious. They bring a big bowl for you, and you explain how the rock gives the stew a special flavor by holding the heat and making all the ingredients cook faster."

Joe dropped the rock into my hand. "You always leave the rock with the family for future use. They buy it every time," he grinned down at me.

Joe stood and stretched. "And don't forget, if it's still raining, you can hint it would be nice if you could sleep in their barn for just one night. It's so wet and cold sleeping on the ground back at the Hobo Camp. Never been turned down yet," he said.

Now, I make Hobo Rock Stew myself. I stole Joe's recipe.

51

Just Fiddling' Around

In the heart of the Depression of the 1930s, we all tried to make a little money any way we could. I lived with my parents out in the Texas boondocks, on a farm, surrounded by woods and streams. It was common understanding in east Texas that if you couldn't ride a bull or play a fiddle by the time you were in your teens, you didn't amount to much.

I cut wood for my Uncle Jess to buy my first fiddle. I learned to play by listening to the other fiddlers. I couldn't practice around my family, especially my brother. He said when I pulled the fiddle bow across the strings, it sounded like two cats fighting. So I went down the hill to the wash bench under the trees to practice. Mosquitoes were thick there, and with one hand on the neck of the fiddle and the other on the bow, I didn't have a free hand to swat them. A few drops of kerosene smoothed on my face cured that.

I'd attended a lot of country dances, going mostly to watch and listen, memorizing the tunes I practiced later at home "for the mosquitoes." With no movies, radio, or television, dances were about the only entertainment we had.

Finally, I decided I was good enough to play for a dance. Along with Mutt Keay on the banjo and Leon Cato on guitar, we made up a band, and on a Saturday night in 1931, we set off to play our first "gig."

Square dancing was the style of the day, and farmers with big houses were in the "dance business." It was a way to make a little extra money. The owner — the House Man — arranged for the band, invited everybody, and cleared two adjacent rooms. We had no amplification, of course, so the band and the caller stood in the archway between two rooms to make sure all the dancers could hear.

The House Man collected the money. He charged "a dime on the corner." Only the men paid, a dime for each set. In order to make any money, the House Man had to be sure everybody got a chance to dance. He kept half of the take and the musicians got the other half. Of course, we three musicians had to split our half three ways. The square dance caller was usually paid by the house. Sometimes there were two callers, so that if one got hoarse, the other could take over.

Musicians didn't have the luxury of replacements. There was no musician's union or ASCAP. We couldn't even take a short break, because two "squares" of dancers were always on the sidelines, waiting for the others to finish. In order to give the dancers their money's worth, he would just keep calling — there didn't seem to be an end to the set.

After we played for about two hours without a break, Leon Cato got mad and left. He said he wouldn't ruin his fingers by picking the guitar all night without a break.

That left Mutt Keay and myself. Now we could split the money two ways, instead of three. The man who owned the house was collecting the money and dividing it up at the beginning of each set. When he came around to pay us, the Guitar Man was gone. "What happened?" he asked.

We told him that his fingers got sore, and they wouldn't give him even a short intermission, so he got mad and left.

"That's too damn bad," he told us, "Now you two will have to play harder, since you lost the Guitar Man. We have to make some money while the crowd is here."

On the next set, I broke an E string on my fiddle. I went into the kitchen and put on the spare string that I always carried. When you tune up a musical instrument in a cold room and return to a warm room, you are out of tune. They always had a big fire going in the fireplace, so we re-tuned and kept right on playing, and the House Man came over and said, "Make that fiddle talk, boy!" then he turned to the man with the banjo and said, "Tromp on that thing!"

He brought a fruit jar of whiskey and poured me a drink in a tin cup. Tears came to my eyes and my hair stood up on my head.

When I told him I broke my last E string and was playing on three strings instead of four, he said, "Keep playing, they will never know the difference."

He was right, they didn't know the difference whether I was playing on four strings or three strings. They were drinking from the same fruit jar. This was the era of prohibition. They made the "rot gut whiskey," also known as "white lightning."

There was a bootlegger who made all the country dances, selling his brew for fifty cents a pint. The dance usually lasted until everybody went broke. If you danced, you had to pay the fiddler. And if you drank, you had to pay the bootlegger. Most of them were broke by one o'clock in the morning.

When the dance was finally over, we counted our money and divided it. We had made almost three dollars apiece. We forgot about the Depression until the money was spent.

The next week, we were invited back to the same house to play for their dance. They were a little too late as we had already agreed to play for another dance further down in the Red River Valley. They had asked us to play because they had a larger house, and more people could dance at one time — and we could make more money.

My partner had an "ancient Hudson automobile." He could only get seven miles to the gallon of gasoline on the muddy roads. Gasoline was about fifteen cents a gallon then.

When we arrived at the house where the dance was going to be, it started to pour rain, with a little hail and wind mixed in.

There was a huge crowd waiting to dance. The caller was already there and so was the bootlegger. They were just waiting for the musicians to arrive.

There appeared to be too many people for the space available for dancing. Some of them waited in the barn for their turn to dance. It was like a semi-barn dance.

In the meantime, the rain continued to fall outside. We were concerned that the creek would get out of the banks and we wouldn't be able to get home after the dance was over.

The host assured the musicians, if the creek got out of the banks and we couldn't cross the creek to get back home, we could stay all night with them. So don't worry, just keep playing. This prompted a square dance song. It went something like this:

> *Stay all night, stay a little*
> longer, pull off your boots,
> throw 'em in the corner. The
> Big Creek's up, you can't get
> over. Don't see why you don't
> *stay a little longer.*

If we weren't the composers of that song, it certainly was apropos at the time. Square dancing is just as popular and as much fun today, as it was in the 1930s.

52

"Love" for Guiness

Ed's girlfriend, Shirley, advised him that they were getting married in June. This date was also confirmed by Shirley's mother. Ed hadn't given his consent, but was aware of the "shotgun" weddings of the era.

The wedding invitations were sent out to everybody in the neighborhood, and Shirley's gown was made by one of the leading seamstresses in the country. It was beautiful, with buttons and bows and a lot of starch.

Shirley's mother handled arrangements for the affair, including the reception at the Community Church. The preacher had promised to be there at two o'clock. Everybody else had arrived, except Ed, the groom.

When the best man went to investigate, he found Ed shooting dice with his friends. He was on a winning streak and couldn't leave.

He sent word to Shirley's mother to just go ahead with the wedding without him, he would be there later. Ed and the minister arrived at the church the same time.

A sixteen-gallon keg of beer was sitting on a platform beside the church house. A bootlegger was present with a supply of "white lightning" liquor. The groom had a bottle in his hand.

The minister was furious. He refused to marry the couple. He gave a short lecture on the evils of alcohol, and advised the crowd not to use the church house for a saloon.

Ed walked up to the preacher, bottle in hand, and explained that the custom in his family was to have plenty of liquor on hand at weddings and funerals. "Going to a wedding without liquor," Ed said, "is like going to a funeral without a corpse."

The preacher wasn't impressed. He mounted his horse, Bible under his arm, and rode off, leaving the couple at the alter — unmarried.

Shirley's mother sent for the Justice of the Peace. While they were waiting, Ed suggested that the waiting crowd should eat now, before the storm hit. The black cloud, with a green and white lining beneath it, suggested hail and wind.

Shirley's mother agreed, saying that rain would ruin the wedding dress.

When the Justice of the Peace arrived in his new Essex, everyone set aside their plates of chocolate cake, and went inside for the ceremony.

The wedding party were formally dressed, but Ed wore his "Payday" bib overalls. One suspender was over his shoulder, and one hung down under his arm.

When the newly married couple left the church, the bride wanted to go with him to her mother's house where they would live.

He said, "I can't stand your mother and you know that. You will come home with me. I'm your husband now, and you will do as I tell you."

"Oh no, I won't! I promised Mother I would never leave her, even if I got married. Anyway, I can't stand your dogs."

"My dogs are not half as bad as your mother," Ed shouted back.

"You can't talk about my mother like that."

"You can't talk about my coon hounds like that either. Besides, I'm catching a freight train out of here tomorrow for California, and I won't be coming back."

"That's fine with me. Just forget that we were ever married. I never want to see you again."

"That's exactly how I feel. Good-bye!" Ed walked off in one direction and Shirley went in the opposite direction.

The marriage lasted exactly twenty minutes.

53

Bryan McKay

Bryan McKay was forced to become a farmer on short notice. He lived in the city with his wife and three small children, and had been a "professional student" for most of his life. He had a Ph.D. in history, and had been teaching only one year when the Depression started in the early thirties. The school funds had dried up and there was a plethora of school teachers and a limited number of positions to fill.

Bryan was an only child and his parents had passed on. He also had a physical handicap. When he was small, he had polio, known then as infantile paralysis. His legs had atrophied, but he could walk up on his toes, with a limp. He was physically unable to do a hard day's work on the farm. He didn't want to leave the city, but his wife insisted they move to the farm where they could raise their own food. She won the argument.

Bryan started in January looking for a place in the country to move his family. His rented house in the city was bought at a tax sale by another family who wanted to move in immediately. He received a notice from his former landlord that his house had been sold and he must move within thirty days.

Snow was still on the ground, and Bryan had no transportation to go shopping for a new place to live in the country. He finally found a farmer who was willing to take him in, and furnish a house and barn. However, business is business, and it is customary that you furnish your own tools and livestock before you can qualify to rent the back forty.

"Where can I buy some mules and cotton seed, and all the other stuff that a farmer needs to get started?" Bryan asked.

"Try the banks," he was told. There were a few still in business, but most of them had been forced to close. ("The banks were busted" was a common phrase.)

He went to the bank to negotiate a deal, and ran head-on into another problem.

The banker's first question was, "Before we can even talk to you about a loan, we have to see a rental agreement signed by you and your landlord, stipulating that you have rented farmland, and that you have agreed in writing to plant a certain number of acres in cotton, and that you will start to repay the bank when you pick your first bale in the fall and . . ."

Bryan interrupted, "I can't rent the land until I can show that I have borrowed sufficient funds to buy all the necessary things I need to farm."

The banker shrugged his shoulders and walked away saying, "It's rough all over."

Now it's March and Bryan is getting desperate. He had no provisions. He needs a "grub stake." In the city he was accustomed to elegant "cuisine." In the country he needed "grub" for his family.

He was advised by a good neighbor to go see the local merchant. The owner of the country store had furnished groceries for some of the farmers until they got on their feet.

When Bryan approached the store owner, he was asked the same questions the banker had asked: "How many acres do you have in cultivation and how many head of cattle and mules do you own?"

"None!" Bryan said. "Looks like I have to prove I don't need the money before I can borrow some."

He was advised by the merchant that his store had to operate a little different in the cotton country than in the coal mining country. The coal miners had to shop at the company store. The company let them work just enough to pay their bills and buy the groceries. If you didn't pay them, you *owed your soul to the Company Store.*

It was a little different in cotton country. You mortgaged all your assets, and signed a note that you would start paying your bills when you got out the first bale. If you didn't — you "owed your soul to the Country Store."

Now it's April. The crops should have been planted in March. The only way Bryan could get a loan was to have his landlord sign the note with him. He couldn't find anyone who was willing to take a chance on him. Finally, he came to see my dad. Dad said he'd never sign another note, because he had been stuck with one that he had had to pay off when the tenant took off and left Dad "holding the bag."

My dad felt sorry for Bryan and decided to take another chance and sign the note. The next time Dad and Bryan went to the bank, they got the loan. The banker would loan only one hundred and fifty dollars.

With that, Bryan purchased a team of mules, their feed, seed for the crop, and groceries until the crop was harvested.

We went back to the field and started to work our own crop. The spring rains had started, accompanied by a few tornadoes and hail storms.

One day, about a week later, it was too wet to plow, and I went squirrel hunting. As I cut across the field, I saw Bryan trying to plow his land. It was a pitiful sight. I stood and watched for a while.

As soon as the bank issued him his one hundred fifty dollars for the year, he went straight to the horse trader to buy a team of mules. The mules were all sold out. However, he just happened to have two good horses, just what you need to pull that plow, he was told.

One of the horses was a saddle horse, the other was a show horse. They both had been retired and condemned. The saddle horse could do a fox trot, a pace, or single foot. The show horse was used in the circus to do tricks. When the reins were tightened up, he would stand up on his hind legs and do a little dance. That's all he knew. The saddle horse wouldn't walk. He wanted to trot and pull the plow. Bryan, with his crippled legs, couldn't keep up with the horses. They were practically dragging him.

The ground was too wet to plow anyway, but Bryan was anxious to get going. The temperature was about ninety degrees and the relative humidity about ninety-five. Both horses had shrunk when they were hitched to the plow. The gun powder they had been fed with the salted wheat bran at the livery stable was wearing off. The horses needed to drink a lot of water. They had the appearance of balloons that had been punctured with a needle and developed a slow leak. They had never been hitched up as a team of horses before. He had the collars on upside down.

I couldn't stand it any longer, and crossed the field to where he and the horses were. I mentioned the upside-down collar.

He said, "No wonder I couldn't get the other things to fit." I knew that the other things are called "hames."

He asked me all kinds of questions about the horses, and how to handle them. I showed him how to put the plow lines around his waist and not around his neck. When you want the horses to go to the right, you holler GEE. When you want them to go left, you holler HAW. But forget that, they haven't been trained for those commands.

He wanted me to show him how to keep the plow in the ground. The weeds were already about knee high, and it was May. I didn't want to discourage him, but I asked if he intended to plant any truck crop? "That's what you moved to the farm for wasn't it?" I said.

"I know. I want to plant something like potatoes and beans that we can eat." Will you show me how to plant a garden?"

For the first time, someone was asking me how to do something, instead of telling me what to do.

"You look pretty young to have studied farming," he asked.

"I didn't go to college. I learned farming the hard way, right here on the farm, not out of a book."

I was a young teenager then, and had been working in the fields from sunup to sundown since I was ten years old. There was no such thing as a child labor law then. All the kids who lived on farms had to work.

When I got home from my hunting trip, I went to our garden and picked some green beans, onion, and potatoes. I put them in a tow sack. I also took the McKay family one of my squirrels. I never told my parents or asked if I could do that — I just did it.

54

The New Deal

In 1934, our new President, Franklin Delano Roosevelt, had a brainstorm. He organized the National Recovery Act, N.R.A. The act provided, among other things, that our government would pay the farmers to plow up their cotton and kill their cattle.

His rationale was to give the farmers a break, to put some money in their pockets.

There was a drought that year. Poor feed crops and the shortage of water made it difficult for the farmer and rancher to survive.

It wasn't compulsory that everybody had to take advantage of the N.R.A. But, if you wanted to get rid of the surplus pigs and cattle, the Federal Government would pay you one cent a pound for the livestock, and seven dollars an acre for the cotton.

The Department of Agriculture was in charge of hiring the personnel to come to the fields, measure the patch of cotton to be plowed under, then come back in one week to make sure the farmer had complied with the law, and give him a voucher for his money.

It was a sad day for the farmer who had worked all year to raise the cotton. Just when it was ready to pick, he had to plow it under. It was even harder to round up the cattle to have them shot.

The law stipulated that the cattle owner had to list all the animals he wanted killed, then notify the proper authorities. They would set a date when they could come. Their job was to kill the animals with a high-powered rifle and let the farmer dispose of the carcasses anyway he chose.

Our neighbor, Mr. Penigar, was a very sensitive man. When they came to kill his cattle, he handed the filled-out card to the man in charge of the massacre, stipulating the number of cattle he wanted killed. When they stood on the rail fence and started to slaughter the cattle, it was more than Mr. Penigar could take. He begged them not to kill his last milk cow.

They looked at his card and said, "We have to kill every animal you have listed," and they did.

Penigar said that cow had furnished milk for all his kids as they were growing up. It made him sick.

The next year, and for several years afterward, the federal government paid the farmers not to raise hogs, cattle, cotton, or corn. They called it the Corn-Hog Reduction Program.

More than a half century has passed, and some of the old farmers are still complaining about having to sell a seven hundred pound steer for seven dollars. That's less than a T-bone steak would cost today.

We have elected ten presidents since the Depression days and the New Deal of F.D.R. in the 1930s. Some are still smarting and blaming the "Damn Democrats."

55

Who Killed the Indian?

It was early summer of 1926 when the Sheriff of Choctaw County, Oklahoma, received an anonymous call.

"An Indian is missing."

So what! There's plenty more.

But the missing man was Tubbs, a prominent Choctaw Indian, who owned the farm in the bend of the Red River. He lived alone, and his nearest neighbor was the Wick Smith family.

The Sheriff summoned a posse and started to search for the lost Indian. He was joined by several volunteers, including Tubbs's neighbor, Wick Smith.

The Sheriff questioned everyone who had any information about the missing Indian. Did he have any relatives he might be visiting? Would he take a vacation and leave his crop to grow up in weeds? No responsible farmer would do that.

One neighbor remembered that Tubbs owned a herd of white-face cattle. They were gone.

"How long has he been missing?" the neighbor asked. It had been at least a month since anyone had seen him.

"A month?" the Sheriff asked. "The field has been plowed just the last few days. The garden has been cultivated too. What happened to all the cattle?"

Nobody had any answers. Not a clue.

The next day, the Sheriff and Wick had a private conversation at the Smith home. They had been searching for five days without results. Wick had always led the posse because he was familiar with the rugged terrain of the Red River Valley.

While sitting in the living room at the Smith home, The Sheriff noticed they had all new furniture. Around the corner he could see a new bed in the bedroom and a new carpet in the hall. That was unusual. Nobody had any money that time of year.

The Sheriff grilled Wick for several hours about Tubbs's fields being plowed and about his missing cattle. Finally, Wick led the Sheriff to the shallow grave of the Indian. He confessed he killed him by beating him to death with a shovel. He had sold Tubbs's cattle to buy the new furniture.

Nobody could believe Wick was capable of doing such a thing.

Wick's case got an article published in the *True Detective Magazine*. It told how he had dug a shallow grave and buried him face down.

Wick was quoted as saying he had to stand on the Indian's back to push him down into the grave.

Wick also got twenty years in prison.

56

Doggone Good Swap

In the early seventeenth century, an Italian, Antonio Stradivarius, made a few violins that are still around today. If you are lucky enough to find a Stradivarius made in 1644, it's worth a pile of money. I always wanted a fiddle, but I knew I could never afford that kind of money. My uncle Jess was a good fiddler, and I wanted to play just like him.

We knew a violin maker in the 1920s named Sam Croy. He could make a violin in just a few days, with his pocket knife and a few other tools. He worked sitting around the fireplace. He used a special hardwood for the back of the fiddle, and a soft wood for the front. This combination produced soft music when the bow was pulled across the strings. Sam told me that most people couldn't tell the difference between the sound of his fiddle and the sound of a Stradivarius. I believed him. "In the dark," he said, "when everybody is square dancing and drinking that bootleg whiskey, they aren't doing much listening. The badder the booze, the better the sound of that fiddle," he said.

"What's the price of a fiddle like that?" I asked.

"Well, I know there is a depression and nobody has any money now, but if you will get me a good hunting dog, I'll swap you the fiddle for the dog. You see this coon hound? I swapped a fiddle for him. And this Irish Setter bird dog? Last fall I traded a fiddle for him, too."

I didn't have any extra dogs at the time, but I went out and found one. Just an ordinary cur dog. I took the dog over to Sam's house to see if he would make a deal with me. He looked the dog over and asked, "Is he a good hunting dog?"

I thought a minute, then made my decision. "As far as I know, he's a good hunting dog," I assured him. I went back to see Sam about two weeks later, and he asked, "How's your fiddle doing?"

"Fine," I said. "How's your dog doing?"

"Laziest damn dog I ever saw. He just lays there on the hearth in front of the fire and sleeps all day long. I took him out in the woods for a little hunting trip the other day, and he was too lazy to chase a rabbit."

"Does that mean you want to swap back?" I asked.

"Oh no, I'll train him when I have a little more time!" he said.

"There's no warranty on the hound dog, and I don't need a warranty on the fiddle either," I reminded him.

"Tell you what you can do for me," he said. "I use a lot of snuff when I'm busy making fiddles. This one I'm working on right now has to be ready by Saturday night for the fiddler's contest. Could you go to the store for me and take a dozen eggs and get me a box of Rooster Snuff?"

I went to the store and got the snuff. When I returned, Sam said he would play a few tunes on the fiddle for me to show his appreciation.

If Sam Croy is still living, he would be more than a hundred years old. I still own the fiddle he made for me.

He was right, it sounds exactly like a Stradivarius. I can't tell the difference. Sometimes on a cold winter day, I'll take the fiddle from the shelf, blow the dust off, and sit in front of the fireplace and play the tunes Sam Croy played for me so long ago. My favorite tune in recent years is: "How much is that doggie in the window?"

57

A Whale of a Tale

We had only one church house for the whole community in our part of east Texas. Several different denominations used the church. It was a first come-first served church. Each denomination held protracted meetings in the summer months. The Methodists usually started in May for two weeks, then the Southern Baptists, the Hard Shell Baptists, the Nazarenes, and those who called themselves Holy Rollers.

In April, services were held outside the church building, under an arbor attached to the church. There were some big wasp nests under the eaves of the roof. We used to go in the afternoon and stir them up and make them fighting mad. When the preacher came and started to get loud, and waved his arms and pounded the lectern during his sermon, the wasps would attack him. It was funny to us kids then. Too late to apologize now.

One time in the spring, a carnival came to town. They had a ferris wheel and the other usual things that go with a carnival. The main attraction was a flat bed truck with a long tank of water. In the tank was a whale. In order to be spectacular and draw a crowd, they had a huge spotlight that shone for miles around flashing on the clouds. This was something new and different. Nobody had ever seen a spotlight before.

The carnival stayed in town about as long as the preacher stayed at the outdoor church. Every night, as soon as it got dark, the whale man would turn on his powerful spotlight at the carnival. It could be seen for several miles flashing on the clouds in a circular motion. It was a mysterious happening.

"What in the Hell is going on up there in the clouds?" someone asked the minister.

The minister explained. He read it from the Bible, and called out to the congregation, "The world is coming to an end — soon."

Some members of his congregation were hysterical. Where could they run? What could they do?

They questioned the minister again, "Are you sure?"

"You don't question the word of God, or argue with the Scriptures," the preacher assured them.

As a result of the preacher's words, some of the farmers wouldn't plant their corn, or even continue to work their fields. "What's the use?" they'd say. "If the world is coming to an end in the near future, why keep on working?"

On Friday of that week, Sam Welch rode into town to get his groceries for the week. He stayed until after dark, and went to the carnival. He found out for sure, where the light on the clouds was coming from. It was the huge spotlight at the whale tank.

He went back to church the next night and told the preacher and all of his congregation what he had found out about the mysterious light in the sky. Most of the congregation was relieved and thanked the man. Some were disappointed because they didn't want to go back to work. They still believed their minister, because he read straight from the Bible about the sign in the sky and the end of the world.

The minister was furious. He thought Welch — a disbeliever — was trying to make a liar out of him, meddling in the Lord's work. "Don't believe anything Welch tells you," the minister said.

The congregation had become disenchanted with the preacher. The question was — To plant corn or not to plant corn?

A few of the members decided to make a trip to town and see whether Welch was lying or if the preacher was right.

The committee returned and made its report that light in the sky was a "whale of a story," a spotlight, like the first man had reported. The preacher's story of doom was a "whale of a tale."

The minister was disappointed and embarrassed. He had two

nights left on his contract, but he wouldn't preach to that bunch of sinners again. He left immediately, but not before telling his congregation where they could go.

58

City Folks vs. Country Folks

As far back as I can remember, when people spoke about us country folk, they called us "just ol' country boys" or "just ol' farmers."

The connotation, of course, was that country people were dumb, stupid, backward — "didn't know nuthin'."

A number of young city people got their "comeuppance" when they lost their city jobs and were forced to move to the country to survive. They had to ask how to set a cultivator, how to feed chickens, and how to milk a cow. They couldn't seem to understand why farmers got up at daybreak.

Riding a Brahma bull, or roping a steer, and baling hay are skills you can't learn from a book. Lots of the city folks seemed to think they could plant an orchard this year, and have peaches next year. It takes several years to grow berries, plums, and papershell pecans — even if you know how to do it.

We always had plenty of company in the good old summertime. Our watermelons were ripe and berries were heavy on the vines. We even had visitors, because peanuts and popcorn were in session. Some of the visitors seemed to think all the things they were eating at our house just grew wild on the farm. They were wrong.

Successful farmers and ranchers are highly skilled and they work long hours. In the winter months, they plow the fields early, getting the soil ready for the next crops. When it's too wet to plow, they mend fences, cut wood, and care for their cattle. Livestock have to be fed the year round, seven days a week.

Beehives have to be moved from one place to another and the fruit trees have to be pruned in the winter months, when the sap is down.

In the summer months, if a storm threatens, the farmers may get out of bed in the middle of the night to haul the hay they'd mowed and baled the day before. They had to get it into the barn before the rain came. If you had peaches or apples drying on the tin roof, you better get them in the house before the rains came. Life on the farm is not "just a bowl of cherries."

Of all the handicaps the farmer had to overcome, including floods, drought, crows and gophers, the worst pests were "fair weather friends," a.k.a. "watermelon friends." They would show up at watermelon season, sponge off us farmers, and move on.

My folks appointed me to put a stop to that practice — and I did.

When the "city slickers" came to our place, I had a price list handy. I ran specials. If they bought ten pounds or more of peaches, they got a price break. If they wanted a gallon of honey, they could have it for half-price, if they robbed the beehive themselves. Not many wanted to do this.

That's how we "ol' country boys" separated true friends from the city moochers.

59

Just Fiddlin' in the Rain

In the early 1930s, ninety percent of the people lived in the country. They were farmers or ranchers. If a young fella couldn't ride a bull or play a musical instrument by the time he was fifteen, he didn't amount to much.

For entertainment, it was a "do it yourself" way of life. The big rodeos and the old fiddlers' contests were the two big events. All the community turned out to cheer on the performers.

Early on, I learned how to ride the broncos and bulls. Now I had to learn to play the fiddle. I practiced hard and played in all the contests, and sometimes I won.

I often beat a good fiddler about my age. His name was Kenneth Rickerson. His mother and sister thought he was the best in the country. After several preliminary contests, I finally got to be one of the ten best fiddlers in the country.

It was summertime, and all the contestants agreed to have the big play-off at Ken Rickerson's house. Actually, Ken's mother, who always referred to her son as "my Kenny," arranged the place and date for the finals. She was Ken's manager and also tried to manage her husband. But he would just light up his pipe and go out to the barn when they had any fiddlin' going on. They had a big farmhouse, with a lot of shade trees in the front yard. They set up a make-shift stadium for the fiddlers, and a special stand for the three judges.

The day of the big contest, it was raining. It had poured all the night before, and the streams were high. I wasn't going to let the rain stop me — "Come rain or come shine." In this case, it got to be "hell or high water." But I wasn't going to miss the old fiddlers contest. To me, at that time, it was like a chance to play Carnegie Hall.

I didn't have a case for my fiddle, so I carried it in a flour sack. To keep it out of the rain, I held it close to my belly and bent forward. I looked like I had kyphosis of the spine. I pulled my shirt around the fiddle to protect it and ran most of the mile and a half to Ken's house.

After I got home, my mother asked, "How come you are home so early — and how did you do?"

"I came in second," I told her.

"CONGRATULATIONS!" she said, as all the other kids came to congratulate me. "WOW! SECOND! I know you should have come in first, but second is good."

"It's time to celebrate," she continued. "Let's cut that big watermelon we've been cooling down in the spring branch."

As we ate the watermelon, my ma asked, "How many played in the contest?"

"This sure is a good watermelon," I said.

"How many fiddlers played in the contest?" she asked for the second time.

"Well, it was raining, you know?"

"I know it was raining — but how many played in the contest?" she demanded to know for the third time.

"Well, actually, it was just Ken and me," I answered.

"Who were the three judges?

"We didn't have three judges, we only had two judges," I said.

"Who were the two judges?"

"Ken's Ma and Ken's sister," I said.

By then we had already eaten the big watermelon and it was too late to retract the celebration.

I rationalized — if it had been a nice sunny day, I would have ten fiddlers to compete with — it's possible that I might have come in tenth, instead of second. Since the judges declared I should win second place, I accepted it.

Ken's mother had been sympathetic. She came over to advise me after the two votes were counted. She said, "If you just keep practicing, one of these days, you will be almost as good as my Kenny."

60

Changing Times

"It's time for a change." That was a familiar phrase in politics, even back in the twenties.

The country was going into the fourth year of the Great Depression and things weren't getting any better. The Depression was pandemic.

Unemployment was still twenty-five percent. In some of the larger cities, it was a high as sixty percent. England and all the European countries were affected. Most Americans had become accustomed to living in poverty. The men who were out of work stole rides on freight trains going to California, or any place, looking for jobs. Stores and shops put signs in their windows, "NO HELP WANTED — DO NOT APPLY." The restaurants' signs read: "NO HANDOUTS."

At soup kitchens all over the country, people lined up to get daily rations. A common sight were the Hoover Huts — temporary shacks or tents. In the depressed communities, they called it Hooverville. People didn't have enough money to buy groceries, much less snuff and chewing tobacco.

Franklin D. Roosevelt, a Democrat from New York, was running for President in the general election of 1932. He won by a landslide and took office in January 1933.

The first thing F.D.R. did was close what few banks were still open.

The government issued script. That arrangement lasted only a few days. When banks reopened, deposits were insured by the Federal Deposit Insurance Corporation (F.D.I.C.). That meant the Federal Government guaranteed the safety of deposits up to ten thousand dollars. That didn't change the minds of some depositors who had lost all their money. They stashed their money in different places, buried it in the backyard, or under their mattresses. They would never trust banks again.

In the meantime, things gradually got better. People in the country helped each other out. They were neighborly.

The prospectors struck oil in east Texas. The towns of Gladewater and Kilgore struck it rich. Oil wells pumped all over the city, even on the courthouse lawn. Talco was another town with "black gold" coming out of the ground. Everybody who owned real estate was trying to sell their royalties. They were dreaming of getting rich, of waking up one morning and seeing a new car in their driveway. It did happen to a few of the lucky ones. Their luck was "a carrot on a stick" for many land owners.

The oil boom opened up jobs for quite a few of the unemployed, but it hardly made a dent in the economy. The oil field workers were called "rough necks." The work was dirty and dangerous, but the pay was good.

Another big project had just started on the Colorado River, near Las Vegas, Nevada. It was the construction of Hoover Dam. As with the oil field jobs, thousands of hands showed up looking for a job. But only about one-tenth of the applicants were hired.

In the early thirties, bank robberies became a fad. There appeared to be a desperado for every bank. The most notorious ones were Pretty Boy Floyd, Machine Gun Kelley, John Dillinger, and Clyde Barrow and Bonnie Parker. They made a game of robbing banks, escaping the police, and hitting banks in other states.

Everybody looked forward to Tuesdays and Fridays, the days the semi-weekly farm newspaper was delivered to the rural mail boxes. Some families didn't take the paper, so they gathered around their neighbors' houses to see what the bandits were doing, and where they had struck last. It was exciting, and it appeared the readers were on the side of the bank robbers.

The fascination and excitement ended one day in east Texas, close to our home, when the last two bank robbers were gunned down.

Bonnie and Clyde had worked as a team for several months. They had engaged in several shoot-outs with the authorities, and always won. They had robbed many banks in five or six states, and killed several peace officers, including two Texas Rangers. The only way they could be stopped was to ambush them and riddle their car with bullets. They died instantly.

Forty years later, Hollywood made an Academy Award-winning movie about Bonnie and Clyde.

61

Quoting Paul

During Prohibition, 1919-1933, the Volstead Act outlawed the sale, manufacture, or transportation of alcoholic beverages.

The bootleggers had a heyday during Prohibition, which ended in 1933, when the law was repealed. For several years afterwards, there were local options, which meant some counties could vote to have liquor, and some not. Counties were either "wet" or "dry." It was very confusing, but it didn't seem to make any difference with the bootleggers. They had their stills in operation, and there was a good market for their product.

Paris, Texas, was the county seat of Lamar County. It was a dry county, and that meant no liquor.

I was approached by my friend Dave, who was about two years older than I. He had a proposition whereby we could make some money if I would furnish the car. He knew where we could buy a gallon of "White Lightning," at the Choctaw Nation across the border in Oklahoma, for three dollars. We could bring it back across the Red River and sell it for a dollar a pint. I was a teetotaler, but this sounded like a good return on our money.

I was kind of the General Noriega of the thirties, and it seemed like a good idea at the time. Dave was a good talker, and he made it sound so easy, I couldn't refuse his offer.

There was one technicality that Dave almost overlooked, money. Who was going to pay the three dollars to the bootlegger for the gallon of whiskey? Dave said he was broke, but if I would go ahead and put up the money, we could settle up when we sold the liquor.

I asked Dave about the car expense. I had to furnish the car, and a trip like the one we were about to embark on would cost money. We would need two gallons of gasoline and three quarts of oil, and that would cost about six bits.

"No problem," Dave said. "Just as soon as we retail the liquor we will divide the money, and I'll pay half the expense."

Dave was always good with figures. He assured me there's no way we would lose on the deal.

We were concerned about the immigration officer at the border between Texas and Oklahoma. We'd heard rumors that guards would stop all cars at the state line. Anyone transporting liquor into Texas from Oklahoma would have it confiscated.

On the way back, we were on pins and needles as we stopped at the guard's booth. He just waved us through and didn't say a word.

We found out later why he didn't inspect our contraband. He had been paid off by the Sheriff of Choctaw County, and the Mayor of Hugo, Oklahoma. The bootleggers had paid the Sheriff and Mayor. It was good business for everybody concerned.

On the way back to Paris, I was driving and Dave was nipping from the jug. I was surprised when he became very quiet and slumped over in the car seat before we got home. I thought he was dead. Then I looked at the jug. It was almost empty — maybe a quart left.

When I roused him, he didn't want me to take him home. He was afraid of his father. I said O.K. I'd wait for him to sober up, but it didn't happen.

When we arrived at his home, he intended to sneak in and go to bed to sleep it off. His timing was bad. It was Sunday morning, and his dad, a deacon of the church, was just coming home and some of the younger children were with him. Dave, the oldest son, was already the black sheep of the family because of his drinking.

When his dad saw his oldest son in a drunken state, he was furious. Dave was a grown man, but his father talked to him as if he were a four year old. Dave's dad got on my case for taking his son out and getting him drunk, and bringing him home still inebriated at ten o'clock in the morning.

His dad ordered me to take Dave to the eleven o'clock church services.

Dave said, "No! I don't like that preacher. He shouts, screams, and gives me a headache, and I already have a headache and a hangover."

"You take this boy to church!" Dave's dad, the deacon growled at me.

"There will be no seats left when we get there, except right in front," Dave complained.

"That's where you belong," his father shouted. "And you listen to the sermon, and don't go to sleep."

At that instant I was ready to sell my car and get out of the free taxi business.

When we arrived at the church, I had to drag Dave out of the car and lead him up the steps. He was mad at the world. Sure enough, the church was packed, and the only seats left were in the front pew. The usher motioned for us to go to the front. Dave was staggering, and I wasn't about to go down the aisle supporting him. The minister was well into his sermon when we arrived. Most ministers raise their voices when they want to make a point. They shout out rhetorical questions, and let them echo throughout the building. Then after a long pause, the preacher answers his own questions.

We were about halfway down the aisle when the minister shouted out, "What did Paul say?"

"Who gives a damn!" Dave shouted back at him.

I immediately turned Dave around and headed him back to the front door.

I could hear the whole congregation gasp. As we left by the front steps, the preacher said, "There goes two poor souls straight to Hell, if they don't repent."

I took Dave to the car, but I was afraid to take him back home. I knew his dad would want to murder both of us. So, I took him down the road to a shade tree and let him sleep it off. It was about three o'clock when I took him home. He wanted me to come in and tell his dad we had gone to church, as he'd ordered.

No way. Good-bye, Dave.

A few months later, the "Feds," or "Revenuers" swooped down on the crooked officials and cleaned house. All the officials went to jail, including the border guards.

I rationalized. Because Dave drank the whole gallon of liquor, and we didn't actually sell any, does that make me a bootlegger? I don't think so, but in spite of what Dave told me about dividing up our profit, I lost.

Dave died at an early age of cirrhosis of the liver and acute alcoholism.

And the preacher? We didn't stay in church long enough that Sunday morning to find out what Paul said. I think Dave had the right answer.

62

Horse Trading

The stock market crash of 1929 was the beginning of the Great Depression of the 1930s.

We didn't lose a dime in the stock market — we didn't have a dime then.

The majority of families lived in the rural area and the minority in urban areas. When the crash came, it left twenty-five percent of the population unemployed for about four years. There were no big factories or big payrolls from any industry.

The small towns and the large cities were all classified then as "country towns." They depended on the farmers and ranchers to keep them in business.

There were no unions or union pension funds, no unemployment insurance, and no Social Security. It was every man for himself. If a person managed to save enough money for a "rainy day" or enough to retire, he was lucky. If had he put it in the bank, he was unlucky as there wasn't any Federal Deposit Insurance Corporation (FDIC). If a man had buried his money in the back yard or hid it in the mattresses, he was lucky. Some lucked and some didn't.

We already lived in the country on a farm. If you lived in the city during the Great Depression, you were at a disadvantage. No money, no job, no groceries. No way to grow any groceries.

Everybody made a mass exodus to the country. The transition from city life to country life wasn't easy. City folks didn't know much about country life and certainly not how to care for a farm. First, they needed someplace to live. If they were lucky enough to find an old farmhouse and could persuade the owner to let them move in and pay no rent, they were off to a good start. Don't expect it to have all the modern amenities you were accustomed to in the city.

Sharecroppers didn't have to pay rent. They did have to agree to rent and work a certain number of acres of land. Usually, at least ten acres of corn and ten acres of cotton. At harvest time, the tenant had to harvest the corn and pick the cotton. He got one half and the landlord got the other half. The landlord furnished all the tools and the mules to make the crop.

The other option was for the tenant to furnish the mules, feed, tools, and all the seed. If the landlord furnished the land only, he got one-third of the corn crop and one-fourth of the cotton crop.

Farm animals were in big demand for a few years when everybody wanted to become farmers. Instead of used car lots, like we have today, they had livery stables in the city where you could rent, lease, or buy the horses and mules. When the supply of livestock got low, the livery stable owner would bring in horses that had been condemned and sent to the glue factory, or to the abattoir for dog food.

The horse trader knew every trick of the trade — legal and illegal. When he found the condemned nags, he put them in a corral and fed them dry wheat bran with gun powder and a lot of salt so they would drink plenty of water and their ribs wouldn't show. When nobody was around, he would get in the corral and beat the horses with a broom handle and yell at the same time. It was a conditioned reflex that he trained the horses to follow.

When a potential buyer came looking for a farm animal, the salesman would strike the side of the corral and yell. The horse would jump and prick up his ears. "See, that's a lively little filly," the salesman would say.

When the "City Slickers" were forced to become "Gentleman Farmers," there was a big demand for horses and mules to pull the plows. Mules made the best farm animals. They were stubborn, but they could pull a plow ten or twelve hours a day, whereas horses were more temperamental and didn't have the staying power of the mules.

At one time the livery stable owner was importing wild horses from the open range of Montana and Wyoming. He paid about twenty dollars a head and sold them for forty dollars. The wild horses could never be trained or broken. It was similar to taking a coyote or a tiger out of the jungle and training him to be a pet. The range horses were high-spirited. They never settled down enough to be of any use to the farmer.

When a prospective buyer came to the lot to buy a mule or horse, the horse trader, always had "just the animal for you." This was similar to the modern day used car salesman who says, "I've got a clean little car for you."

As one horse trader was describing his competition, he said, "That man can sell you a dead horse and make you believe you got a bargain."

63

The Great Depression Is Getting Worse

Now it's 1931 — it's worse than 1930. What will 1932 be like? Can't get any worse, but it did. More banks were going "busted," more people were losing their homes and farms, and more people were out of work. There was no money in circulation. Everything was on the barter system. Cotton that sold for twenty-five cents a pound a few years before was worth only five cents a pound now. If you farmed the creek or the river bottom, the crops were washed downstream by the floods. If you farmed in the fields not threatened by the floods, the soil was poor and so were the crops.

In 1931, Henry Ford was paying his employees at the Ford Motor Company in Detroit five dollars a day for piece work. They were turning out cars at the rate of two a minute. When the rest of the country heard about the big money, they loaded up their belongings and headed for Detroit. But few people could afford to pay four hundred eighty-five dollars for a Ford. Sales stopped, and the plant shut down. That left Mr. Ford with a big inventory.

In the cities, especially Detroit and most other big towns, people were literally starving to death. They had soup lines set up to feed the hungry. Families were better off in the farm country. Farmers had plenty to eat, but no money.

Matt, one of my friends in the country, wanted to make some money, so he sold out "lock, stock, and barrel." He didn't know where he'd find a good job, but he finally decided to steal a ride on a freight train and go to California. Everybody else was leaving for somewhere, looking for "greener pastures."

Matt had never been away from home. The night before he was to leave, he came to say goodbye. He went with me to feed the hogs and cows before dark. When we finished the chores, we sat on the rail fence to talk.

Matt said, "Do you think it's safe for me to be out here in the dark with all this money on me? I sold everything I owned and have all the cash right here in my pocket."

I assured him there was nobody around to rob him.

A few minutes later, he went through the same thing again. "Do you think it's safe out here in the dark with all this money on me? I don't feel comfortable."

Again I assured him that he was safe, and we talked some more.

About fifteen minutes later, he got restless, and for the third time, he asked, "Do you think I'm safe with all this money on me?"

"How much money do you have?" I asked.

He looked over his shoulder both ways, leaned close, and whispered in my ear, "Thirteen dollars and twenty cents."

64

"Beds, Twenty-five Cents"

During the Depression, I went to Dallas looking for a job. Already thousands were ahead of me, looking for any job to make some money.

At midnight, I was still on the streets. I couldn't afford a dollar for a hotel room. I strolled into the ghetto section of town and saw a sign: "Beds 25¢."

I walked up a long flight of shaky stairs and opened a cracked glass door into a dimly lit room. Sitting behind a small desk was an unsavory character wearing horned-rim glasses and smoking a cigar.

As I approached his desk, he said, "Yes?"

"I just happened to be in the neighborhood and saw your sign. Do you have any rooms left?"

"How old are you, boy?"

I lowered my voice an octave and raised my age two years. "Eighteen," I said.

"Got a quarter?" he asked. "Sign the book here and I'll show you the restroom at the end of the hall. When you get through, you just pull this chain and the water dumps right down in the commode." He pulled the chain to demonstrate, but the commode was stopped up, and the water went all over the floor.

"Well, I guess one of the drunks threw the Dallas Morning News in the commode again. Frankly, I never cared for all this new-fangled plumbing myself. I prefer the old-fashioned out-house." He waded through the water, rolling empty wine bottles out of his path with his foot.

"Which bed is mine?" I asked.

"The only pad left is this one between these two guys."

"Don't you have any cots?"

"Oh no, they're all sold out. Up in the deluxe section, they rent for thirty-five cents a night."

"How many people can you sleep here? They all look drunk. Is that right?"

"They're all winos. They have to get off the streets at night or the cops will take them to jail, and they don't like that. Bill, over in the corner, has been here three days. He really 'hung one on' this time. He'll probably sober up enough to leave tomorrow. I can't go to sleep myself. They smoke and set the mattresses on fire sometimes. Taking care of thirty drunks is no fun," he said.

"Don't you have any pillows?" I asked.

"What do you expect for a quarter, kid, the Waldorf-Astoria? Just put your fist under your head for a pillow, and don't take your shoes off."

He had already told me three times, "Don't take your shoes off."

The temperature was about ninety degrees and the building had no ventilation. The stench was nauseating. The grunting, groaning, snoring, and teeth grinding made sleep impossible. My bedfellows were a weird bunch.

Even the cockroaches walked funny. They didn't run across the floor. They just meandered. I think they'd inhaled too much of the alcohol fumes.

When daylight came, I caught the first Greyhound bus home, but I vowed to return, as soon as I made some money.

65

And the Band Played On

The 1930s was the Big Band era. It was also the hey-day of ball-room dancing. Arthur Murray, who standardized and popularized American and Latin rhythms, had a chain of franchised studios from coast to coast.

All the big hotels had huge ballrooms, used for dancing, unlike to-day.

One hot steamy Saturday night in July, I boarded a Greyhound bus and went to Dallas for a night out on the town. Benny Goodman was playing at the Adolphus Hotel.

When I walked up to the front entrance, the doorman said, "You can't come in here in your shirt sleeves."

"I'm wearing a clean shirt," I told him.

"I'm sure your shirt is clean, but you have to wear a coat, too."

"I'm not cold, honestly," I said.

He gave me a cold stare, and said, "Why don't you go down to Neiman-Marcus and get you a nice suit, like this one I'm wearing, then come back next Saturday night?"

"O.K., I'll buy a new suit and I'll see you next Saturday night." I did go to Neiman-Marcus, but those nice suits cost ninety-five dollars. I went to Sears and bought a suit for $29.95 that looked exactly like the ninety-five dollar one. The only difference was the absence of a Neiman-Marcus tag in the collar.

When I went back to the dance the next Saturday night, the same man was at the door wearing the same suit. He recognized me and said, "I see you went to Neiman-Marcus and got you a suit, but where is your dance partner? No stags allowed, only couples," he said.

I went out on the street to find a dance partner. On the corner of Commerce and Akard, I saw a beautiful, statuesque blond. She gave me a big smile as I walked up to greet her. I asked if she would like to go to a dance with me.

"Oh, yes," she said in a sexy voice. "Where?"

"Across the street at the Adolphus Hotel."

"Oh, no! I can't go there."

"Why?" I asked.

"I'm a hooker," she said. "But thanks for the invitation."

There I was, all dressed up, and no place to go. I strolled down the street to the *Baker Hotel*. A sign in the lobby read: "Arthur Murray Dance Party."

I took the elevator to the top floor ballroom, alight with fancy chandeliers.

When I opened the door, nobody questioned my presence. Instead of throwing me out, they pulled me in and made me feel welcome.

I apologized for not bringing a dance partner. They assured me I didn't need a partner at the Arthur Murray Party. "This is a metal ball. We give trophies to the winners."

The hostess showed me the trophies for the tango, samba, waltz, and fox trot.

She said that all the big bands came to Dallas. Even Guy Lombardo left the Waldorf-Astoria Hotel in New York to play a week in Dallas. "Last week," she said, "we had Wayne King and the week before Glenn Miller."

The girls all wore beautiful dance gowns and the men wore tuxedos and tails.

When they turned the lights down low and played a Viennese Waltz, I would swear their feet were not even touching the floor.

I thought, *this is for me!*

The Arthur Murray instructors are not only good teachers, they are also good sales people. The hostess wanted to dance with me. That was her job. The idea was to show the new student how much fun he could have. They wanted to get you "hooked on dancing." I expected the teacher who wanted me to dance with her would want to sell me dance lessons, but she didn't. She wanted to sell me a contract to become a teacher. She told me I would make an excellent teacher. She said I looked good in my Neiman-Marcus suit, and I was light on my feet and . . .

She even had me believing that line. I told her she didn't have to sell me — I was already sold after watching the dancers perform. I didn't sign a contract that night, but later I did.

The only time I've stopped dancing since then was just long enough to take a drink of water and change shoes.

66

Nine Votes

Roy Caviness was a successful farmer and rancher. His spread was in the creek bottom, next to ours.

He was an honorable, honest man, but wanted to get into politics. In Texas, we had four country commissioners.

Mark Kennedy was his opponent. On the first try, Kennedy won by eighty votes. Two years later, Caviness ran against Kennedy and lost by fifteen votes. The third time he was sure he would win. He knew that several of his friends would vote for him, if they could get to the polls.

That's when Roy asked me to take over his campaign. I knew several of the voters and with a little campaigning, I could win them over to the Caviness side.

I agreed. My job was to be sure that all potential voters who didn't go to the polls to vote in the prior election had an opportunity to vote this time. I was to furnish transportation to the voting booths.

At that time, Texas had a poll tax of $1.75 to vote. That was a lot of money. Many voters rebelled against the tax. They equated it with bribery.

Women's suffrage was relatively new then, and more women were becoming interested in politics. We calculated that if I would just get twelve voters who had not voted the last time, we could win the election.

Roy gave me the names of several voters and their addresses. He advised them in advance that I would be picking them up on election day to take them to the polls. He wasn't sure they wanted to vote for him, but it was my job to convince them on the way to the polls.

June 6 was the Democratic primary. In the case of the commissioners, there would be no run-off. Only two were in the race. The polls were open from seven a.m. to seven p.m.

I needed to get at least fifteen people out to vote that day. If they voted for Caviness, he would pick up enough votes to put him over the top.

I set out early to pick up the first voter, Mrs. Johnson. I arrived about seven a.m. The family was expecting me. They were very nice and asked me to have breakfast with them. I had already eaten and explained I was gathering up a load of voters who didn't have transportation. The husband at this farm had to plow cotton that day, and could not go to vote.

We then drove down a narrow lane to another potential voter named Beulah. Things were not going well at this household. A family feud was in progress. I explained who I was and what I was doing there. They finally quieted down. The fact that their neighbor, Mrs. Johnson, was in the car made them a little more comfortable. Just as we were about to leave, her husband remembered he hadn't paid his poll tax, and couldn't vote. He didn't want his wife to go vote unless they could go. The wife didn't like that arrangement, and told him so. The husband blew his top. He shook his finger in her face and told her he was the "man of the house" and whatever he said was law. He sounded like Jackie Gleason telling Alice that he was the boss. The wife just walked away from the argument and got into the car.

I had room for one more passenger. I asked the two ladies if they knew of someone else that needed transportation to the voting booth. They suggested Emma, their closest neighbor, about two miles back in the woods.

When I saw Emma, I immediately thought of my weak tire on the right rear side. I judged that Emma would tip the scale at about two hundred and eighty pounds. She wanted to vote, but first she had to get ready. She said she had just washed her hair and "couldn't do a thing with it." I told her to hurry, that the other two ladies had to get back home as soon as possible. After a long wait, Emma came out and asked if we could wait while she gathered up the eggs to take to the store. I agreed to wait, if she would hurry.

When she came back with the eggs in a paper bag, she said, "I better run to the outhouse one more time, as those roads are bumpy, you know, and I don't want to have an accident."

When Emma was finally ready to get in the car, I wanted my first passenger to move over and let Emma sit on the side that had the good tire. That was the sunny side. The first lady didn't want to move over, so we got off to a bad start.

When all three of the ladies arrived and voted, I wanted to take them back home as quickly as possible, so I could get another load of voters. But Emma had to take her eggs over to the store and sell them so she would have some money to buy needed bobby pins.

One of the other ladies wanted to get ten cents worth of ice to make ice tea for dinner. The third lady wanted to buy some groceries across the street. After they all had time to do their shopping, I started to round them up. I helped one load her groceries and went to look for another. I found her and brought her to the car. The first one had left again.

"Where is Emma?" I asked.

"She came back to the car, but left again, because it got too hot sitting in the car."

I went to look for Emma and found her at the check-out line, showing the girl at the cash register pictures of her grandchildren. Five people were in line behind her, waiting to pay for their commodities. I approached Emma and told her that the other two ladies were sitting in the hot car, waiting for her. She did not seem to be concerned, and snapped at me for interrupting her.

The girl at the cash register was not too interested in her pictures, but was too polite to say so.

Just as Emma got through with that batch of pictures, she turned her purse around and got out another fistful of snapshots. "Now this is little Billy," she said. "This is my stepson's oldest boy by his second wife. This looks just like him, don't you think? He's a cute little bugger, ain't he?"

By now eight people were in line waiting to check out. The clerk was nearly in tears. I went over to apologize for holding up the line, and she said, "That's all right. Why don't you and your mother wait over by the door? I'll look at the rest of her pictures when I get the rest of the people checked out."

When I finally got Emma out to the car, the other two ladies had left. They were standing in the shade of the chinaberry tree, fanning with a folded newspaper. I got all three of them loaded and was ready to go, I thought.

Then Emma spoke up and said, "I'd better go to the restroom one more time before we leave, you know it's a long drive and.—"

"I know, I know, bumpy roads."

The other ladies wanted to go back to the shade tree, but I persuaded them to remain in the car and fan with newspapers.

Once we got on the road, I brought up politics again, and asked each who they voted for. All three had voted for *MARK KENNEDY*. When I asked them why they did not vote for Roy Caviness, one said, "We never hear anything about that Caviness man, but Mark is always getting his name in the papers."

"That's because he is the incumbent," I said.

"He's what?" one of the ladies asked.

"Incumbent! I thought he was a Baptist."

I asked Emma why she voted for Mark Kennedy.

"He's got such a nice smile," she said.

It was then that I came to the conclusion: If you want to be elected, you have to have a big smile and a lot of hair. Things like "honesty" and "integrity" are a handicap to a politician.

During the conversation about the difference between the two candidates, Emma said that Mr. Kennedy had saved the county a lot of money by using his head. I asked how he had saved all that money.

She said, "He was far-sighted, and he knew the price was going up on all materials that would be needed for the next year, so he bought a large supply of lumber and nails and bridge planks. It was in the paper."

The fact of the matter was, he thought he might lose the election, and he spent the money in advance. That is called deficit spending. Instead of buying the hardware and lumber from one of the two big stores in Paris, John House or Johnson Billingsly, he bought everything from his store, co-owned with his brother-in-law. Conflict of interest hadn't been thought of at that time.

With my second load of voters, I changed my strategy. I polled them first. Asking someone who he intends to vote for is personal and confidential, but it is politically expedient. If he answered "Kennedy," I would tell him, "Mr. Kennedy is sending someone to pick you up." Then I went to another house and asked the same question. The voters were just about equally divided between the two candidates.

I didn't feel good about saying the Kennedy car would come to pick up the voters, but I was beginning to discover that to be a good politician, and to get elected, you had to lie a little. I rationalized that maybe Kennedy's helpers were actually coming to pick up his voters.

The next house I went to, the lady was ready to go, but she wanted to take all her kids along. She volunteered that she was going to vote for Roy Caviness. So I had one solid vote and three extra kids to haul.

Later in the afternoon, with more than twenty miles round trip to make, I went to a farmhouse to pick up a man and his wife. A neighbor was visiting them. I asked if she intended to vote for my candidate. She said it did not matter who one votes for, just as long as you vote.

On my last trip, just before the polls closed, I ran into more trouble. An elderly couple had been sitting on their porch since seven o'clock in the morning, waiting for me. They let me have it "with both barrels" for keeping them waiting all day. I tried to explain that I had been working all day, and had made many trips to the polls.

When I asked who they intended to vote for, the lady said, "I'm not voting for Hoover again, that's for damn sure."

I told her that Hoover was not on the ballot. "We have a new President now, Franklin D. Roosevelt." When I asked who she wanted for commissioner, she did not know who was running. I suggested that my candidate, Roy Caviness, was a good man to vote for.

"No young whippersnapper is going to tell me how to vote," she informed me.

I will never know how she voted.

When the polls closed, the votes were counted and transported to the county seat in Paris to be recounted and posted. All the country folks gathered at the plaza where a big fountain cooled the air. A huge blackboard sat on a ladder on the platform. Votes were erased and updated every few minutes.

It was like the county fair. People crowded to get a look at the board. A man sold ice cream cones from a cart. The votes kept coming in from the remote precincts. Kennedy and Caviness were nip and tuck all evening. About midnight, it was all over except for the votes from two precincts. These were the precincts I had been working all day.

Garrets Bluff and Chicota were the holdouts. When Chicota delivered its ballots, Caviness was ahead by five votes. We stood by and waited until the last precinct came in. This was the batch of votes from Emma and about fifteen other people I had taken to the polls that day.

I was sure we had it made. They erased the blackboard and posted the final votes for the evening. It was a tense moment.

It was almost two o'clock in the morning. The fog was rolling in, and everybody had left.

I started to walk away, then turned and looked at the board one more time. I could not believe it. The man that I had worked so hard to get elected had lost again by nine lousy votes.

67

Social . . . What?

Chuck arrived in town with a wagon load of wood. Joe brought produce — watermelons, peaches, and vegetables. There must have been fifty wagons parked on market square that Saturday morning in 1935.

All the farmers arrived early while it was still cool. They lined up their wagons to display what they raised on the farm — corn, blackeyed peas, fryers, sometimes tomatoes.

The city folks showed up to bargain with the farmers for the best deal they could get. There were no fair trade laws, parity, farm labor unions, or price fixin'. It was "open season," every man for himself. The sellers wanted a nice Sunday dinner. If they sold their produce for a decent price, they could bring home a few store-bought victuals. Maybe they'd buy a twenty-five-pound block of ice and crank out a freezer of homemade ice cream for a Sunday treat. The buyers wanted the same thing, at the best price they could get.

During a lull in the buying, Chuck, a wagon away, said to his neighbor, "Joe, what do you think about Social Security?"

"What'n hell is Social Security?" Joe growled.

"You mean you never heard of Social Security? You been hiding under a rock down there in the creek bottom for the last year?"

"Listen Chuck, I don't have time to bother with that sort of stuff. I'm out in the field every day, trying to scratch out a living for my family."

"Don't you ever listen to the radio? You never listened to F.D.R.'s Fireside Speech?"

"I ain't got no radio, but the Little Woman and the kids want me to get one. They say everybody is getting a radio now. I sort of half-way promised I would get one when we pick the first bale."

"Well, you still take the newspaper, don't you?"

"Naw. I stopped that when Will Rogers and Wiley Post got killed in that plane crash in Alaska. I always read his column and the comic strips. I like Maggie and Jiggs and Popeye, but I can't afford $1.50 a year for a paper that comes only twice a week. But what's this about that social thing? What did you call it?"

"Social Security. The Federal Government holds out one percent, one penny out of each dollar you earn. It goes into your Social Security account, and when you reach age sixty-five, you get it back with interest. You could actually get as much as twenty-five or thirty dollars a month when you turn sixty-five."

"Sounds more like socialism to me. That F.D.R. has already made me plow up my cotton. Paid only seven dollars an acre. Killed my cows and gave me a penny a pound. Now he wants to take one percent of my wages and pay it back when I am sixty-five?"

"Joe, whether you like it or not, it has already passed and they've started to take out the one percent this year. I think it's a good deal.

Joe waved his hand in denial, then hefted a watermelon for a customer and dropped the nickel into his overall pocket. Turning back to his friend he said, "What makes you think we'll live to sixty-five? If this depression don't end, we'll all starve to death before we reach 65. DAMN DEMOCRATS!"

68

"Weathering the CCC"

The Civilian Conservation Corps was established in 1933 for men between the ages of seventeen and twenty-three. F.D.R. was our new President, and he wanted everyone to have a job. The unemployment rate was about thirty percent. There was no social welfare then. If a family didn't have a job, or any source of income, they could apply for relief, or get in the "soup line," if they could find one.

I couldn't apply for any kind of relief, because we lived on a farm and had plenty to eat. I couldn't get into the CCC for the same reason.

I applied anyway, in Paris, Texas, and arranged to have my money sent to a cousin. He agreed to keep it for me. I would get it all when I'd served six months, the minimum time we could sign up for. We were paid thirty dollars a month. Twenty-two dollars was to be sent home to parents. The cash I received was eight dollars a month.

Actually, I didn't see any money. I got a "canteen book" with eight dollars worth of coupons worth five cents each. That paid for cigarettes and candy or anything I needed from the canteen.

The Civilian Conservation Corps was organized to preserve the forest. Naturally, we were called "tree monkeys." Our job was preventing and fighting forest fires.

The day we left Texas, on the train, we thought our destination was somewhere in Oregon, but at the last minute, they told us we would be going to San Bernardino, California. "Never heard of it," someone growled.

Two hundred and ten men left Paris, some of them for the first time. We were on the rails two days and two nights in first class. Accomodations included upper and lower sleeping berths on the train, the classiest ride I ever had.

Our C.O. was an Army captain. The company doctor assigned to the unit was also a captain. Each received a salary of one hundred and fifty dollars a month. The doctor, we learned later, had lost his license to practice medicine. Apparently, he had been taking too much of his own medicine, and was also an alcoholic. Not only did the doctor sample his own medicine frequently, he had one glass eye. He didn't have to be licensed by the state to get a job with the United States government.

While traveling on the train across the Arizona desert, we had to take our second shot for smallpox and typhoid fever. The doctor was going through the coach giving everyone his shot. An orderly helped him by carrying a tray with all the paraphernalia. He had exactly the right number of vials of serum counted out and ready for use.

Bracket, a small blond boy of sixteen who had lied about his age to get into the CCC, was asked to stand and roll up his sleeve for his shot. The doctor turned to the orderly and picked up the vial and needle. When he turned back, he asked Bracket to stand a second and he gave him another shot. Bracket thought he was supposed to get two shots.

The orderly reminded the good doctor that he had already given Bracket his shot. It was too late.

The doctor apologized to him and continued down the aisle, playing "dart" with the needle. When he got to the end of the train, he had no shot left for the last boy, as he had given it to Bracket.

A few hours later, Bracket became deathly ill. He had a high fever and looked as if he wouldn't make it to California. The doctor ordered ice packs for his head, and begged the guys not to tell the company commander about his mistake. Bracket survived. Later on, we had occasion to be grateful to this same doctor.

When we finally arrived at the Santa Fe Railroad Station on Third Street in San Bernardino, a crowd waited to greet us. They asked, "Are all of you from Texas? Where are your boots and spurs? Where is your guitar?" Apparently their only knowledge of Texas came from ten-cent Western movies.

We climbed aboard trucks covered with tarps. The backs were left open so we could see out as we headed up the mountain road. We all tried to look out the back of the truck to see the lights of San Bernardino, disappearing as we headed for Crestline. For a bunch of kids who had never been away from home, and who had lived where land was flat with lots of wide open spaces, this was scary. When we got to Crestline, we went down a very steep grade toward Lake Gregory. The driver put the truck into low gear to save his brakes. The truck made so much noise, we thought we had lost control, and it was running away with us.

We went to a camp in Miller Canyon, where Silverwood Lake is now. It was October 1936, and the San Bernardino National Forest smelled like pine trees on that clear cold night.

Later that winter, the snow got pretty deep. The old timers said it was the most snow that had fallen in the mountains in several years. Some of the guys got "cabin fever" and went "over the hill" — that's AWOL— absent without leave.

The rest of us were on twenty-four-hour fire watch. One day, while we were fighting a fire in a canyon, the wind suddenly changed and trapped a company of men. One of our men was burned to death and several others were scorched.

The Forest Rangers trained us to adapt to any job pertaining to the National Forest. We cleared buck brush and piled it in fire trails several feet wide to stop the blaze. The fire break wouldn't stop a fire if it was driven by high wind. The buck brush was cut and piled up in the fire breaks. The only time it could be burned was when it was raining. Then they used a gasoline torch to light the brush pile.

One cold windy night when it started to rain, sleet, and snow, it was an ideal time to burn the brush.

About two o'clock in the morning, our company was ordered to get out of bed and put on our heavy clothes and raincoats. We were going to burn the brush we had cut and piled up earlier. Several truckloads of men were waiting to leave when we were saved by the old one-eyed doctor who had been a bane to us in the past. He came out to the trucks and ordered the company commander and the chief Forest Ranger to unload the men. He said it wasn't fit for man or beast to be out in that kind of weather. Some of the these men, he said, just got out of bed with the flu. They could all come down with pneumonia, and he would be responsible for their health. This was one time the doctor outranked the company commander and the Forest Ranger.

When we unloaded the trucks, several of us went over to the old doctor's office and thanked him for coming to our rescue. He was gloating when he said, "How'd you like the way I handled the company commander tonight?"

One of our jobs was building spike camps to house tools and equipment. One of the buildings I helped build is still standing. The Mountain Community Hospital has since been built close to it. We also built an ice skating rink at Blue Jay. It was later torn down and a new one built.

Horsethief Canyon was in a desolate area of the rugged San Bernardino Mountains. Many years ago, the old timers told us, horse thieves would steal the horses and stake them out in the canyons during the day, then at night, they would move them across the country to auction. They made big money until they got caught. Some of them were hanged.

The Cleghorn Truck Trail was just a trail in 1936. The Tree Monkeys made a paved road out of it by blasting rock with dynamite and using a jackhammer and bulldozers through Horsethief Canyon. The road came out into Cajon Pass. It is now the Cleghorn Road.

Several movies were shot around Lake Arrowhead in the 1930s, and several Hollywood celebrities lived in the area. Some still live there. The big dance bands played in the village. I used to go dancing every Saturday night at Crestline or Lake Arrowhead.

69

Brother, Can You Spare a Dime?

My "salary" from the CCC was eight dollars a month, which was actually canteen coupons, not real money. To make a little extra, I set up a barber shop in the latrine, and charged twenty cents for a hair cut. I was the only barber in the camp.

After a few weeks confined in the San Bernardino Mountains, we were allowed to go to town.

The chaplain and the company doctor took us into the recreation hall for a lecture. They told us where the trucks would park, and when we would return to camp. They said San Bernardino had a population of forty-six thousand people (it's one hundred and eighty thousand now), and they didn't want any of us to get drunk and get lost. One place for sure we shouldn't go was the red light district. It was on "D" Street, starting at Third and going all the way down to Rialto Avenue and across the railroad tracks.

The doctor described the terrible diseases we might catch if we patronized the girls. The chaplain backed him up by reading scriptures from the Bible. After the lecture, they asked if we had any questions.

One guy raised his hand and asked, "Could you give me the address of that red light district again?"

We parked our trucks by the Municipal Auditorium, and went in different directions. I stopped and counted my money. After all that barbering, I had almost thirteen dollars in cash — a small fortune in those days.

As I walked down "E" Street, I was stopped by a disreputable looking man. He asked if I could spare a dime so he could get a hamburger. I gave him a dime and went on my way.

A few steps farther, another guy asked if I could let him have a dime for a bowl of chili. He said the Kansas dust had run him out of his state. He couldn't find a job and had not eaten in two days. I gave him a dime for a bowl of chili, and he asked if I could give him another nickel for a cup of coffee.

The next guy told me the Mississippi flood waters had washed everything he owned down the river. He was cold and hungry. Could I help him by giving a little money to get something to eat?

When I got to Third Street, I turned right toward "F" Street. The bums were getting in line to hit me up for more money. Remembering how it was in Texas when I left, I always helped anyone who was hungry.

I went into the drug store on Third Street to take inventory of my cash. I had eighty-five cents left.

The man behind the counter asked, "What's the matter kid, the Winos getting all your money?"

"They are hungry. I was just helping them buy something to eat."

He laughed. "Don't give those guys any more money. They are not looking for a job and they aren't hungry. They're alcoholics, bums, and winos. They only want money to buy more wine."

When I went back out on the street, a guy walked up to me and opened his mouth to speak.

I stopped him. "I'm working this side of the street," I said. "You go over on the other side."

70

Cool Clear Water

In the mid 1930s, Peaches Mahan, Henry Morgan, and I pooled our money and bought a 1928 Model-A Ford. We wanted to travel in class. Since everybody else was going somewhere, looking for work, we planned our trip from Dallas to California.

The first six hundred miles would be the hardest. If we could make it to El Paso, we would be halfway to our destination. The highway along the Mexican border was two lanes wide. There were miles and miles of nothing, from Fort Stockton, Van Horn, and on through the Big Bend country.

We could always find a nice motel — they called them "Tourist Courts" then — for a dollar and a quarter per night.

Along the way, it was common to see cars on the side of the road, their hoods up, smoke and steam coming from their radiators. Flat tires also were a frequent reason for roadside stops.

We were advised by some of the local people that this part of the country was having a two-year drought. Tumbleweeds scattered across the road and clouds of dust swept before us.

When we got to Ysleta, our car was smoking and the gas tank showed empty. But we were in luck finding a Texaco station at the side of the road where several smoking cars waited for attention. A huge sign read: "Gasoline 13¢, Water 15¢." The attendant wouldn't let us put water in the radiator. He was afraid we would spill a few drops. The station, like all others in that part of Texas, hauled its water by the barrel from the Rio Grande River.

After buying gasoline, we took inventory to determine if we had any money left from that day's budget. We had just enough to buy a dime bowl of chili or a hamburger for each of us.

In El Paso, we saw a Mexican restaurant with the parking lot full of cars. The attraction was a band, the Sons of the Pioneers, featuring Roy Rogers. They were singing for their supper. The restaurant owner gave them stale pies and pastries from the back room. He also paid them some money if they attracted customers. Roy was young and not yet "King of the Cowboys." A few years later, he was making western movies and riding his horse, Trigger, through the sagebrush.

Some of the songs they sang always made me thirsty. They were: "Drifting Along With the Tumbling Tumbleweeds" and "Cool Clear Water."

71

Social Security Card

In the summer of 1938, I read an article in the Paris (Texas) *Morning News,* stating that the Rural Electrification Act (R.E.A.) needed a few good men to run a power line five miles out in the rural community. They also advised it was a temporary job, lasting only a few weeks.

At that time, only the city folks in east Texas could afford electricity in their homes. The families in the rural areas used kerosene lamps. Some owned Coleman lanterns, which had to be pumped frequently.

The article further stated the job paid thirty-five cents an hour, or $3.15 for a nine-hour day. That was good money at that time.

Wanting to be first in line, I left immediately to get in on that big money. Even so, when the hiring office opened at seven a.m., a huge crowd had gathered. I was at the end of the line. One by one the applicants stepped up for a few words with the interviewer. He would order some of the men to get on the truck. Others who didn't qualify left.

When I finally was second in line, the man ahead of me was greeted by the interviewer. "You got a Social Security card?"

"Have I got a what?"

"This is a Government project, and you have to have a Social Security card to work," he was told.

"What's a Social Security card?"

The interviewer explained what a Social Security card was, and told him where he could go to get one.

After hearing the lecture given the man ahead of me, I didn't want to appear uninformed.

"I was on my way to the post office to get my Social Security card, and just—"

"You go get your Social Security card first, and come back tomorrow, and I'll talk to you!"

The next morning at seven a.m. sharp I was there with my brand new card in hand, and went through the same procedure as the day before. When I got to the window, he took my card without comment and started to write something on the form. Then he looked up at me. "Are you married or single?" he asked.

"Single," I said.

"This office is hiring only married men," he said.

I turned away in disgust, but he called me back.

"Tell you what," he said. "You come down here tomorrow, bring your lunch and wait. It may not happen tomorrow, but one of these mornings someone out of the twenty-five hands we hired will get drunk and won't be able to make it to work on time. If you are here with your lunch packed and ready to work, we'll put you on the truck."

I took his advice. The next morning I packed a peanut butter sandwich and waited. All twenty-five men were present. Wednesday morning, the same thing. Thursday morning, I was getting anxious. I was running out of peanut butter.

On Friday morning, he called one man's name three times. No answer. The supervisor looked at me, winked, gave me a thumbs up sign, and pointed to the truck.

When we got to the job site, the crew chief gave me a pick and shovel, and told me the power line poles would also double for telephone poles. The holes had to be dug five and a half feet deep. It had been a dry summer, and the ground was as hard as concrete pavement.

"How many holes do I have to dig for a full day's work?" I asked.

"The other guys averaged about three and a half holes a day," he said.

"How can I dig a half of a hole?" I asked.

After pondering the question, he said, "I don't know, but why don't you just imagine you are a gopher, and start to dig?"

After one week, the funds for the job had been used up. No money, no work. They told us we would be notified when they received another grant. We didn't complete the five miles as scheduled.

When I got paid, the government held out one percent on the dollar. I still have the voucher stub to show that I paid the first nineteen cents into my Social Security account in September 1938.

72

Checking Out

"If you can't 'cut it,' move over and let someone else take your place. There's no shortage of people looking for work." These were statements often heard in the San Joaquin Valley in the 1930s, Depression years. People from as far away as Florida came in "limping" Fords and on motorcycles looking for jobs. I was no exception and was there in 1938.

Some ranchers in the valley owned a section of land, six hundred and forty acres. They raised a variety of crops — cotton, potatoes, alfalfa, and several kinds of fruit.

To assign jobs for the most able and dedicated fruit pickers, one of the regular ranch hands would drive a pickup truck load of buckets into an orchard. He would throw two or three buckets under each tree as he drove by. Another truck behind him would throw off step ladders. The mad scramble started. Whichever worker grabbed a bucket and ladder first was hired.

After two or three hours passed, a straw boss would come by with a writing pad and take the name of each man who had managed to get a ladder and fill his bucket. That way the boss knew who was on his payroll.

Potato harvest was a little different, and my buddies, Joe Jones and Hank Collins, and I arrived in time for it. After the potatoes were plowed up, they were sacked and lined up in wind rows. I drove a truck along the rows, going no faster than five miles an hour. I was ordered never to stop. Joe and Hank rode on the bed and grabbed the seventy-five-pound sacks pitched up to them by the two guys on the ground.

Besides catching the sacks, it was my buddies' job to keep them upright on the bed so as to get maximum use of the space on the truck.

We really earned our thirty-five cents an hour, especially Joe and Hank.

We had no lunch break, but the driver who hauled the potatoes to Wasco and Shafter, always stopped on the way back from delivering a load and let the crew get a loaf of day-old bread for five cents and a quart of milk for ten cents. We hauled several loads each day, unloading at about the same speed as we had picked up the sacks in the field.

After the potato harvest was over, I got a job hauling alfalfa hay. The bales weighed about eighty pounds, and they were packed so tight that stabbing them with the hook was like trying to pierce a brick.

After working by the hour, my buddies, Joe and Hank, and I wanted to do our own contracting, and work at our own pace.

We made a deal with a farmer, Mr. Hack, to "chop" (thin and weed) ten acres of cotton for fifty dollars.

He hesitated, but told us we could have the job, provided we would start on the side that had the most grass and weeds. We agreed.

Starting on Friday and working 'til dark on Saturday, we had completed the hardest part. We intended to come back Monday morning and knock out the other five acres. Maybe we could finish in one day if all three of us worked until dark.

When we returned to the field Monday morning, a bunch of Mexicans were already working on our project.

"Hey, you Hombres are in the wrong field. That's our project," I said. They just kept working. I finally found one who could understand a little English. "How much did Hack pay you for this job?"

"Ocho dolores."

"Eight dollars?"

"Si."

We tried to find the owner, but he was over at his other spread.

"He'll be back tomorrow," his assistant told us, "but he is not hiring right now," he added.

We went to the other acreage to find him and told him what happened. He wasn't concerned. "I didn't know whether you guys would be coming back. I can never depend on you migrant workers. The Mexicans came looking for work early this morning, and I told them to go ahead and finish that patch."

We asked about the fifty dollars he owed us.

"I'm not gonna pay you guys, because you didn't finish the job, and I only pay my hands on Friday nights anyway!" he said. "If I fire you, I'll have to pay you on the spot, but if you quit, you will have to wait 'til Friday."

Cesar Chavez wasn't around to help us, so we had to do our own negotiating.

After an argument, he agreed to pay us twenty-five dollars for our part of the five acres.

We hurried to the bank in MacFarlane to cash our check. When the doors opened, I was first in line with the check and my I.D. in hand.

"This check is no good," the teller said.

"Why?" I asked.

"It's dated Friday, and this is Monday. Mr. Hack owns most of this bank, but he never pays his hands 'til Friday. Come back then."

I went back to the car where my two partners were waiting to get their share of the twenty-five dollars. When I told them what happened, they blamed me for not noticing the date on the check.

"You know we want to go to San Jose to get in on the grape harvest as soon as we get our money," Joe said.

"We are not going to hang around here 'til Friday, and we are not driving back down here from San Jose just to cash that check," Hank added.

They told me I'd better do something in a hurry.

I waited 'til the bank was crowded, and sneaked in without the first teller seeing me. A girl at a window at the far end of the bank was a "plain Jane." Her name tag said, "Ruby."

As I stepped up to her window, I said, "Hi Ruby, what a pretty dress you are wearing today! Who did your hair? I've never seen you looking so good."

She gave me a big smile and without looking at the date on the check or my I.D., she shelled out twenty-five dollars.

As I pushed my way through the crowd to leave, she was still smiling.

When I got back to the car, I flashed a twenty and a five.

"How'd you do it?" Joe asked.

"Its easy if you know Ruby," I said.

73

Kansas Bread

We felt we'd picked all the prunes and grapes in California when we headed eastward for the wheat harvest in Kansas. Our Model-A broke down in Reno, Nevada, delaying us two days. When we finally arrived in Hoxey, Kansas, at about four p.m. on a hot windy day, we drove out to the wheat fields.

We knew the wheat harvest lasted only about ten days. If it wasn't harvested within that time, it was often lost. Wheat was subject to many hazards. If a sand storm blew in, the whole year's crop was destroyed in a few hours. Sometimes grasshoppers leveled the entire acreage. Fire, too, could be a threat. At harvest time, the farmers worked from daylight 'til dark, including Sundays and the Fourth of July.

So, the boss we talked to had work for us. He was a Russian named Blankenski. When he and his family came to America, they legally changed their name to Blank. He explained that wheat harvesting was much more difficult than handling hay. He handed each of us a pitchfork, sized me up, and told me to "get on the header barge." I didn't know what a header barge was, but pretended I did when he pointed to a wagon. Then he left us to our job and went on to supervise another unit. We hadn't had any lunch or dinner because we'd been traveling all day. Anyway, we didn't have any money for food. We'd spent it all on repairing our Model-A in Reno.

We set about our jobs, doing the best we could. The combine did the cutting and threshing at the same time. Another machine, the unit we worked on, was a little different. A mowing machine cut the wheat and a belt threw it on the header barge. When this machine started up, the straw was filling my wagon, the header barge. It was about fifteen feet long and ten feet wide. I had to move my pitchfork hard and fast to keep from being buried in the straw. We began work about 4:30 p.m. and by dark, at 8:30, when we stopped, I was dehydrated and weak.

Blankenski came up to me with a grin on his face and asked, "Well, how did you do?"

Wanting to keep my job, I said, "O.K."

"Did you know there was supposed to be two men on that barge instead of one? You did the work of two men. I think you are going to work out all right."

The oldest son of the Blank family was about thirty-five. He was a medical doctor and had an office in Kansas City. He told me the story of their family history. His dad had died at an early age, and left a wife and five boys. His family had immigrated from Russia about two generations ago. They had settled in that part of Kansas, between Grainfield and Hoxey. He graduated from medical school, and left the farm to the younger brothers. He still had an interest in the farm, and watched over the younger boys. He didn't trust them to take complete charge of the harvest. He was losing money by closing his office and returning to the farm. It would only take about ten days, maybe two weeks to harvest the wheat, and that was more important than keeping his office open.

He explained that the farmers got only one good crop of wheat about every two or three years. If they had a good crop every other year, they could survive. But if they had two bad years in a row, they were out of business. The banks would move in and foreclose on the farm. F.D.R.'s New Deal had a system called the "ever normal granary." They had a "parity" on corn and wheat. If you didn't think the price was right at harvest time, you could store the wheat in a grain elevator, and hold it until the price went up. The U.S. government always guaranteed a set minimum price.

The good doctor also explained that some of the farmers would make a "bumper crop" of wheat and turn it into cash immediately. They would go out and buy a lot of farm equipment, such as combine tractors and trucks. They would make a small down payment. If they had two dry years in a row they were in big trouble.

It was dark when we finally left the field and traveled about one mile to the big farm house, and a huge barn for the horses.

Dr. Blank was definitely in charge of the operation. He showed us a little building, like a smoke house, where we could sleep. He pointed out where our shower was. The shower consisted of a barrel on a platform about ten feet off the ground. The barrel had to be filled in the morning so the water could get heated by the sun during the day. A bucket with nail holes punched in it acted as a shower head. A faucet on a pipe turned the water into the bucket. A yard-wide piece of canvas wrapped around the base of the platform maintained some privacy. The Kansas wind blew the flap of the "shower curtain," and it was pretty cold.

The mother of the clan was huge, like all of her sons. She spoke with a Russian accent. Sometimes she would talk in Russian, especially when she didn't want us to know what she was saying.

We were introduced to a young girl, name Evesta. She helped cook during the big harvest. She was young, big, and tough looking. My sidekick, Peaches, said he thought she could have been a quarterback for a football team. She didn't talk much, she just supplied the grub for the hungry hired hands.

The next day, the doctor, fearing it was going to storm before the wheat was harvested, needed more hands. He sent his youngest brother to town to wait 'til the freight trains came through. Hobos always stole rides on the trains going west and Blank said, "Don't come back without some men who are willing to work, even if you have to offer them three dollars a day."

This fifteen-year-old brother wasn't back by quitting time, and the doctor was fit to be tied. Just as we were leaving to go home, we saw a cloud of dust down the country road. We waited. The brother explained that four freight trains came through the town, and only two stopped. "There were hobos all right, a lot of them. When I told them about the jobs I had waiting for them at three dollars a day, they just laughed at me and stayed on the train."

We worked on Sundays and the Fourth of July and were making progress in the harvest. About three p.m. on the twelfth day, a black cloud rolled in from the northwest. It looked ominous. The doctor gave orders to work faster. "What I always fear is a dust storm," he said. The dust started to blow. The sun at three p.m. looked like a full moon. The sky grew darker by the minute. The doctor ordered us to keep working. Finally, we couldn't see the sun. It was dark, although it was only about four p.m. The dust was so heavy it seemed like midnight.

From the barn where we took the mules to unharness and feed them, we couldn't see the house which was only about fifty yards away.

Mrs. Blank and Evesta had the kerosene lamp in the kitchen. It gave very poor light, and there was about as much dust in the house as outside. When they put supper on the table, the hungry guys went for it like they were starving to death.

They made their own bread and sliced it with a big butcher knife. The bread was white, but the dust made it look like whole wheat. The butter was brown with sand, but we all slapped the butter on our bread and ate it.

One of the hands laughed, "Eat up. A little dirt won't hurt you. After you've been in Kansas a while, you'll get used to it."

Mrs. Blank served iced tea to drink. The ice was cut from the lakes in the winter time and buried under the house in a special bin. It kept through most of the summer months. The tea was strong and laced with sand.

The next morning, the storm had blown over and the sun was shining bright and hot.

In the kitchen, the women swept up buckets of sand that had blown into the house. They explained that most of the farmhouses were built to keep out the rain, but the blowing snow and dust could not be kept out.

The next day we went to the fields, but there was nothing to do. The wheat wasn't vertical, it was horizontal. It couldn't be harvested in that position. If the storm had waited one more day, we would have finished the job.

The doctor shook his head. "We were pretty lucky to save most of the crop. It's time for me to go back to Kansas City and take care of my patients."

We all went back to the house and he paid each of us in silver dollars. Thirty-nine big ones each for thirteen days work. We took our money and *blew* town. We'd had enough wind.

I still think twice before I order brown bread.

74

Man of Means

I checked every car on the lot. It was still 1939, but the 1940 models were out. The Chevrolet pick-up was the one I was interested in.

It was a cold Sunday morning and the east wind blew right through my body. That's probably the reason there were no salesman on duty. Over on the corner of the lot was a small, windowed cage-like building. I could see a man sitting inside reading the newspaper.

Because he wouldn't come out, I decided to go in to get some information. The cigarette smoke and the fumes from the Coleman kerosene heater made breathing difficult.

As I walked in, the man didn't look up from his paper or say good morning. He was mumbling to himself something about the football scores. Apparently he had lost a bet on some college football team.

"How much is the 1940 Chevy pick-up?" I asked.

"Oh, you can't afford a car like that," he said.

"Well, how much is it?" I asked.

"Six hundred twenty-four dollars, but I'm sure you don't make that kind of money. Are you working at all?"

"Of course I'm working."

"What kind of work do you do?" He continued looking at his newspaper.

"I'm a barber," I replied.

"Oh, barbers don't make any money these days. The depression is not over yet. How much money do you make?"

"I make fifteen dollars a week," I told him.

"Fifteen dollars a week? You make fifteen dollars a week?"

He immediately stood up and looked at me for the first time. Dropping the newspaper at his feet, he fired up a Chesterfield cigarette, zipped his jacket up under his chin, and said, "I've got a clean little car out here I think is exactly what you are looking for."

"No," I said. "I'm looking for a new 1940 Chevy pick-up. I'll just go down on Elm Street and buy one from the other dealer."

He not only lost his bet on the football game, he also lost a sale on a new car. He failed to recognize a Man of Means.

75

"Clipping" Around Texas

I had been barbering several years in government installations when I wanted to get a license to barber in civilian shops. Some of my best education for life came during my barbering days.

The first day in school, they start you off in the "bull pen." That's a one-chair room. Most of the new students stay there two or three weeks before graduating to the big shop with thirty-six chairs. I stayed half a day in the bull pen.

When they enrolled a new student in school, they notified the hobo camps. The winos came on down for a free hair cut. They were dirty, smelly, and never got a haircut until a new barber started at the school. Some of the students quit the same day they started.

"I didn't know it would be like this," I've heard new students say.

Mr. Cox was the student instructor. He told me I shouldn't be giving away my services to the bums in the bull pen. If I wanted to make some money, he would promote me to the front chair, and I could be in charge of the cash register, and I would get one-half of what I took in. He also advised me that I would get better tips working the front chair. A student tip was a nickel.

"You are a good barber," he said. "But you are doing it wrong."

"Why?" I asked.

"You are shaving necks all the way around. You should just shave down the sides and feather the hair in the back."

"I thought everybody shaved square across the back of the neck. That's the way I've always done it."

"Oh no, did you ever notice how Tyrone Power, Henry Fonda, and

Clark Gable's hair looks in the movies? They don't shave all around, they shave down the sides of their neck," he insisted. "Everyone in Dallas has the new modern look."

While we were discussing hair styles, a tall guy with a ten-gallon hat and shaved neck, squared across, walked by the window.

"Look, that man has his neck shaved all around," I said.

"Oh, he's not from Dallas, he's probably from Ft. Worth, or somewhere out in the country. Ft. Worth, is called a 'Cow Town' because they have the biggest stockyard south of Kansas City. Dallas is a sophisticated city, an eastern City. Ft. Worth is out where the West begins.

"When Amon Carter, who owns most of Ft. Worth, comes to Dallas, on business, he won't eat in our restaurants. He brings his lunch from home, in a brown paper bag, and sits down on the curb to eat his lunch. There's always been rivalry between the two cities. I don't think they really mean it, though."

"There's one thing Ft. Worth, has that Dallas, doesn't have."

"Yeah, what's that?"

"A beautiful city, just thirty-two miles away."

Mr. Cox, after convincing me to shave down the sides, also told me how long the sideburns should be. From the lower part of the ear lobe toward the end of the nose. He said sideburns were named after General Burnside, a famous Civil War general. They later revised the name to "sideburns." Some referred to long sideburns as "lamb chops."

Since that time, we had a war and the "G.I." hair cut was a flat top. Then, in the sixties, men let their hair grow long. They were called "hippies." Some didn't get a haircut at all. The barbers almost starved to death during that fad.

If Mr. Cox knew what they were doing to his tonsorial efforts, he would turn over in his grave.

After completing barber college and taking the state board, I'd passed it and was ready to go just about anywhere to get a job. Transient barbers were free to travel and "clip" their way from one town to another. We were also known as "boomer barbers."

If there was an oil boom or a job with a big weekly payroll, we barbers would be there.

On Saturday afternoon, I was working in a three-chair shop. One of the barbers was on vacation and his chair was vacant. A "boomer" with a three-day beard came in. He looked as if he had a hangover. He carried his barber tools in a briefcase and asked if he could go to work on the vacant chair.

The shop owner told him the empty chair belonged to a barber that was on vacation and had been working that chair for ten years.

"Oh, that's all right, I'll just work today, I don't want to take his job."

"Well, I don't know," the owner hesitated. "I don't think so."

"Oh, come on," one of the waiting customers said. "Let him work the rest of the day. I've been waiting here for almost an hour. I need to get home early. I promised the little woman I would take her out for dinner tonight. There's still four men ahead of me, and I only want a shave."

"O.K., but just this Saturday. My regular barber will be back Monday," the owner said.

The big guy jumped into the barber chair and said, "See I got you a job, I should be your manager, you better give me a good shave now."

The new barber took his tools from his bag, placed them on the stand, hung up his razor strap, put the chair in the reclining position, and lathered his customer's face. He then put a big hot towel over the lathered face to soften his beard.

Slowly, he strapped his razor, then sat down and stared out the window. While seated, he took off his shoes and socks, went to the lavatory, wet cleaned the black curd from between his toes.

In the meantime, other customers were coming in. Some walked out, looking back over their shoulders in disbelief. The rest of us were virtually holding our breaths, wondering what he would do next. We didn't say anything.

When his customer, under the hot towel, began to snore, the "new barber" slowly packed up his tools and walked out the door without saying a word. The manager appointed me to take over the unfinished job.

I shaved the customer and woke him up to let him out of the barber chair.

"What happened? You're not the same man. Where's my barber?" he inquired.

"I heard you are his manager. I guess you'll have to find him," I said.

After barbering in Ft. Worth, Austin, and Brownwood, I went west to Pecos, three hundred miles away from any big cities. It was a famous frontier town where Judge Roy Bean had presided. His court was known as the "Only Law West of the Pecos."

After returning to San Antonio, to a big shop, I worked with a barber who had been studying in a Seminary to become a minister.

He didn't say, but from some of the things he said, I think he had flunked out of school, or was expelled for giving too much "counseling" to the wife of one of his parishioners.

He was talking to one of his customers while giving him a shampoo. "At that school, they furnished me a house to live in, all the utilities paid, and most of my groceries. I thought that was pretty *damn good.*"

A man in the next barber chair overheard the conversation. "Can preachers use those four-letter words now?"

"Oh, hell, I don't know, I'm not going back there anymore," said the barber preacher.

At six o'clock Saturday night, some of the barbers left the shop. Some had to work until ten p.m.

In the dressing room, the de-frocked minister came in to change his clothes. It was quitting time for him. He took off his white barber smock, hung it in his locker, put on his coat and tie, reached back into the locker, and took out his Colt .45, held it up to the light to check the chamber, stuck it in his belt, reached back in the locker and took a pint of "Old Crow" whiskey from the shelf. He shook it and held the liquor up to the light. "It's half full," he said.

The last thing he took from the locker was the Holy Bible, which he put under his arm as he walked out the door, and said, "See y'all Monday."

One morning when I was working at my barber chair, a well-dressed man walked by, looked in, and saw thirty-six barbers working. He felt his face with his hand, and dashed into the shop for a quick shave. He said he had just ridden into town from Chicago, on the train, and had to attend an important meeting in thirty minutes. He said he really needed a haircut, too, but wouldn't have time for it.

I assured him I could give him a haircut and shave, and have him ready for his meeting in less than thirty minutes.

"O.K., go ahead," he said.

When he got out of my barber chair, I gave him the ticket for twenty-five cents. I was at the front chair, and operating the cash register.

He looked at the ticket and did a double take. "You must have made a mistake. This says twenty-five cents. You mean a dollar twenty-five don't you?"

"No, twenty-five cents is correct," I said.

"My barber in Chicago has taken care of me for the last twenty years. He charges $1.25 for a shave and a haircut, and it takes him forty-five minutes. You did it in fifteen minutes for only twenty-five cents?"

"We do everything quicker and cheaper in Dallas. Besides, this is a barber college."

"It's a what? A barber college? You didn't tell me that before I got in your chair!"

"There's a big sign on the window that says 'American Barber College.'"

"Well I'll be damned. How could I have missed it?" He handed me the ticket and a quarter. "You got a mirror so I can see the back of my head?"

He turned his head from one side to the other, pulling his ears back as he held the small mirror to inspect his new haircut from all sides. He handed the mirror back to me and reached for his wallet. "That's a much better job than I get in Chicago," he said, and handed me a dollar bill, grabbed his briefcase, and rushed out the door, looking back to read the Barber College sign on the window as he ran his hand over his chin.

The other barber students, hearing the conversation and witnessing the dollar tip, left their chairs and came over to me. They wanted to see the bill.

One said, "If he's from Chicago, I'll bet he is one of Al Capone's partners. The bill is probably counterfeit. Nobody gives a dollar for a twenty-five cent job. That's a day's work."

"When you guys get to be as good a barber as I am, you, too, can get a tip four times the size of your bill," I gloated.

Everyone doesn't have the temperament to be a barber. The school is the proving ground, where the students get the "acid" test. If they can't "cut it" (hair, that is) they should find another job.

The union barber shops in 1940 charged thirty-five cents, but very few belonged to the union. The so-called "scab" shops charged twenty-five cents. The barber college charged fifteen cents for a haircut. We had more customers than we could take care of. Our customers were the down-and-out hobos, bums, families with several small children, and people who were broke. We also had people with money who were frugal — that's the reason they had the money. They didn't particularly care how their hair looked if they could save ten or fifteen cents.

The streetcar operators had a strong union. One of the drivers came in for a haircut, and some Vitalis for his hair. He looked sharp when I got through with him. He went back to the train depot and told all his friends about the barber he had found, and how much money he saved. The next day, all the streetcar drivers lined up, waiting for me. They wouldn't let any of the other students work on them.

When the union officials heard about it, they threatened to picket the street car headquarters.

One barber student came from Winters, Texas. Everybody called him "Winters." He had a wooden leg and the state was paying his tuition at the school.

Winters had not only lost his leg, he had also lost his compassion, his temper, and a few other things. He didn't like kids, and wasn't too crazy about grown-ups. In barber school, each customer took a number and waited his turn. The barber couldn't choose his client; he had to take his share of kids.

One day he got a small kid in his barber chair. That's when the trouble started. We could predict exactly what he would say. It was always the same words with the kid crying, rubbing tears and snot mixed with hair into his eyes and mouth.

First: "Hold your little head up, son."

Second: "Hold your head up, boy!"

Third: "H-O-L-D T-H-A-T G-O-D-D-A-M-N H-E-A-D U-P, K-I-D!"

At this point, everybody in the shop laughed.

Winters would throw his comb and scissors down and stomp off with his peg leg jarring the floor. He would stay in the men's room until the instructor got the kid quiet, cut his hair, and apologized to the mother.

She would never mention the episode to Winters. At our price, she knew better.

76

How-Now-Brown-Cow

Mrs. Gayle ran a boarding house in Dallas.

I was a student in barber college. The owner of the college advised me that she had a friend who wanted tenants for her board and room house. She charged five dollars a week, and that included two meals at her house and she would pack a lunch for them.

She had a special rate for the barber students. She would let them wash dishes morning and night to pay half their board and room.

My friend, the owner of the barber college, advised me that none of her students had ever lasted more than three weeks at Mrs. Gayle's place. I asked why?

"She's overbearing, opinionated, a bully, and just plain mean."

"Sounds like someone I can get along with," I said. "Give me her address."

I arrived just in time to wash the dinner dishes. Mrs. Gayle was everything that I had been told, plus she was stingy and nosey. She was a huge woman with a voice to match.

Mrs. Gayle formally introduced me to her husband, Ray, and told me he was a postman, and had killed a man a few years before. She seemed proud of him for what he had done. I got the impression she was bragging and warning other people to watch their step around him.

Her husband was about half her size, and obviously scared of her. He wore thick-lens glasses, and never looked you in the eye when talking to you. He just mumbled and looked down at the floor. Ray never ate at the table with the other members of the household.

After dinner, when it was time for me to wash the dishes, he would gather up all the scraps, especially the bread heels from the table, put the mixture in a big bowl, and pour milk over it. That was his dinner. I would have to wait and wash his dish after I was through with the other dishes.

One night while washing pots and pans, it was eight o'clock, and time for the Craft Music Hall with Bing Crosby and Bob Burns. I brought my little radio in the kitchen and set it on the refrigerator to listen to the program.

Mrs. Gayle stormed in and turned my program off. She said I couldn't concentrate on my work if I was listening to those girls. Those girls were the Andrews Sisters. They were singing, "Don't Sit Under The Apple Tree With Anyone Else But Me."

Ed, another boarder, worked for the Otis Elevator Company. He had been living at the boarding house longer than any of us. One night at dinner, he came to the table late. He went to the refrigerator and poured a tall glass of milk.

"No," Mrs. Gayle said. "You are allowed one small glass of milk each meal, not one big tall glass."

"The short squatty glasses hold more than the tall slim glasses," Ed argued.

"No they don't," Mrs. Gayle said. "You think I'm stupid."

"I can prove it. Let me show you by measuring one of the small glasses filled water, then I'll pour it in the tall slim one. See, the glass runs over. You've been cheating yourself all these years."

Ed was right, and Mrs. Gayle was furious. She had been wrong and was embarrassed.

Russell, a streetcar operator, had been a boarder long enough to have learned to be quiet. He knew to be in bed at ten p.m., up at six a.m., and pay the five dollars a week board and room. He didn't fill the bath tub more than one-third full, and was sure to turn off the lights in the room. And he didn't "talk back."

Ray Lee Fortner was the problem tenant. I felt responsible for him because he had been a friend for several years. I thought I would do him a favor by getting him a place to live at Mrs. Gayle's. She gave me fifty cents for bringing her a new tenant.

Fortner had beautiful curly hair. It wasn't blonde, but canary yellow. He would spend hours in front of the mirror caressing his hair after a shampoo, putting every hair in place. Jack May, a mutual friend, would sneak up behind him and muss-up his hair. Fortner hated that, but he was shy and never fought back.

Fortner had come to Dallas to get a job as a radio announcer. He was promised the job if he would train his speaking voice. The manager had written out some key words for him to practice at home before the mirror — in the bath tub, or just anywhere. He was to speak from his diaphragm, and learn to roll his vowels. And practice, practice, practice.

Fortner wanted the job and was willing to do anything he was told.

One night, after ten o'clock, he was in the bath tub, running water, and practicing his voice lessons over and over. He was saying: HOW-NOW-BROWN-COW. Mrs. Gayle barged in without knocking, turned off his bath water, pulled the plug from the tub and screamed at him for using too much water, and disturbing everyone in the house. She woke the rest of us sleepers. We got out of bed to see what was happening. It was a shocking sight.

Fortner was standing at attention in the bath tub, with water dripping from his body, with his hands cupped over his head to protect his hair. Mrs. Gayle was "preaching" to him about breaking her house rules. She looked over her shoulder and saw three of us tenants standing behind her. She treated us like three-year-olds, by wailing and telling us to get back to bed where we belonged, and to mind our own business.

The last thing Mrs. Gayle told Fortner was, "If you don't straighten up, I'll pack your bags and put them on the porch and throw you out with them. And another thing, I don't want to hear anymore about that 'Brown-Cow.'"

For the next few days, when the boarders met Fortner in the hall, they would say in a low voice, "How-Now-Brown-Cow."

He couldn't take it any longer. One Saturday morning in the spring of 1940, he packed his bags, combed his hair, took his brown cow and never returned.

77

World War II

As early as 1938 and for sure 1939, I knew the U.S.A. would be in another war — soon.

Everybody was telling me that World War I was the war to end all wars. They also quoted President Roosevelt (F.D.R.) who said in his first campaign speech, "If I'm elected President, no American soldier will ever shed a drop of blood on foreign soil." But when Hitler ran roughshod over Poland, Czechoslovakia, Austria, and Hungry, the handwriting was on the wall.

He marched through France in 1940, and had already begun bombing London.

Hitler's slogan was: "Today Germany, Tomorrow the World."

That would have happened too, if the U.S.A. had not jumped in, and we were almost too late.

When I got my draft notice for my physical examination, the doctor classified me as 1-B. "You have flat feet. You could never be a soldier because you would be required to hike ten to twelve miles with a full field pack and a rifle. You couldn't keep up," he said.

I knew he was wrong, because I was reared on a farm, and I had walked behind a team of mules and plowed ten acres of cotton or corn in one day. That equaled about twenty miles of walking in twelve hours. In the evening I would walk five miles to a country dance, then walk home.

I didn't tell the doctor about that. He had classified me 1-B. I was glad I wasn't classified 4-F. They were the ones who couldn't pass the physical and never had to go to war. The popular accusation was that they were staying home to "take care of the girls."

The doctor who gave me my physical was a civilian doctor, and he told me they would be "taking all the women and children in the service before they'd accept me."

I told the doctor, I was engaged to be married in one month.

"What? You want to go to war and get killed, and leave a widow?"

A short time later, the Japanese bombed Pearl Harbor, and destroyed most of our ships on the first raid. We were losing an island a week in the Pacific, and we had just declared war on Germany, and I had just gotten married.

They called a few more million men up to be reclassified. I went from 1-B to 1-A. The final physical examination was given to six men at a time, all lined up against a wall. The first order was: "bend over, wiggle your fingers, read the letters on the wall, raise your right hand and repeat after me."

Congratulations, you are now a soldier, for the duration, plus six months.

One guy tried to fake blindness when the doctor asked him to read the letters.

"What letters?" he asked.

"The letters on the chart," the doctor told him.

"What chart?" the man asked.

"The chart on the wall!"

"What wall?"

It didn't work.

Next we went to the supply sergeant to get our uniforms. ("If it fits, take it back." That's suppose to be a G.I. — Government Issue — joke, but it was more like the truth.)

We were supposed to get seventeen weeks of basic training, but since they needed troops in a hurry, they cut the time down to thirteen weeks. We trained long hours, and very hard. By the end of the thirteen weeks, some had dropped by the wayside. Some had epilepsy, some had heart problems, and some had psychological problems. Of course, some simply could take it and some couldn't.

Staff Sergeant Willie D. Brown was a peace-time soldier. He had been in the Army for several years, and had been stationed at several different bases in the U.S. and at Scofield barracks in the Philippine Islands. He was about six feet four inches and weighed two hundred and eighty pounds. He had been assigned as part of a cadre to train the new recruits and get them ready for combat. He had a voice that could be heard all over the base, and the tone was authoritative. He could send chills up your spine. When he shouted a command, the new recruits responded immediately or suffered the consequences.

I had known Sergeant Brown when I was a civilian, running a P.X. barber shop on the base, at Camp Bowie, in Brownwood, Texas. When I was drafted, I was assigned to Camp Bowie as a new recruit.

Colonel Hunt and Major Holloway were still there. They welcomed me and said they had not had a good haircut since I left. Both of the field officers were West Point graduates.

When I was their barber, as a civilian, we were good friends. We talked and socialized. But, when I came back as a buck private, they treated me differently. I had to salute and say, "Sir."

(Ironically, I took Major Holloway's place on the battlefield in Normandy two years later, when he was blown to pieces. At that moment, it didn't matter that I wasn't a West Point graduate.)

Sergeant Brown, like the commissioned officers, could not show any favoritism, nor did I ask for any. When we were several weeks into basic training, Sergeant Brown picked out a few of the most promising soldiers to promote to corporal. One hot afternoon, we were in drill training when Sergeant Brown ordered one of his potential corporals to take charge of the platoon.

Of course he wasn't a real corporal yet, he was just acting as a non-commissioned officer. His name was Private Wilson.

The guy was scared of the sergeant, but he wanted to make a good impression so that he'd be in line for his first stripe.

As he walked out in front of his troops, he said in a high-pitched voice, "All right, men, fall in, please."

Sergeant Brown walked over to Wilson, towering above him, and said, "Did I hear you say, fall in, please? Fall in, please?" Then he raised his thunderous voice and shouted, "Soldier, you are in this man's army to learn how to fight and kill. You are not teaching Sunday School. From now on, you will knock off that *please* stuff. Is that clear?"

"Sir, yes sir," Private Wilson said.

He did make corporal, and before we went into combat, he made buck sergeant. He was burned to death in a tank at the Normandy invasion.

I can still hear Sergeant Brown's voice in my sleep sometimes saying, "You are not teaching Sunday School, you are in this man's army to learn how to fight and kill."

At Camp Walters, close to Mineral Wells, Texas, we were training in close order drill under Sergeant Levy. He was a hard boiled drill sergeant, and had no patience.

A "blue darter norther" was blowing in from the Panhandle, kicking up a lot of dust.

In our company was an odd thirty-year-old guy named Frederick, who didn't know his right foot from his left. However, his biggest problem was that he was totally deaf in one ear and couldn't hear well out of the other. He had passed his physical without his deafness being detected. The Sergeant didn't know he had a hearing impairment. He had been giving Frederick a hard time for not following his commands, for not standing up straight, and for not swinging his arms in the military fashion. They were getting on each other's nerves, and Sergeant Levy wouldn't let up on him.

The Sergeant gave the command,"Forward march, by the left flank march, by the right flank march, to the rear — march."

Frederick didn't hear the command, "To the rear, march." He kept marching straight ahead, with his gut in, his chin up, and his arms swinging in a military fashion, just like he was ordered to do. The only problem was that Frederick was marching West, alone. The other thirty-nine men were marching in formation. The next command was, "To the rear — march." By this time, Fredrick was about a hundred yards ahead of everybody else, marching into the wind, all alone.

The Sergeant gave the command, "Company halt." He yelled at Frederick, "Halt. Come back. Stop!" Frederick heard nothing and kept right on marching, in a military manner with his gut in, and his chin up.

Close order drill is a serious business. Nobody talks or laughs, or even grins. If you do, you fall out and do twenty push-ups, or fall on your face. But as we saw Frederick marching away, nobody could keep from laughing.

This infuriated Sergeant Levy. Military regulations prohibited putting a hand on a soldier. You could get up in his face, nose to nose, and shout as loud as you wanted, or call him any name in the book, but you couldn't touch him. A soldier was not allowed to talk back. That was insubordination, and he could be court-martialed for doing so.

In this particular instance, the Sergeant had to stop Fredrick. He ran after the guy like a collie dog rounding up sheep. We thought he would have to tackle Fredrick, but he would have violated military law by grabbing him.

Fredrick didn't know what was going on. He had looked straight ahead while marching, just as he was taught, and thought the other guys were marching along beside him. He was surprised and scared when the drill Sergeant appeared in front of him and marched him back and got him into line. We stopped laughing.

The first lieutenant was giving a lecture on the Sherman tanks we would be using in combat. It was about 104 degrees, and we wore full field packs and steel helmets on our heads.

A recruit named Meisner, who was of German decent, was sitting on the ground. He spoke better German than English. He came from one of the Texas German settlements, New Braunfields, San Marcos, or Killeen.

The menus in all the restaurants in those towns were written in German. The newspaper was in German. The English translations were in fine print. In some of the settlements, the Germans threw rocks at our tanks when we were on maneuvers. They were still loyal to their Mother Country, even though they didn't like Hitler.

Meisner was dosing off to sleep while the lieutenant was giving a talk about how much the tank weighed, how long and how wide it was, its maneuverability and capability, speed, etc.

The Lieutenant stopped talking and started to ask questions. His first question was directed to Meisner. "Stand up," he yelled.

Meisner stood up and stood at attention. He was scared as he looked straight ahead.

"How long is that tank, soldier?" the lieutenant shouted.

After a long pause, Meisner said, "One hundred feet long, sir."

That infuriated the officer (The tank was actually twenty-six feet long).

"Look at that tank, look, look, you say one hundred feet long? What's wrong with you soldier? Now how long is that tank?"

After another long pause, Meisner was staring at the tank and all the other men were holding their breaths.

Again the officer shouted out, "How long is that tank, soldier?"

"Three feet long, sir," Meisner said.

Everybody tried not to laugh, but we couldn't control ourselves. Meisner was not trying to be funny. He just didn't understand English very well, and furthermore, he had been dozing instead of listening to the lecture.

When we were training at Camp Hood, Texas, we had to go on a bivouac in the woods, just as if we were in actual combat. The first thing we did when we stopped was to dig a "fox hole" for protection from "enemy fire." We had no protection from ticks that infested the woods and the greater job was protecting ourselves from them. We had to detick each other frequently, because you could get Rocky Mountain Spotted Fever from them. Lyme disease was unheard of then. (It wasn't discovered until forty years later.)

Maneuvers or bivouac lasted about a week at a time. We got to play war games with our tanks. We had the light tanks that weighed thirteen tons and the big Sherman tanks that weighed twenty tons. The small tanks had a three-man crew, and the big ones a five-man crew. We didn't have the modern equipment then. The tanks were equipped with a periscope for the driver to see out through the little "cat eyes" in the tank's turret.

The tank commander stood up in the turret of the tank to give signals to the driver. By pressing on the driver's right shoulder with his foot, he indicated the driver was to turn right. If he wanted him to go left, he pressed on the driver's left shoulder with his foot. If he wanted him to go faster, he would tap his foot on the driver's helmet with his foot. If he wanted him to stop, the tank commander pressed straight down on the driver's head.

One hot Saturday morning we were simulating a battle with the enemy. The battleground was several thousand acres of ranch country. Abandoned homes and barns dotted it. The U.S. government had confiscated the land, and paid the ranchers a small sum and gave them ninety days to sell their livestock and get off the government property.

Some of the buildings left behind were expensive and had been the homes of real people. It was our aim to destroy the property and level every building that was standing.

While I was a tank commander, I also had to train to be a tank gunner and tank driver. It was my turn to drive on that attack. The commander, Erlickson, was standing in the turret giving the signals, having me drive in circles, tearing down small trees, fences, and "battling" other "enemy tanks." It was dusty and the sound of all the tanks was deafening. I couldn't see where I was going. The small opening in the driver's seat, and the periscope sight were shot out by the "enemy."

Erlickson was a huge soldier, about six feet four inches. He was chewing gum, and the faster he made me drive, the faster he chewed.

The roar of all the tanks and the sound of the .50 caliber guns didn't bother me, but his gum chewing was driving me crazy. He was a staff sergeant, and I was still a buck private. He wasn't allowed to smoke in the tank, but he could chew gum.

As we circled in the tank, we tore down the smoke house and the yard fence. The next round we got the rest of the smoke house and part of the back porch. Then we headed into the screened back porch, and the commander was tapping on my helmet to make me go faster. All of a sudden he started to press straight down on my head with his foot. That meant stop. He pressed so hard on my helmet with all his weight that he pushed my head down between my shoulders. He yelled to the crew, "Get out quick!" As we scrambled out of the tank to see what had happened, we kicked each other in the face.

We were surprised that behind that screened back porch was a cistern. A cistern is sunk in the ground and walled like a dug well or a reservoir. Rain barrels under the eaves of the house caught the run-off from the roof and the water was piped into the cistern. Every farmhouse had one. We had broken the top of the cistern with our tank. The tank had partially dropped down, and was lodged against the rock wall of the cistern at a slant. When we stuck our heads out of the turret, we were looking down into the water of the cistern. The "enemy" tanks shot our crew when we tried to get out of our tank. We had been defeated and had to drop out.

Sergeant Erlickson was still smacking his wax.

On manuevers, we had the red army and the blue army. The training lasted six weeks. About half of the training was at night. That meant no lights. We used flashlights with a red piece of cloth over the lens to keep the glare down.

In the meantime, we had to combat the snakes, mosquitoes, and hurricanes. On manuevers, we didn't come in contact with any civilians for six weeks.

Later in the war games, we were shipped to Louisiana, to train in the swamps and pine trees. We deliberately got the tanks stuck in the swamps so we could learn how to extricate them from the mud. We had to learn how to "throw a track" on a tank, then get out and fix it by getting the track back on. All of this was under the "fire" of the "enemy."

We had an alcoholic in our company named Eubanks. It was difficult for him to stay away from booze for very long. He conned his commanding officer into letting him volunteer to haul our drinking water in five gallon G.I. cans from a distant well. The company commander congratulated him for working on his own time to supply fresh water to the troops.

The real reason, however, was that Eubanks wanted to find a bootlegger. Alcoholics have a way of finding booze if there is any in the vicinity.

He wasn't the only ingenious booze finder. He had a drinking buddy by the name of Pop Baines. Anybody over thirty-five years old was given the rank of Pop. Baines had lived a hard and fast life. He looked sixty years old. He was like a mascot to the tank battalion. Everybody liked Baines, and he liked all the G.I.s.

When I was stationed in the barracks with Baines, both of us were cooks. He always insisted that I go home to see my family on the weekends and he would work my shift. The main reason he always volunteered to help everybody was that he knew he would be needing someone to help him when he got drunk and was unable to function for two or three days. Who could refuse to help him? After all, didn't he pull a weekend shift for you? We felt obligated to help him.

One time at Camp Hood, I was leaving on a weekend pass, and Pop Baines was taking over my cooking shift for me. I was getting everything ready before I picked up my pass and signed out. Cauliflower was on the menu for dinner. I took a ten-gallon aluminum boiler and washed the vegetables, put them on the burner and covered the pot. When I raised the lid, to my chagrin, I saw millions and millions of tiny lice coming out of the cauliflower. They obviously had been buried deep in the head, and ordinary washing would not reach them. But the heat ran them out. I looked around to see if anybody else had seen anything. I reasoned that if the lice had been eating cauliflower, they also should be edible. I yelled at Baines to take over and I took off. That was in 1943, and I didn't get any complaints, but now it can be told after fifty years.

When we were in Louisiana on maneuvers, I was the head cook. We were in the swamps — like a rain forest. It was five minutes 'til chow-time. Meals had to be served at noon sharp. All the G.I.s were lined up with their mess kits.

All military rations were powdered or dehydrated. For dessert we had butterscotch pudding. The field ranges burned gas and had to be pumped frequently. We lifted a twenty-gallon boiler of hot butterscotch pudding off the fire and entered it at the end of the chow-line for dessert.

Out of an oak tree above us fell a huge lizard or salamander into the boiler full of hot pudding. He tried to swim or crawl out, but all the skin burned off his body, and left a green trail in the yellow pudding. I grabbed a spatula and dipped him out. It was too late to substitute another dessert for that meal. The terrestrial creature lost his life in the deal. That was in the summer of '43. No complaints yet.

The mosquitoes were almost as big as our tanks. At night we had to rub kerosene all over our bodies and faces, and saturate a rag with kerosene to hang over our heads to help keep the mosquitoes away.

We had to walk a few miles to a farmer's house every night to buy kerosene from him.

One night a hurricane blew in. A tall dead pine tree uprooted and fell within three feet of my head while I was sleeping in the pup tent.

When six weeks of maneuvers were over, we got to turn on the lights in our vehicles, and also got a one night pass to celebrate in Alexandria, Louisiana, on the Red River. It was a small town, and about fifteen thousand G.I.s got a pass to go into town for one night. We had to be back in the woods by eleven p.m. The town had bars and there were some bootleggers supplementing the supply of liquor. It was a wet town, but it was dry when we left.

The captain came over and said, "Holding, I know you are the only teetotaler in the company, you will have to round up all these drunks and get them on the truck. It's after eleven p.m., and they aren't all here."

That was a difficult assignment for a sober guy of my rank.

When our division was stationed at Ft. Jackson, South Carolina, I was promoted to P.F.C. — private first class — with one stripe. For the first time, I out-ranked somebody — all the buck privates on the base. They were at the end of the "totem pole," the "bottom of the heap" or the lowest in the "pecking order."

A private first class had rank and could give orders to the "yard birds."

After completing a twelve-mile hike with a full field pack, on a hot summer day, I was exhausted. It was almost chow time, and I thought I could take "ten" before I did anything else. I went into my pup tent and stretched out on a G.I. blanket.

A voice from outside my tent shouted, "Holding, the colonel wants to see you."

"Send him in," I answered.

"Holding, come out of that tent!" an angry voice demanded.

As I went out, there stood a second lieutenant, with his brass bars shining in the sun.

"Holding, you don't talk to an officer like that," he said, as he reached over and ripped off my P.F.C. stripe.

"Now you get down to Colonel Hunt's tent and give him a haircut, on the double." (On the double, in military jargon, means trot, don't march).

When I got to the colonel's tent, I told him what happened.

That's not his business to demote another soldier," he said. He called to his runner (that's a messenger) and told him to go bring that second lieutenant to his tent "on the double."

The second lieutenant is the lowest in rank of the commissioned officers. They feel that they are more important than a general. They are always bucking for a silver bar that a first lieutenant wears.

The second lieutenant came running into the colonel's tent, saluted, and stood at attention while the colonel dressed him down.

It was well worth losing my stripe to hear what the colonel said to the junior officer. Any minute, I thought the Colonel would rip the brass bars off the lieutenant's shoulders, but he didn't.

The colonel ordered the captain of the company to re-issue me my stripe immediately.

78

The London Blitz

Long before the U.S. was officially involved in World War II, we were supplying guns and planes to Britain.

Hitler had been building up his armed forces for several years, and had already overrun most of the European countries. His next target was England. After Dunkirk, he thought London would be a pushover. He was wrong.

When Sir Neville Chamberlain, the Prime Minister of Great Britain, returned from his infamous conferences with Adolf Hitler, he stepped off the plane in London, and proudly announced he had negotiated with the Fuhrer and was assured by the dictator that he didn't want any more territory, and there would be no war with Britain.

London was bombed again that night. Hitler's word was worthless.

When Winston Churchill took over as Prime Minister, the English people got behind him. He had been a soldier in World War I, and fighting Germans was nothing new to him.

He admitted, later, that his country didn't have much more than a sling shot to fight off the air raids every night. As soon as darkness arrived, the bombing would start. Wave after wave of planes would come across the English Channel over the white cliffs of Dover, dropping their bombs on London, at random.

The Germans had strategic bombers, dive bombers, and fighter planes. They aimed at train stations and airports, and they were right on target sometimes. They also bombed churches, and the residential sections of London, killing men, women, and children. When the London fog rolled in, it was impossible for the anti-aircraft guns — the "ack-ack guns" to shoot at the bombers, which couldn't be seen through the dense fog.

The German pilots dropped incendiary bombs to burn the city and to furnish light from the fires for the next wave of bombers. They knew there would be firemen on the ground fighting the fires. They became targets for more bombs. If they could eliminate the firemen and engineers, that would be a successful raid for the Germans. If they bombed the railway stations and airports, transportation in and out of London would be stopped.

Since all lines of communication were cut off, that meant no sugar, citrus, and tropical fruits from other countries. Everything was rationed. Each person was allowed one egg and one ounce of cheese per week. Milk was limited to babies only. The main diet was potatoes and a few vegetables grown in victory gardens.

Because London was bombed two or three times every night, the English had to use their subways, which they called the "tube," for bomb shelters. The bombing destroyed buildings, and sometimes clogged up the exits and entrances to the subways, trapping thousands of people.

The military authorities didn't want the civilians to use the tube as a bomb shelter, but the people used it anyway. Those in the suburbs had their own bomb shelters which they used every night. The beds in the houses were seldom used. The people wouldn't dare go to sleep and get killed. (In the winter months, it was dark at five p.m. and daylight at eight a.m.) The shelters had no sleeping accomodations, nor any heat. People slept sitting up.

Americans were sending clothes and blankets to the bomb victims. Knitting in the U.S. provided hand-knit sweaters. Americans were "Knittin' for Britain."

Many families sent their children to the British countryside for safety. Some of the more affluent families sent their children to Canada and the U.S.

I had been listening to war information on the radio for the past four years. The foreign correspondents who brought us the news were H. V. Kaltenborn, John Daly, Edward R. Murrow, and Gabriel Heater.

Murrow was the daring reporter. He went out on the streets of London during air raids, picked up the sounds, and transmitted them to the U.S.A. by radio. There was a lot of difference between listening to it on the radio and being there. I was there.

When our tank battalion landed in Wales, we went into training immediately. After a few weeks, I got a three-day pass and went to London. I found a place to stay for two nights, in a combination hotel and store. My room was upstairs over a barber shop. As soon as I got into bed, the sirens started to wail. With lights off, I moved the blackout curtains and peeked out. The German planes were dropping incendiary bombs as well as the conventional ones. I put on my shoes and rushed down the long flight of stairs to the barber shop. Two barbers were working and a few customers were waiting and reading magazines. I was non-plussed.

"What do you do in one of these air raids?" I asked.

"Well, you can go outside and take a chance on getting hit with shrapnel, or you can go back to bed and take a chance on getting a direct hit," he said, as he continued to clip his customer's hair.

The planes were flying over, and we heard a bomb whistling through the air. It hit close.

"Wow! That was a blockbuster," he said.

"What's a blockbuster?" I asked.

"It destroys a whole block."

"We are going to have a lot of people to bury tomorrow," one of the waiting customers said. "We can't give them a decent burial because the mortuaries are all full, and they have been bombed, too. The hospitals are also full, and we need medical supplies."

One turned to me and said, "We are glad to see you chaps over here and ready to help us. The American planes we are getting now and your trained pilots are a big help."

"The average age of our pilots is nineteen. If we can hold out 'til the ground invasion starts, we'll be lucky."

All the waiting customers got in on our conversation. They were speculating when the big invasion of France would start. The Germans had taken over France four years ago, and the German troops were dug in and waiting for our arrival.

I told them when I studied geography a few years before, London was the largest city in the world and New York City was the second largest.

They said London wasn't the largest now, because a lot of people had run to the country, and eighty-nine thousand people had been killed by the bombing.

The all-clear signal sounded. "What's that mean?" I asked.

"That means they have dropped all their bombs and have headed back to Germany for another load. They will be back again just before daylight for another raid. You can count on it."

I went outside to see what was happening. The street was full of debris and the jeeps they were using for ambulances had the top half of the headlights painted black, so they wouldn't shine upward.

They were picking up the injured and the dead. I walked about two blocks down the street and found a pub open. Customers were all drinking beer and playing darts as if nothing had ever happened.

I walked another block, and as I crossed the alley, I heard a sound "Psssst. Psssst. Hey, Yank, you want to do it standing up for a shilling?"

"Not right at this time," I said.

I went back to my hotel and waited for the next raid.

The barber shop man was correct. Just before dawn, the Germans struck again. I felt like a veteran by then. I didn't even get out of my bed.

We in the U.S.A. have had some senseless bombings recently, at the World Trade Center in New York, and more recently in Oklahoma City. If we multiplied our loss by ten, or fifteen, or twenty, it wouldn't equal one night's bombing in London during World War II.

Fifty years later, the Britons are dancing in the streets of London to commemorate the end of World War II.

They are still playing: "There'll be Blue Birds over the White Cliffs of Dover tomorrow when the world is free."

79

Going My Way?

It was 1942, and everything was rationed, especially gasoline and tires. The U.S. had lost several islands in the Pacific to Japan, including the ones that produced rubber. We hadn't yet learned to produce synthetic rubber.

To conserve the short supply of automobile tires, the federal government passed a law that applied to all forty-five states. The maximum speed limit on any highway was thirty-five miles per hour. They reasoned that a tire would last twice as long at thirty-five miles an hour as it would at seventy.

Before the war was over, the U.S. was making its own synthetic rubber tires. These weren't as resilient as the natural rubber tires, but during the war we had to substitute many things.

The U.S. stopped making cars in 1941 and didn't start up the automobile plants again until 1945. The manufacturing lines were converted to building tanks and planes. There was also an urgent demand for ships, guns, and ammunition to fight the war. The plants back home were working three shifts. The workers were called, "the man behind the man behind the gun." Women, for the first time in history, were working alongside men in the shipyards and other defense plants.

Each automobile owner was allowed two gallons of gasoline for each car per week. They had "A" stickers on their windshields. If they worked in a defense plant, they were allowed four gallons a week, and had a "B" sticker on the windshield. The defense workers also car pooled. The defense department had signs posted in all public places and in the mess halls that read: "Is this trip really necessary?"

"Black market" gasoline was available if you could afford it. Pleasure or vacation travel were put on hold for about four years during World War II.

I was stationed at Camp Walters, a training base near Mineral Wells, deep in the heart of Texas. This was in 1942. I wanted to go to town, but didn't have a car. Anderson was one of the few men who owned a car and he kept it on the base. He had been a bootlegger in civilian life and was having a hard time fitting into the military life. We new recruits had just got our first weekend passes and were trying to get rides into town.

Anderson was a temperamental, hard-boiled, selfish type. I didn't understand it when he asked me if I wanted a ride to town.

The cold north wind was blowing and it was almost dark. As we drove out the guarded gate, Anderson stopped to pick up another hitchhiker. We both recognized him as a man from our barracks. His name was Farrell.

He got in the back seat, and never stopped talking. He asked the driver how long he had owned "this old car."

"I bought it in the spring of '35 from a bootlegger," Anderson answered.

After a few miles, Farrell asked, "Don't you have a heater in this old car? It's cold back here."

Anderson didn't answer, he just kept driving.

The next question from Private Farrell was, "It seems you have a broken spring, or you need new shocks on this old car. It rides like a log wagon."

Again, no answer from Anderson.

Another mile down the road Farrell said, "This old car really smokes, I think you need a ring job. Don't you ever change the oil?"

This time Anderson answered by pulling off the road and demanding, "GET OUT!"

"What?" Farrell asked.

"You heard me — get out now! All you've done since you got into my car is make fun of it. Now you get out and catch yourself another ride or walk!"

As we drove away, leaving Farrell standing beside that desolate road in near-freezing temperatures, I wondered if I would be next. Things were quiet as we chugged along. Finally, I said, "You know Anderson, you've got a pretty damn good car here. I like the way the motor hums, too."

He looked at me with a sardonic smile and said, "Shore beats walking."

80

"Cutting Up" for the Colonel

Colonel Hunt was a West Point graduate who believed in military discipline. He seemed to be more interested in having his men learn how to salute, keep their shoes shined, and get their haircut every ten days than in teaching them how to survive in combat.

It didn't bother him to order his troops to load up with full field packs and sit for three hours waiting for the order to move out. The only hours we could call our own were from taps at ten p.m. until reveille at six a.m.

We all went to the firing range together to practice shooting the 0.30 rifle and the Colt .45. Colonel Hunt shot a score of ninety out of a possible hundred. I shot ninety-eight out of a hundred. Of course, I'd been shooting all kinds of guns since I was ten years old, back in the Texas woods, where a sure shot was the main way to get meat for the table. A poor shot didn't eat very well.

When I outshot the Colonel, he was embarrassed. He congratulated me and awarded me a "sharp-shooter" medal and promoted me to "acting" sergeant. Sergeant's pay, however, did not come with the "promotion." He was forever upgrading me to "acting" something but it didn't include more pay. The real reason for this was that I would be making more money than the colonel — not from my military pay, but because I was doing barbering on the side, on my own time.

When we got to the United Kingdom, we found that electricity was delivered at 220 volts. In the U.S., of course, we use110 volts. That didn't bother me, because I didn't need electricity to cut hair. I'd brought my hand clippers along.

On our British base, however, there was another snag. Military regulations there stipulated that a soldier could not charge another military person for cutting his hair on the premises of a military installation. Our men liked this regulation. They didn't have to pay. Tipping was optional, of course, and helped increase my "take."

The colonel had to comply with the regulations and issued his order that there would be no barbering in the barracks or tents.

He was the first one to violate his own orders. He sent for me to come to his tent to cut his hair. Right away, remembering all the "acting advancements" he'd given me, I saw an opportunity to even the score a little.

I took the new blades out of my hand clippers and put in old ones that were dull, even a little rusty. When I got to the colonel's tent, I wrapped the towel around his neck and began to clip.

With the first pass, he jumped out of the chair. "Are you pulling my hair out by the roots?" he growled.

I showed him the blades and told him how they'd rusted coming across the Atlantic.

"You cut my hair on the ship coming over. The sea was rough. We even got sick, but your hand clippers worked fine then, didn't they?"

"Maybe you were too sea sick to notice, sir?" I suggested.

"Can't you buy some new blades in the village?"

"The only place I can get new blades is in Birmingham, sir." That was a three-hour journey.

"You know the 'Krauts' are bombing Birmingham every night, don't you? It would be dangerous to go there."

"I know, sir, but for you I would be willing to take the chance."

He wrote me a two-day pass and told me to finish his haircut as soon as I got back with my new blades.

In Birmingham, I visited one of my friends in business there. He showed me around, and we had a good time. Yes, we were bombed, but took no direct hits.

Oh, about the clipper blades . . . I didn't bother to shop for them, as I had a new pair back at the camp.

81

D-Day

While we waited in England for the Big Event, the allies continued to build up enough supplies and trained enough men for the invasion. We didn't know the exact day.

For a week, we sat waiting, not knowing if we were waiting to die. On June 5th, we were standing by, but the storm held us up. The channel was too rough for a landing.

Finally, before dawn on June 6, 1944, the first Allied troops headed out across the English Channel for the beaches of Normandy, France, to take Europe back from Adolf Hitler.

During the next two months, two million men would follow. But on that first day, D-Day, a force of 156,000 invaders were sent through blockaded waters, across mined beaches and into the teeth of German gunfire.

I was a member of a tank battalion. We were among the seventy-three thousand Americans to hit the beach that day.

I don't think it was one day. It was more like three, all run together. The fighting was continuous.

The Germans had been waiting four years for us. They were prepared. They had "pill boxes" walled with five feet thick concrete, impregnable to artillery fire or bombs. Finally, a lucky hit from the battleship U.S.S. Texas, put some of them out of business.

Inside the bunkers were the heaviest of guns in the German battery.

We landed on Omaha Beach, where the day's worst casualties occurred. The number of dead was estimated at two thousand to three thousand. A high bluff topped with German artillery crews and snipers had been untouched by allied air strikes, so the American troops whose boats had lucked through the blockaded waters, were sitting ducks on the beach.

But the U.S. landing force kept coming, by sheer force and numbers pushing its way through gaps in the bluff.

Our battalion hit the beach at midday.

There were tanks ahead of us, but a lot had been destroyed on the beach or sunk in the water. Dead soldiers were everywhere.

We had to keep pushing on because more tanks and men were coming behind us. We headed around the bluff and moved inland.

The allies had sent paratroopers ahead the night before. We saw some of them hanging from trees, shot dead.

Because of the heavy casualties, General Bradley had considered pulling the troops out. Firepower, determination, and brute force made us continue forward. But it was a recipe for disaster.

Omaha Beach was littered with burned-out trucks, wrecked tanks and the scattered bodies of G.I.s. Immediately after landing, hundreds of men were cut down at the water's edge by intense fire from the Germans.

Our orders were to keep pushing on until we established a firm beach head. Hitler's orders were to push the Americans, British, and Canadian soldiers back into the English Channel. He didn't succeed.

During combat, we were flooded with three days of heavy rain. We had to stop our advance, and dig fox holes. The water ran into them, but they protected us from the enemy's small arms fire. However, a fox hole would not protect a soldier from the bombs. If a bomb landed close by a fox hole, it might cave in and bury a soldier alive. If he were lying flat on the ground, the concussion might rupture his stomach or spleen. To prevent that, he did not lie flat. Instead, he knelt with his body weight on his knees and elbows, helmet in place. It was weird, but not funny.

By July 1944, the allies had pushed into the hedgerows of Normandy. We were on the offensive, but the going was slow, and the casualties high. During the first thirty days of combat, we lost half of our men, and two-thirds of our tanks.

Replacements were hard to come by, and so were tanks. Of course, the U.S. was also fighting a war in Japan, and this other front had to be supplied with ships, tanks, guns, ammunition, and men.

But we were lucky because the Russians were our allies then, and they were fighting the Germans on the Eastern front.

82

"Dear John . . ."

John Wallace was a nineteen-year-old kid from Kansas. He lived on a farm with his family, and had never been out of his county. He had just finished high school, when he was drafted for military duty.

Being a farm boy who was accustomed to operating heavy equipment, he was selected to serve in a tank battalion. That was a good choice. Of course, a tank is not a combine or a tractor and they were used for entirely different purposes.

John was an excellent warrior. He had to be to survive. When a crew is assigned to a tank, it becomes their "fortress, weapon, and home."

We were allowed to put our wives' or girlfriends' names on our tank, if they corresponded with the company's "letter." We were in company "B." John's girlfriend in Kansas was named Betty. He had the honor of naming the tank Betty. We lost that original tank to the Germans, and we didn't want to lose another one. When we brought up a reserve tank from the rear, it was named Betty 2. We three tank crewmen lived in our tank until there was an air raid. Then we headed for the fox hole, pronto.

The infantrymen didn't like to be close to our tanks. Tanks drew fire from the enemy. We kept our tanks camouflaged whenever possible.

John was the nervous type who had to be moving all the time. In his constant movements, he beat a trail around our tank. He'd pace around and around until we had to jump into it and move out in a hurry.

He was concerned about his mail. If he didn't get a letter from home every few days, he was depressed. The mail would catch up with us about once a week, if we were lucky. We could not write letters home. The war department did let us use V-mail, but it was censored by the commissioned officer before being sent. The pre-printed letter had about twelve or fifteen lines.

Each line was marked with a little box. The statements asked: "How are you? Put an x in the box to say you are fine." The soldier couldn't use his own words to make any mention of what he was doing or what country he was in, for fear of giving away our location. We had to get rid of all our personal belongings before we went into combat. The only exceptions were we could keep a picture of our wives or girlfriends. I had a picture of my wife and a two-year-old daughter. I'm sure they helped me get through the war.

When John got a letter from Betty, he always let me read it. I was his mentor. John also showed me a picture of Betty and said they'd graduated from high school together and planned to get married as soon as he got home from the war. In one of her letters, Betty wrote: "Why don't you write long letters anymore like you used to?" Obviously, he couldn't explain to her why. V-mail was all he could use to communicate.

One day at mail call, John opened a letter from Betty. I could tell from the tortured look on his face, there was something drastically wrong. I thought he had been hit in the heart by a sniper's bullet.

"What's wrong, John?" I asked.

He handed me the letter and slumped to the ground, holding his head in his hands. He was speechless.

It was a short letter from Betty:

"Dear John, I know you won't mind, but things have changed. I met this cute guy, named Frank. The draft board classified him 4-F because he was an alcoholic. He said he was just a social drinker. I know you would like him if you met him. He said you probably had one of those French girls anyway.

"Frank said you probably would never get out of the war alive, and if you did come home you would be in a wheel chair for the rest of your life.

"Frank said he was married once before for a short time. He said his wife never did understand him. He is ten years older than me but that won't make any difference. Once we get married and settle down, I'm sure he will stop drinking or cut down. He is not working now, but he's looking for a job.

"Well, John, I guess this is the last letter I'll be writing to you, but I want you to know it was nice knowing you."

I persuaded John to see the Chaplain because he threatened to turn the machine gun on himself.

The Chaplain read a few passages from the Scriptures and assured John that everything was going to be all right. He said the Germans were wrong and the Americans were right, because they were Christians and the Germans worshiped Hitler. His conclusion was, "Just trust in the Lord and no harm can come to you."

John was not satisfied with that answer, although the Chaplain did all he could.

When we walked back to our tank, John told me we would have to get another tank driver, as he wouldn't be coming back. I talked to him, but he would not change his mind.

The Germans were dug in just over the hedge row. We could hear them talking. He took his Tommy gun and a pocket full of hand grenades and jumped over the hedge row and started to spray bullets at the Germans. We could hear the return fire from the enemy.

I'm sure he didn't last long. We retrieved his body a few days later. He was already "dead" before he made that one-man attack. The Germans didn't kill him, the "Dear John" letter from Betty did.

83

The Lull Before the Storm

The Germans fought a psychological war as well as a shooting war. While waiting for supplies to catch up and reinforcements to build on the allied side, the Germans were doing the same on the other side of the battle line. But we had no rest at night.

A Piper Cub plane we called "old bed-check Charlie" flew over our territory looking for any sign of movement or light. If someone struck a match for a cigarette, it could be seen by Charlie. In a matter of minutes, all hell would break loose. The heavy bombers and fighter planes would pay us a visit.

One G.I. said, "They're throwing everything but the kitchen sink at us." All night the heavy artillery pounded us. At one point, we were surrounded in a pincers movement by several divisions of Germans. We never knew exactly where we were, but when the enemy made a dawn attack, we were forced to capitulate.

The Allied forces never retreated. They re-marshaled their forces and "fell back to new positions." That's the way the generals rationalized it.

Often times when we were pinned down and communications cut

off, we didn't know our position or whether our comrades were lost, captured by the enemy, wounded, or dead. Then a swarm of U.S. planes would come to our rescue. When we saw them coming, someone would say, "That's better than a letter from home."

We did get real letters from home, infrequently. Sometimes the folks would send newspaper clippings, showing a map with a line indicating our position. "It's wonderful, you're almost to Paris," the letter would explain. They knew more about our position than we did.

We had a visitor, an entertainer, every night for about three hours. Her name was "Axis Sally." She had a counterpart in the Pacific War, named "Tokyo Rose." These girls were propaganda ministers, who interrupted our radio sets to bring bad news. They spoke near-perfect English, and played records featuring American music. Their purpose was to sell the G.I.s a bill of goods. "Why don't you lay down your guns and go home to your family? Your wives and girlfriends are cheating on you. You will all be killed before the war is over. Go back to your country."

She was convincing. After hearing the same line over and over, no doubt some of the guys believed her. Most didn't.

The Stars and Stripes was our official newspaper for the front line troops. The reporters got their information from the G.I.s, under dangerous circumstances most of the time.

Bob Considine was a front-line reporter. My favorite reporter was Ernie Pyle. When he wrote his column, you could almost see, hear, and smell the war. He made it through the war in Europe without a scratch. When the war was over, he went to Japan as a reporter. He was cut down by a sniper's bullet just before the war ended in Japan. They made a movie about his life as a reporter.

Andy Rooney was young when he got his first assignment with *The Stars and Stripes*. He said writing was difficult. As far as I know, he's the only one of the World War II bunch left. He appears on "60 Minutes" every week.

It's hard to believe that Andy Rooney was ever a kid.

84

St. Lo, Breakthrough

After we took St. Lo in the daytime, the Germans would take it back at night. When we finally took over after two weeks of fighting, there was only one building standing, a small church with a steeple. A German sniper was hiding in the steeple. He had picked off several of our men before we got him.

All the church houses in the French countryside had a graveyard next to the church. Some have been there for hundreds of years. The bombs, dropped by both sides, had literally blown the corpses out of their graves.

Bastille day in France is July 14. That was the day in 1789 when the Bastille was stormed. Some of our generals thought it would be a moral victory for France and the other allies if we could get to Paris and free their city from the Germans by Bastille Day. It didn't happen, but we did get there later.

After the Allies, including the British, Canadians, and Americans, launched their second offensive, we reached Paris on August 25, 1944. In the offensive, the U.S. had lost more than fifty thousand men and two hundred thousand were injured.

In my company, practically all the men had been killed or injured, including the commissioned field officers. Major Holliday, second in command of our battalion, was killed. There was no one to take his place.

Colonel Hunt called me, "Holding," he said, "This time, I'm not calling you for a haircut. Major Holliday is dead and we need someone to command ten tanks."

The colonel said he knew I could do it. We didn't have ten tanks then, only seven, but reserves were being brought up and we were getting more troops.

A bunch of seventeen-year-olds who hadn't finished their thirteen weeks of basic training in the states were among the new troops that were being sent to the front lines.

"They are going to need a lot of help. An order just come down from General Eisenhower to take Paris at all cost. Hitler has sent an order to his troops to hold Paris at all cost. That's going to be plenty of cost on both sides."

"But Sir, I—"

"That's an order, Major, over and out."

When a soldier gets an order like that from his superior officer in combat, he doesn't defy it, and I didn't.

About the only thing Colonel Hunt had ever said to me in the last two years was, "Take a little off the top." Now he is begging, asking, ordering Private Holding, acting Sergeant, acting Major, to take over. He seemed like an injured animal, trapped.

Actually, that was about right. If you are a commissioned officer, you are not allowed to fraternize with the enlisted men. On the battlefield, when the medics had more dead bodies than they could handle, G.I. trucks came in to help with the evacuation. They picked up charred bodies that had been hit with artillery and bombs. These were thrown onto the trucks like cord wood and hauled away. Some bodies were enlisted men, and some were officers of different ranks. It didn't matter now. Death is a great equalizer.

At this stage of the war, troops and supplies were getting low for both sides. The whole world was at war. Troops were spread thin on some fronts.

Switzerland was the only country that managed to stay out of the war. The average American G.I. was not a professional soldier. Most of them came from small towns and the country, because in the 1940s, that was where most of the people lived.

They didn't like war, and had not given much thought to being in the military. They had rather be home plowing corn or squirrel hunting. However, the German soldier was born and bred to be a professional soldier. They were trained in parochial schools that taught Nazism. They were known as "Hitler's Children." Since 1933, when Hitler took over as dictator, he put all of Germany's resources into the war machine for World War II.

The U.S. was ill-prepared for war, compared with Germany. However, the U.S. built a war machine and trained about eighteen million troops in less than two years.

When the German soldier lost his superior officers, he couldn't function on his own. He was used to taking orders from a superior officer. They belonged to a "superior race."

The American G.I. was never exposed to the kind of propaganda given the German soldier. When Americans lost a superior officer, each man below him knew how to take care of the situation. They were independent and didn't like taking orders from anyone. I think we had the better trained men. Of course, I was prejudiced.

As we pushed on toward Paris, the Germans were dug in and waiting for us. When Germany took over France in 1940, they just marched right into Paris with no resistance. The French didn't fight back.

Paris is known as the most beautiful city in the world. I will agree. Neither side wanted to see those beautiful buildings destroyed. Hitler thought that Paris would belong to Germany now and forever.

In 1944, when the Allies came to run the Nazis out and give Paris back to the French, the Germans still didn't want to scar Paris, so they took their last stand in a circle at the edge of the city.

I didn't get to Paris, but I could see the Eiffel Tower from the suburbs. About three p.m. on August 25, 1944, we encountered the heaviest fighting. A thunderstorm had struck, and with all the heavy artillery, the machine guns and the roar of tanks, made communication almost impossible. I was glad none of my crew was chewing gum. That would have driven me crazy.

When the dive bombers were attacking our tanks, I gave orders to park and camouflage. My tank crews were all new recruits, just arrived from Ft. Benning, Georgia, and Camp Hood, Texas. They had just finished a crash course in tank maneuvers. One said he had only recently got his driver's license. None of them had ever been in combat. They were all sent directly to the front line to fight in the biggest military operation in history.

They were well disciplined and took military orders seriously. Although they were inexperienced and scared, they were good soldiers. Like all of the other men, they were afraid of dying.

My new tank driver was a red-headed seventeen-year-old kid from Arkansas. As I was directing him, he got the signals mixed up and backed the tank over me. I was pinned under the belly of the tank for several minutes. I could not breathe, and I could hear the crew trying to get help from the other tank crews, but they were all busy trying to stay alive. I think they were looking in the soldier's handbook to see how to get a man out from under a tank. I was in and out of consciousness. They couldn't decide whether to drive forward or backward. When I finally was freed, they shot me full of morphine and put me in a half-track to evacuate me to a field hospital.

The U.S. Army didn't have helicopters then. Our half-track was bombed and strafed on the way to the evacuation center. All the huge field hospital tents had white crosses on top to indicate they were not to be bombed. But the German planes dropped flares to light up the ground, and strafed the line of vehicles waiting with wounded soldiers.

Inside the hospital tent, cots were placed so close, a man could not walk between them. The legs of the canvas cots sank into the ground and the canvas bottom rested into the mud. When the bombs dropped and shook the ground, the cots would sink farther in. The aisles of the hospital tent were filled with stretchers. Doctors were treating only the men they thought had a chance to live. The others? Why waste time on a soldier who would probably die anyway.

I was in that category. They said I was bleeding internally, but they couldn't give me any water. The nurse gave me a small wet rag to put under my tongue. She said, "Maybe tomorrow, if you are still alive, we can give you some water." When daylight came, I could see a line of stretchers outside, waiting to get in. The dead ones were carried out of the tent to make room for the live ones. While I was unable to move, I remembered what some wise people had told me about war.

Sergeant Brown in basic training: "You are not here to teach Sunday School, you are in this man's army to learn how to fight and kill."

Our company commander: "There's going to be a hell of a lot of you men that won't come back."

And my Grandmother Holding, when I was about five years old, told me stories about the Civil War when she was a young teenager.

I asked her if I could go to the next war if they had one.

"No! You don't want to go to the war."

"Why?" I asked.

"There's nothing worse than war," she said.

These advisers were right. By now I agreed with them.

Once when I was knocked out on morphine, I heard Glenn Miller playing "In the Mood." I woke up. The same thing happened again later that day. I felt as though I were coming back from death.

Glenn Miller was a popular Big Band leader, who was on a tour, playing USO shows for the troops behind the lines. His plane went down over the English Channel before Christmas of 1944. They never did find him or the plane. It's still a mystery.

On the third day in the field hospital, the doctors took me out and ordered x-rays. I overheard two doctors discussing my x-rays. I had two crushed vertebra, transverse processes of the fourth and fifth lumbar, fractured and crushed rib cage, and ribs torn lose and puncturing my lungs. I had a pneumothorax and was losing air from my lungs.

One doctor said, "Nah." The other shrugged his shoulders, "Nah, Yeah, well, maybe. Let's give him some plasma and glucose and see what happens." They left me on a table and hung a bottle of plasma in a dogwood tree, put a needle in my arm and I could watch the bottle emptying into my veins and I could feel life coming back into my body. For the first time in two days, I knew I was going to live.

For my future funeral, I have made one request. I want them to play the original Glenn Miller's "In The Mood." If I don't rise up, go ahead, close the coffin. That's the end.

85

Medical "Practice"

After three days, I was moved to a military barracks hospital in England for further treatment. I spent several months there before being transferred back to the states.

The Germans had lost most of their planes by that time, but they were sending over the V-1 bombs or robots and later the V-2 bombs. They were destructive, but there was no way to know when one was being launched from across the English Channel, because they made no noise.

The American and British planes had a base not far from the hospital. When the planes roared off for a mission to Germany, some of the G.I.s would jump out of their hospital beds from force of habit and try to dig fox holes in the slab floor. They were on sleeping pills and pain killers at the time.

The most critically ill patients were housed together in long barracks in double decked beds. I thought I was in serious condition until I raised my head enough to look down the aisle. On both sides were patients in full body casts, some with bandaged heads, and missing limbs — arms and legs. At least we were still alive. I felt much better after comparing my problem with theirs.

Most of the doctors and nurses were young. Some had been in practice a few years. Several were just finishing medical school and serving their internships in England. They had plenty of patients to practice on. For many of the young doctors, the U.S. government had financed their medical training and given them the rank of first lieutenant in exchange for their services taking care of the wounded G.I.s. They didn't always get instructions from older and experienced doctors. All they knew was what they had read in books.

One such young doctor was assigned to the intensive care barrack where I was. A master sergeant was checked into the bunk bed above me, the only ambulatory patient in the barrack. He had been trapped in the "Battle of the Bulge." The snow was deep and the temperatures dropped to near zero at night. Each man was issued one blanket and one pair of shoes and socks. The sergeant's feet were frost-bitten and his toes had developed gangrene.

It was obvious that the young doctor assigned to him had never treated such a case before. First, he told the sergeant that it was his fault his feet had frozen. He should have had sense enough to keep them clean and dry and should have put on dry socks every morning.

The old soldier became more agitated.

The lieutenant treated him as though he were a juvenile delinquent. In the military, you can't talk back to a superior officer, especially a medical officer. If you address the officer as "Sir," you may be able to disagree with him and not be charged with insubordination. Maybe.

The doctor gave the soldier an order. "Sergeant, you will report to the surgical barrack, next door, at seven o'clock tomorrow morning. We are amputating both feet at the ankles. Is that clear?"

The Sergeant jumped off his top bunk, came to attention, and said, "Sir, you son-of-a-bitch, you are not cutting my feet off. Is that clear?"

After the doctor came out of shock, he said, "You are talking to a medical officer. You are just a sergeant, I'm having you court martialed."

The sergeant said, "Go ahead, sir."

The lieutenant sent for the commanding officer of the hospital.

Major Fronenberg, a forty-year-old medical officer in charge of the base hospital, arrived, bringing the sergeant's medical records with him. Now it was time for the first lieutenant to salute and stand at attention while the major pulled rank.

The commanding officer read aloud from the staff sergeant's records. He had been wounded and hospitalized three times. Battle scars were all over his body, and he still carried shrapnel in his back. He had received the Purple Heart, the Oak Leaf Cluster, and several other medals. His "hash marks" extended from shoulder to elbow.

Major Fronenberg told the young medical lieutenant that they had a barracks half full of victims with frostbite from the Battle of the Bulge. He explained that the Americans were trapped and snowed in and some of the wounded had frozen to death.

After explaining "The War" to the lieutenant, the major invited the sergeant to the "frost bitten" barracks to recover.

About ten days later, the sergeant came back to see me. He took off his shoes to show me his feet.

"They are as good as new," he said. He was ready to go back to the front line to fight and to see his buddies.

When I improved, they moved me to another barracks with the paratroopers. All had much the same leg injuries. If they didn't get shot out of the air before reaching the ground, they would often fracture a fibula bone just above the ankle or sometimes just below the knee, an especially vulnerable part of the anatomy.

I listened while the young doctors, some serving their internships and some their medical residency at the army barracks, discuss the different methods they used on knee surgery. One technique left the paratrooper with a stiff knee. If they cut the cartilage, the synovial fluid would be lost, and nature does not replenish it. There has been a big improvement in knee surgery since 1944. They do it with a hollow needle now.

When General Patton, "Old Blood and Guts" came to visit the wounded troops, he was a tough talker. One soldier was suffering from a physical wound as well as "shell shock," AKA Psychoneurosis. When the General was reprimanding him, the kid started to cry. General Patton slapped him.

None of the patients or nurses would report the general. He was a three-star general, and there was no one to report him to. Who would believe them? It was several months later when a G.I. was transferred to another hospital and leaked the information to a reporter. He was afraid to print the story, because the papers were censored by the allied forces. We didn't exactly have freedom of the press then.

The story finally hit the papers in the U.S., but nothing ever happened to Patton.

We got information about it from the states, but it was never reported in *The Stars and Stripes*.

In the winter of 1944-45, the casualties continued to come in. The Army barracks in Britain were overflowing with casualties. General Eisenhower asked for permission to admit osteopaths and chiropractors to the medical staff. President Roosevelt approved. Both he and the general had been chiropractic patients in the past. The M.D.s said, if you let quacks come into the hospitals, we will walk out.

The President received the order saying, "It's the wrong time to have the doctors go on a strike when they are needed most."

Penicillin was new. They were giving me forty thousand units a day. They thought that was a big dose. Now they give two million units. Sulfa drugs had been replaced with penicillin. A few months before, they were using all the various sulfa drugs. One day an order came down from the surgeon to throw all our sulfa drugs into the commode, and "don't forget to flush."

Patients were getting adverse reactions. When sulfa drugs are taken orally, the patient had to drink plenty of water or the medication will clog the kidneys. We were limited to one canteen of water, less than a quart, a day. That was our ration for all our water needs.

The favorite drug for pain was codeine; for infection, penicillin. If those didn't work, surgery was the next step.

I saw patients come to the hospital barracks twisted up in pain like a pretzel. They got the routine treatment and nothing else.

For me, personally, I have no complaints. The doctors helped save my life. Most were caring and patriotic. Some were not. There's more politics in the military than in civilian life.

After spending ten months in four different hospitals, I was sent to Camp Carson in Colorado Springs, Colorado. That was a convalescent hospital, and it was crowded with disabled veterans waiting to be discharged.

While in that hospital, several G.I.s with worse injuries than mine went downtown to a chiropractor. One morning at reveille, the captain came out, and said, "At ease men." Then he made an announcement. "It has come to my attention that some of you men have been going downtown to see these so called 'QUIROPRAKTERS,' and if you are caught, you will be court martialed. These guys are not doctors, they never even went to medical school, and they are dangerous."

I could hardly wait 'til five o'clock to go for my adjustment. When I arrived at the doctor's office, several patients from the hospital unit were waiting. Some were on crutches and some in wheelchairs.

When you are in the military, you have no rights. You belong to Uncle Sam. These guys were willing to risk a court martial to go to a doctor who would help them.

Two doctors on Colorado Boulevard in Colorado Springs, stayed open until ten o'clock every night to take care of the veterans stationed at Camp Carson. They would never charge anyone in uniform for an office visit. One doctor told me he had two sons in the service. One was injured in the South Pacific, and one was in the military hospital recovering.

I asked the doctor if the base commander had ever sent MPs out to check on his patients.

He said, "Yes, but they didn't arrest anyone. They took that street off-limits to the G.I.s, but it was never enforced."

When I asked the doctor if some of the things the captain said about him were true, he showed me his Ph.D. diploma in chemistry. He said he had been in practice for twenty-two years and a lot of military people were his patients. Some patients had been discharged, but still came back to his clinic for physical therapy and chiropractic adjustment. He showed us x-rays of veterans with spines twisted up like pretzels, that he had treated.

At Camp Carson, only the men with one hundred percent disability were discharged. It was a memorable day and also a sad one. Everyone had feelings of guilt for the thousands of buddies left behind. They wouldn't be coming home. Never.

Adjusting to civilian life, for some, was difficult. Nobody is ever the same after going through a war. I saw a nineteen-year-old soldier "turn forty" after only three years in the war. Some turned gray at the age of twenty-two.

Everything, after the war, seemed anticlimactic. You got the feeling if you could go through a war and come out alive, you could do anything. No matter how hard any new task, it was easy by comparison.

It takes a while in civilian life to become accustomed to driving your own car down the road and not be concerned that a land mine will blow you up. In an airplane, there's the constant fear you will be shot down.

After months of sleeping on the ground, in a fox hole, or in the mud in wet clothes, with a machine gun at your side, and a Colt .45 strapped to your hip, sleeping in a real bed with sheets felt pretty good.

My suit left behind four years ago was too small now. Probably, it just shrank, hanging in the closet. The moths had made several meals from the suit, too.

At chow time (dinner), I now sat down at a table with real china and silverware. I didn't have to wait for a whistle to blow before I could eat. Tumblers of water stood beside my plate, not just one canteen full to last all day. No more "K" rations — a small can of hash or spam. No more "D" rations — a compact bar loaded with vitamins, minerals, and calories (it looked and tasted like a board).

Now that I was a civilian again, I could walk out of my house, go anywhere I wanted, stay as long as I liked and never had to sign out or in. I didn't have to report to anyone where I'd been, except that I was married, and it seemed a good idea to tell my wife.

A small minority couldn't handle civilian life. They couldn't adapt.

Veterans' hospitals were full of physically and psychologically disabled patients. Some were rehabilitated. Some could never be.

Forty-six years later, I volunteered to go to Desert Storm and drive a tank.

The recruiting office said my military record was impressive, but they couldn't take anyone over the age of fifty-one.

Uncle Sam didn't want me. It's good to know that I can take my medals and a dollar to get a cup of coffee anywhere in town.

86

San Antonio

When I moved to San Antonio, Texas, after the war, I knew I would need a job to work my way through four years of school.

Dallas Turner, one of my best friends from early school days, arranged an interview with one of his associates at a radio station. Dallas had a terminal case of tuberculosis and was forced to retire at twenty-eight.

The interview went well, but the new manager at the radio station said my voice was too soft. He advised me I would make a good doctor, because I had a good "bedside manner."

I told him I would be a doctor in another four years, but in the meantime, I needed a job.

He agreed to give me a job as a radio announcer, if I would go to their special school for six months. He said, "Who knows, you might become another Gabriel Heater or Walter Winchell."

I could not accept his offer of schooling, because I was already in school full time at the Texas Chiropractic College, so Winchell would have no competition from me.

Instead I went to the St. Anthony Hotel barber shop looking for a job. Elmer Doolittle was the manager. Two of his brothers barbered and his sister Mary, was the cashier. It was a big shop with fancy manicurists and two shoeshine boys, it was a busy shop.

I told Elmer that I was in school from eight a.m. to two p.m. everyday, but I could work from two 'til ten and all day Saturday.

He said he needed a full-time barber.

I asked, "What happened to the barber on the tenth chair?"

"He starved to death," Doolittle said with a wink. Then added, "I'm kidding." He had cirrhosis of the liver, due to drinking over the years."

After discussing my credentials and the number of years I had barbered, Elmer said, "Well, I don't know, you have been cutting the G.I.s hair, and giving them the military flat top style. You can't do that in this shop."

He continued to tell me all the reasons why I wouldn't be the right barber for that vacant chair.

All his barbers had been here for several years, and they had their own clients, he explained. "We work by appointments only, like a doctor's office." He said I looked too young and this wasn't a union shop. "That's the reason we can charge six bits for a haircut."

The union shops had gone up to sixty-five cents recently, and most of the scab shops were still charging fifty cents. The type of clientele Doolittle had didn't mind paying seventy-five cents for a haircut, and they often tipped twenty-five cents.

I knew this was the best hotel in the Southwest. All the traveling people stayed here, and several of the rich cattle barons had suites reserved in the St. Anthony Hotel. They only dropped in every two or three weeks to occupy their rooms.

When the interview was over, and I started to leave, Elmer said, "Why don't you come down and work a few days. You are wearing a nice suit, and you look and talk professional. Maybe you would fit into this elite crowd of millionaires, socialites, politicians, and dignataries."

I did try out for the job. I had no problem fitting in with the clientele, as I already knew how to talk cotton, cattle, and oil. I stayed four years, until I got out of school and took the state board exam in chiropractic.

The other barbers came over to my chair to see what I was doing. "How do you cut a head of hair in ten minutes, when it takes us twenty?" They watched how I used my clippers over the comb, instead of scissors. They had to admit I gave a better haircut.

A barber shop is a clearing house for first-hand information. Many good rumors start there, too. No matter how many times I heard the same joke, I was polite and pretended it was the first time I'd heard it.

One time a man came in and asked, "Have you heard the one about . . .?"

I held up three fingers to indicate I had heard it three times. He went ahead and told it anyway.

One morning when I was at my barber chair waiting for my first customer, and reading *Gray's Anatomy* between time, in came a tall guy, all dressed up in Western attire. He saw me lay down my book as I got up to greet him. He picked up my book and looked at it, and asked, "Are you a doctor too?"

No, I told him I was studying to be a doctor, but I was only in my first year. I was barbering my way through school.

He proceeded to tell me about his medical problem. He was in town to see a medical specialist. His small-town doctor in Kerryville couldn't help him. He had a huge cattle ranch in the hill country, and employed several cowboys to help run the ranch. After telling me what a huge spread he owned, and all the cattle and sheep he had to take care of, he got off the subject of his physical problem.

"What is your physical problem?" I asked.

He said, "I have a splitting headache I've had for two weeks. It won't go away. I went to my family doctor. He tried all the usual medicines, but it didn't work. I went to another doctor, he gave me the same thing. It didn't work either. Then I went back to my regular doctor, and he told me I might have a brain tumor, and made an appointment to see a specialist in San Antonio."

"What does he specialize in?" I asked.

"Oh, hell, I don't know. I think he is a neurologist or a psychiatrist or some kind of head doctor."

When I got through cutting his hair, I asked, "Do you want a shampoo before you go see your doctor?"

"Oh, I know my hair is dirty, but I've been afraid to wash it, because of this headache. Do you think it will hurt me to have a shampoo?"

"No," I told him. "It may even cure it." Of course, I needed the six bits that the shampoo cost.

"Well, go ahead," he said. "It couldn't make my headache any worse than it is now."

I used Fitch shampoo, massaged, and manipulated his scalp with my finger tips. Then I rinsed his head with warm water, and did more manipulating of the scalp. When I got through and dried his hair with a towel, and gave him his ticket to pay the cashier, he said, "By God, I don't have a headache now."

He came back to my barber chair, after he paid his bill, and gave me a generous tip. After about two hours, he returned and said, "This is the first time in two weeks that my head is not hurting. Do you think I should still go see that doctor at two o'clock?"

I advised him that if he didn't intend to keep his appointment, he should call and cancel it, as doctors have to charge for their time.

He went to the front desk and phoned and cancelled his two o'clock appointment. He came back to my chair and asked to see the book I was reading when he came in. I let him look through *Gray's Anatomy*. I had to reassure him that I had three and a half more years to go before becoming a doctor.

What I had done for him was form of hydro-therapy, physical

therapy, and reflexology. I was not treating his headache, but only washing his hair. Curing his headache was incidental.

"You must have magic in those fingers," he said. "You cured my headache."

For the next three years, the rancher never failed to come in and see me when he was in town. He thanked me, and said if he ever had another headache, he would know where to come.

Buford Juster of Texas was first a Railroad Commissioner, then he was elected Governor in the 1940s. I cut his hair when he was Railroad Commissioner. After he was elected Governor, he still came from the state capital in Austin to San Antonio for me to cut his hair. He was a good politician, and I promised to vote for him for a second term.

A few days before the election, he stopped in San Antonio for a "stump" speech, and to get a haircut. He had fine, blond, curly hair, which is hard to cut. He knew I was a student in chiropractic college. He encouraged me and said he planned to sign our chiropractic bill if we got it through the legislature. He went to see his chiropractor every week, he told me.

He was riding the train, in a Pullman car that had "V.I.P." posted on it. By traveling this way, he could get his sleep and not be bothered by people asking for special favors.

He boarded his Pullman coach about eight p.m., headed for Houston, where he was to make a political speech at ten a.m. the next day. He had left word not to wake him too early, as he needed his sleep.

At ten o'clock the next morning, he was still asleep. His aide didn't want to wake him. About 10:45 the Mayor and other officials were waiting to greet the Governor. His aide admitted the Governor had been drinking a little, and would not be too happy if awakened. When he entered the Pullman, Buford Juster wasn't sleeping. He was dead. I'm sure that my haircut was not the cause of death.

I didn't get to vote for him, nor did he get to sign our bill.

Early one Saturday morning, Red Berry, one of my regular customers, dropped in to get his usual shave. He said he was on his way to the City Hall to turn himself in.

"What happened this time Red?" I asked.

"I shot a man last night," he said.

"Did you kill him?"

"Oh, yes. He's dead all right, but I have already called the police and told them what happened, and asked if I could wait until morning to come down to the courthouse. The beds are so hard in that jail. I told them I would check with my lawyer, and we would post bail tomorrow."

City Hall said, "That would be all right. We know you are a man of your word."

The Mayor and City Council knew all about Red. He helped them get into office. He had a clan he controlled, a regular "One-Man-Mafia."

When Red talked, everybody listened.

All the movie stars stayed at the St. Anthony Hotel when a premier of their movie came to town. Instead of coming down to the barber shop for a haircut or shave, they called for room service. Usually they wanted a manicurist, as well as a barber. Most of the time they were good customers, and gave generous tips. They were often a little drunk and would talk about their careers and all the Hollywood gossip. However, when the liquor wore off, and they were plagued with a headache and a hangover, they could be very grouchy, and the tip was lousy.

One time the manicurist and I got a call from a well-known movie star to send up a barber and a manicurist. Other customers were waiting in the shop, but we put them on hold, and went up to the suite to accommodate the "big shot" movie star. He was talking on the telephone when we arrived. He motioned for us to sit down, but continued to talk on the telephone for almost twenty minutes. When he finally hung up, he didn't apologize for keeping us waiting. He was very grouchy. After the manicurist and I had finished our job, he gave us the smallest tip we had ever received. When we returned to the barber shop, our regular customers had got tired of waiting and left. We worked by appointments only, and we lost money because of that guy.

The hotel had to cater to that type of clientele. Everybody that came to the barber shop had plenty of money, or tried to make us believe they did. A few blocks from the St. Anthony, across the river, was a skyscraper, the Nix building. On the top floor was the hospital. Several of our barber customers were patients at the hospital. When they were unable to come to the shop because of illness, they called for a barber to come to them.

One day, a call came from the hospital to send over a barber to shave one of their patients. He had been a regular customer at the shop and insisted he wanted a barber from the St. Anthony shop.

Since I was the newest barber, the manager gave the assignment to me. On the top floor of the building, I found the old man with pneumonia and a high fever. I lathered his face, but he was so hot with fever, the lather dried before I could strap my razor and start to shave him.

A few days later, someone from the Nix building hospital called the barber shop and requested the same barber that had worked on their patient before, to hurry to the hospital.

I gathered up my tools, and hurried as fast as I could. I was too slow and too late. The patient was dead.

His next of kin and a nurse were present. They insisted I go ahead and shave him, because that was his last request.

I refused, initially; that was a job for the mortician, and they should get the body to the morgue before rigor mortis set in. When I returned to the barber shop and told Elmer what had happened, he said, "Did you get paid for your call?"

"You can't collect from a dead man," I told him.

87

Friend or Con Man

I had a customer named York. He was a small man, about a hundred and thirty pounds and five feet six inches tall. He had an eight-year-old son. They always made Saturday afternoon appointments with me for their barbering. Both wore expensive, tailor-made clothes. They even wore handmade cowboy boots, and Stetson hats.

York was in the investment business with some of the wealthiest people in San Antonio as his clientele. He explained that he was not a banker or in the savings and loan business, but worked for individuals who wanted to get the most interest on their money. He worked on a percentage basis.

He had a good line and made it sound as if he were doing the investors a favor by taking care of their savings, by using his experience. To me, it sounded legitimate.

One of his clients, Doctor Ross, was a famous surgeon. He turned over his entire life savings of three hundred thousand dollars to York, which would be equal to at least three million today. Doctor Ross had been the York family surgeon for several years. He had operated on York's wife and mother-in-law several times. They attended the same church.

One fine day, York broke the news to Doctor Ross, that he had made a bad investment, and lost all the three hundred thousand dollars entrusted to him.

The next Sunday, York loaded all his family in their new car and went to church. Six of them, Mr. and Mrs. York, the mother-in-law, a twelve-year-old daughter, an eight-year-old son, and a five-year-old daughter.

Doctor Ross was waiting for the York car at a stop sign on a country road. He had a double-barreled shotgun which he fired, reloaded, fired again, and reloaded. When he finished, he thought all six were dead. They were, except for the twelve-year-old girl who leaped from the car and ran down the road. He shot her, like a rabbit as she was running. She fell, critically injured, but survived.

Doctor Ross turned himself in to the sheriff. His attorney got a change of venue, and Ross was tried in a small town outside of San Antonio, about one year later. He had no money left to hire an experienced criminal attorney. He was represented by a public defender, who pleaded that Ross was insane at the time of the multiple murders.

The district attorney was a tough one. The state could always get the best investigators and psychiatrists at the taxpayers' expense. The defense had to pay for their own. The fact that Doctor Ross was in the medical field enabled him to find a psychiatrist to testify in his defense. The trial lasted several weeks. There was no television in 1945, but the trial was carried live on radio. We brought a small radio to the barber shop so we could listen.

The radio announcer described Doctor Ross as a man who appeared to be in a trance. He had let his hair and beard grow long. He sat at the table with his defense attorney, reading the Bible and not looking up throughout the trial. We listened to the jury as they were polled. Then they read the verdict: Not Guilty By Reason Of Insanity. Ross was institutionalized in the psychiatric hospital at Terrell, Texas.

I knew York and his son to be very personable. I had been their barber, and learned much about their family, and personal lives, as he always talked about them. I will never forget the details.

Doctor Ross lost all his money and the York family lost their lives over money.

88

Wrong Place—Wrong Time

Her name was Rosa. She's gone. His name was Juan. He's dead.

Zarzimoria Street in San Antonio had many night clubs, a.k.a. honky tonks. That part of the city had a high crime rate. Every evening the ambulances converged on that section of town. Some kept their motors running, as they knew it wouldn't be long until a call came from one of the night clubs reporting that someone was injured.

One Saturday night, an ambulance was called to a crowded night club. The club owner explained he didn't know what had happened. While the Mariachi band played Tex-Mex music, someone on the dance floor collapsed and the crowd scattered. The manager didn't hear any arguments or gunshots. There was no sign of injury or blood on the victim, and nobody came forward to identify him or admit to being an eyewitness.

The ambulance attendant pronounced the victim dead. The body was taken directly to the morgue by passing the hospital.

The coroner was on a long weekend quail hunting trip to Padre Island. When he returned to his office on Wednesday, he had several bodies in cold storage waiting for autopsies.

When the coroner did a post-mortem examination on Juan, he found that he did indeed die from a heart attack. The heart was "attacked" with an ice pick from the rear, between the ribs, and straight into his heart. The puncture wound had closed, leaving no sign of blood.

Now it was time for the detectives to solve the crime. Several days had passed since the murder was committed. After interviewing several people, all of whom disclaimed they were at the dance, most said, they "didn't know nuthin'" and they didn't see "nuthin'."

Finally, one girl came forward to tell what had happened. She knew Juan and Rosa. They were both illegal aliens from Mexico. They had been in San Antonio for only a short time. On the dance floor, Juan had found a new girl, and was dancing too close to her while he left Rosa — standing alone.

The small room was not well-lighted, and was full of smoke. The dance floor was crowded. When Rosa had an opportunity to dance close to Juan, she took from her bra, an ice pick, which she always carried, and without anyone noticing, fixed Juan so that he would never dance with that stranger again.

The informant was asked, "Where is Rosa now?"

"She headed for Mexico that same night."

Case closed.

89

The Senator Filibustered

When I was a student at Texas Chiropractic College in San Antonio, we didn't have a state law regulating our profession. We were considered outlaws.

Every year for the preceding six years, we had introduced a bill to license our profession, but it was narrowly defeated each time. The reason was, we were out-numbered eleven to one — in dollars. The medical doctors were subsidized by the pharmaceutical companies, and they didn't want anybody cutting in on their territory.

About five hundred students were enrolled at the college, most of them disabled veterans recently discharged from the military service.

We didn't have legislative advocates then. They were called lobbyists. I was appointed by the student body to represent our school. I was the "little lobbyist to the big lobbyist."

After spending some time in Austin, talking to our legislators, especially the ones on the health committee, I returned to school with a positive report. Everyone on the committee I talked to said they would surely look into the situation. They even took pads from their pockets, asked questions, and made notes. They never promised to vote for the bill, but gave me every indication they would. When someone agrees with you, there's nothing left to discuss or argue about.

But when they voted, it was against our bill.

Can you trust a politician, even if he agrees with you?

One of my best friends, George Watson, was discharged from the army about the same time as I. He ran for state representative. Although he was only twenty-three, a few years in the war had made him appear much older. Naturally, knowing him for several years, I campaigned for him and helped him get elected. He promised to vote for our bill. He voted against it.

When I asked why, he said his mother operated a convalescent hospital in Paris, Texas, and it had to be inspected and given a clean bill of health before her license could be renewed by the City Health Department. George was advised that if he voted for our bill, his mother would lose her license. They would close her down. The Health Department had the authority to condemn her establishment.

George told me that his mother and some of her patients were getting chiropractic adjustments. That would have to stop. George apologized, but said he couldn't let his mother lose her business. He knew the medical doctors had a monopoly. They were the "only show in town."

In the next session of the legislature, we were back again. We brought up our "heavy artillery" and so did the medical association.

Their strategy was always aimed at their superior knowledge and education. That's what they wanted the general public to believe. It backfired on them. It gave us an ideal opportunity to answer their charges. The curriculum to complete for licensing was about the same number of hours for medical doctors, osteopaths, and chiropractors. Actually, you could get a medical license from Johns Hopkins University in forty-five hundred hours. Texas Chiropractic College required 4,708 hours to get a Doctor of Chiropractic degree. The same standard textbooks were used in all three schools.

To get a Doctor of Chiropractic degree, we had to have more hours in anatomy, neurology, and chiropractic adjusting techniques. The medical school taught more hours in chemistry and pharmacology. A candidate is either professional after getting the basic degree, could specialize by taking additional classes — additional hours, and taking another state board exam.

Bills in the legislature are usually passed in a "smoke-filled room" a few days before they came to the floor for a final vote. They called it "swapping off" or "you scratch my back and I'll scratch yours."

Senator John Marsh, who was carrying our bill, had been a district attorney in Monahans, a small west Texas town. A few years before, his wife had a serious illness and was treated by several medical doctors, then went to a prestigious clinic in another state. She was treated and sent home. Her prognosis was a fatal illness.

The senator had spent all his savings on doctor bills. One of his friends suggested he take his wife to a chiropractor. He did, and after a few treatments, she was in good health and working again.

The senator knew, first hand, what chiropractic care could do. He appreciated what the doctor had done to help his wife. He had plenty of enthusiasm for our cause, and was eager to help us get the bill through the legislature.

We had a public hearing at the State Capitol. I got about three hundred and fifty of the disabled veterans who were in school with me to go to the hearing. About half of the student body brought their wives along for moral support.

When the chairman called the committee to order, our senator made a brief opening statement. Then he asked for the opponents of the bill to make their case against the proposed law. The spokesman for the medical doctors made some derogatory remarks about our profession. He also made some personal insults. His argument was that chiropractic students did not go to school long enough to learn anything. Furthermore, the State of Texas should not license a bunch of "untrained quacks" to treat sick people. He said if chiropractors continued to treat sick people, and called themselves doctors, they should be locked up. At this point, all the chiropractors' wives let out a "boo." They were reprimanded.

Marsh challenged the medical doctor. He asked, "Have you ever studied chiropractic?"

"No!" was his answer.

"Have you ever had a chiropractic adjustment?"

"I should say not!" he answered.

"Do you know that the chiropractic schools use the same textbooks that you use in medical schools, and do you know that it takes as long to get a chiropractic degree as it does a medical degree?"

"I don't know anything about their school and I don't want to know!" was his reply.

"Well, doctor, you have just admitted you know nothing about chiropractic schools or what they teach, and you never studied chiropractic, or had a chiropractic adjustment. You are here representing your group. If they have selected you to represent them, then they don't know any more than you do. I move that this hearing be adjourned."

The session lasted less than fifteen minutes. A few days later, our chiropractic organization won in the house by a small margin.

When it was time for the senate to vote on the bill, the next week, we hoped we had a chance, but knew it would be a close call.

On the day of the debate and final hearing, our Senator Marsh was ready to take on the opponents of the bill. When the opposition leader got through blasting us and urging the full Senate to vote against our bill, Marsh started to talk. It was about eleven a.m. Senators are permitted to filibuster. Marsh took the floor to speak. He could talk as long as he wished. No one could interrupt the speaker. The senator was talking to a full Senate. A vote on a bill can be taken any time a quorum is present. If the majority votes in favor, the bill becomes law, after the Governor signs it.

Senator Marsh had eaten breakfast, but he was on the floor talking at noon, so he missed lunch. In the meantime, the other senators came and went. It is to their advantage to be present, in case there is a roll call. The senator talked all afternoon and right through dinner time. His only "breaks" were to drink a little water at frequent intervals. Midnight came and went, and he was still filibustering. One o'clock, two o'clock, three o'clock — still talking.

At 3:15 a.m., about five of the senators needed coffee to stay awake. A little restaurant stayed open all night, several blocks from the capitol. They thought the senator would still be talking when they returned.

After they were gone about five minutes, another senator who was co-sponsoring the bill, took a quick head count, and did a little arithmetic. He calculated that the five senators who went for breakfast were in opposition to our bill. We were pretty sure we had enough votes to put us over the top if the roll was called NOW. A quorum was present. The vote was called. We won by two votes. When our opposition returned about thirty minutes later, the voting was over.

They were "fit to be tied." One senator was so mad, he threw his hamburger on the floor and stomped it. But the vote was legal and the opposition could do nothing about their loss.

The senator who had sponsored the bill and filibustered until the right moment to take a vote had won.

The press stayed on the job that night. The next day, the headlines in the San Antonio paper read: "What A Hell Of A Way To Pass Legislation."

90

The Miracle of the Violin Case

My friend knew I was a fiddler and one-time member of a string band. That was why he was sure I'd be interested in a true story that involved a violin case. The year was 1950, and he showed up at my office with a piece of birthday cake. It wasn't my birthday, and it wasn't his, but the cake was brought from a family celebration he'd just attended, and he wanted to share it as well as his story.

It had begun one hundred years before. In the early 1850s, twelve families of a small Pennsylvania community, like thousands of others in the East, decided they would seek their fortunes in California. They were filled with wanderlust.

They loaded their wagons and headed west. They had no map or compass to guide them, they just used the setting sun for a beacon. They had well-traveled roads in the eastern states, but eventually, they ran out of road — there wasn't even a wagon trail. There was no Barstow or Las Vegas to use as a landmark. There were no signs of civilization — only wild animal tracks. As with all pioneers, they suffered many hardships, but were fortunate that their covered wagons were not attacked by Indians. As they traveled, the land became more and more barren — so unlike the green land they had left.

When they reached California, like the Donner party before them, they found themselves crossing the forbidding, below-sea level valley we now know as Death Valley. Ahead lay the formidable Sierra range, topped by nearly fifteen thousand foot high Mt. Whitney, the highest peak in the continental United States.

They passed through the hot valley. At its lowest point, two hundred and fifty feet below sea level, temperatures reached a hundred and thirty degrees in the summertime. As others before them had found, water was the most critical commodity they carried. They managed to cross this wasteland into the slightly higher, but still hot, Mojave Desert.

One young woman was pregnant when they left Pennsylvania. All were confident they would be settled somewhere in California before the baby was born. However, the severe conditions of travel contributed to the premature birth of the tiny baby, a girl, who weighed only four pounds. She lived — but only for three days. It was the mother's first child, and she was, of course, heartbroken.

Funeral arrangements were discussed as the caravan came to a halt. One man offered to donate his violin case for a casket. Another fashioned a grave marker with his pocket knife, carving on a small board the date of birth of tiny Amelia and her death, only three days apart.

The fifty-five members of the caravan prepared to take part in the ceremony. They dug a grave beside a Joshua tree, and were about to place the child in the violin case coffin in the earth when one of the party suggested the hole must be deepened, as coyotes would surely dig it up.

Finally, the infant was placed in the improvised casket. The marker was driven into the ground at the head of the tiny grave site. All members of the party joined hands. Under the blazing desert sun, they sang "Rock of Ages" and offered prayers. It was time to close the violin case, but the mother asked if they would sing just one more verse before they closed the lid of the violin case.

During the singing, the weeping mother suddenly cried out, "I saw her little toe move. She is still alive!"

The elders of the group insisted it was just her imagination. But another woman spoke up. "I think I saw her foot move too!"

The mother bent over the coffin, grabbed the tiny Amelia and ran to the shade of the wagon. Hysterical, she massaged the baby and asked if someone could get water. An emergency supply was kept, carefully guarded, in the lead wagon, and a young boy was sent to get some.

The young mother's friends and her husband tried to reason with her, insisting she was having hallucinations, that they must complete the ceremony and continue their journey. But she would not listen to them. She clasped the baby to her bosom, rocking as she wept.

As soon as the young boy returned with the tin cup of the precious water, the mother poured it over the face of the baby. Little Amelia cried out and all gathered began to weep with joy.

The violin case was retrieved by its owner, and so was the grave marker. The empty grave was filled. They loaded up and continued their westward journey. In a few miles, they found wagon tracks which led them southward and west as they meandered through Cajon Pass and to water in the welcome green of the San Bernardino Valley. Mormon families already settled there befriended the newcomers, and they decided this was the place to settle.

Besides bringing me a piece of her birthday cake and sharing the story of Amelia, my friend said that sixty people representing five generations had gathered that day for the birthday party.

On display was a diary, written in pencil on a writing tablet — a day-by-day account of their travels west. The tablet had turned brown after a century. The grave marker was a testament that Amelia had missed, only by seconds, being buried alive in the Mojave Desert.

He told me proudly that Amelia — at one hundred years — was still in good health, and did all her own house work, raised chickens, and worked in her garden.

In appreciation for the cake and his story, I got out my fiddle and played "Rock of Ages" as a tribute to Amelia's hundredth birthday.

91

Going Home

Wright's Chapel was well attended. Everyone dressed in his finest clothes.

After Sunday School and church were over, the brothers passed the hat for the offering. The "hat" was not just a figure of speech, but a real hat. It was usually a ten-gallon Stetson, but it never filled up.

One Sunday morning, when the usher came down the aisle with the hat, everyone scrambled for his wallet and dug out a nickel or dime for the collection. That was pretty big money then.

One older teenager, sitting next to me, reached in his pocket for his money and dropped a condom out of his wallet. It was not wrapped and rolled down the aisle toward the podium, spun around, and stopped beside one of the parishioners. It looked as big as an automobile tire. Everybody turned around and looked at me. If they weren't looking, I imagined they were.

The congregation filed out of the church, but nobody picked up the offending rubber. Whoever picked it up would be admitting guilt. Everyone stepped over it or walked around it, and I felt everybody was looking at me.

About sixty years later, I went back to the community where I was reared. There's a saying, "You can't go home again." I did, but I couldn't find it. While I was there, I borrowed a car and asked my cousin, Troy Wright, to be my guide. He had lived near Wright's Chapel all his life and kept up with what was going on. I told him about the condom incident, asked if he would take me to the old church house, as I wanted to see if it was still lying there or if someone had picked it up.

He said, "It's not there anymore." But we went anyway just to see. When we got there, he said, "Well, here it is."

"Where?" I asked.

"I told you, it's not there anymore."

"I thought you meant the condom is not there anymore."

"Oh, no! I meant the church house is not there anymore. They tore the church house down as well as the school to make room for Camp Maxey. Uncle Sam confiscated ten thousand acres of land. All this land was used for tank maneuvering and for an artillery range. This ground we're standing on now belongs to Uncle Sam. We are trespassing," Troy said.

On the ground where the church once stood now stand huge trees, hickory and oak, some ninety or one hundred feet tall. I went over to the side and tried to find the tree where I used to tie my horse. Then I remembered, I didn't own a horse then. I only had a "rent-a-mule" for a one-night stand.

As we stood and talked about old times, and the old gang we used to hang out with, everyone I asked about was either dead or moved to Houston, Dallas, or California.

We used to have a homecoming here every five years. The crowd kept getting smaller and smaller. We finally stopped having them. Then I asked, "Do you remember a girl they called 'Two Ton Tony'?"

"Oh, yeah — sure. She married that no good bastard. Can't think of his name now. He wouldn't work. He was a bootlegger and stayed in jail half the time. They had ten kids. One of her boys got tangled up in drugs. I think he's spending ten years in the Texas Penitentiary at Huntsville. Tony finally divorced her husband and married another guy. Now they are divorced. I don't know where she is now. I think she moved to California. Do you ever see her out there?"

Then we went back where the church stood, and I looked up in the tall oak trees. The mockingbirds were flying from one treetop to another, singing and building their nests. I remembered how I used to play "Listen to the Mockingbird" on my fiddle. I think they were mocking me that day. I felt that I was standing on hallowed ground as I looked up through the treetops into the white clouds. I imagined I could see ghosts of the past ministers and the people I used to sit in church with. I had an eerie feeling. "Let's get out of here," I said.

As we drove down the blacktop road, which used to be a narrow dirt road, I could see tracks where the tanks had been playing war games several years before.

Troy pointed out the place where Hubbard Cato had lived. "You remember him, don't you?"

"Of course I do. He used to pick the banjo and Mutt Key picked the guitar, and I played the fiddle. We made blue grass music for the country dances during the Depression. What happened to Hub?"

"Oh, he went nutty as a fruit cake. You know he tried to kill his family? I think he went to the insane asylum in Terrell, Texas. They call it a psychiatric hospital now. I think he finally died there, but I don't remember."

Another quarter of a mile down the road was J. J. Killman's store in the 1920s, but its gone now. Jess Killman had some sort of paralysis of his legs when he was a kid. He walked on his tiptoes and looked as if he was about to fall forward. He took advantage of his disability by having his wife wait on him. One day he was sleeping in the hack under a shade tree at his country store. It was a hot day, and when the sun moved, the shade moved also. He was left there in the hot sun. He called his wife and asked her to pull his hack into the shade. He never moved.

The whole Killman family has passed on in recent years.

The store was located in Dead Man's Hollow. It was a spooky place with a small stream surrounded by thick brush, willows, and birch trees. When I was a kid, I used to walk down the narrow road late at night. When it was cloudy or foggy, it was so dark I could hardly see my hand two inches in front of my face. I was the only kid brave enough — or stupid enough to walk through there all alone.

92

Mable the Mourner

Mable never misses a funeral. I've known her for twenty-five years. She attends at least one a day, sometimes two.

The Greater Los Angeles area has a population of more than fifteen million people, so some of them are sure to die every day. If you don't believe it, just read the obituary column. That's what Mable does.

She picks one dead person who lived on the "right side of the tracks," a prominent individual who likely has a lot of friends. The bigger the crowd at the funeral, the better. No matter whether the deceased was a man or woman. He or she is always about the same age or older than "Mourner Mable."

She always carries a newspaper clipping from the obituary column in her purse, with all the vital statistics. If she is ever asked a question about he deceased, she can answer with some authority.

Maybe she "worked for him several years ago," or he was "her second cousin," or she went to the same grade school with him. No, she didn't know any of his friends or relatives, since it had been "such a long time." If she can't answer all the questions, she becomes emotional and reaches for her Kleenex. Who's going to cross examine her on a delicate subject of death?

She always wears black and a black veil that covers her face. Her sunglasses protect her identity. She pretends to sign the guest register, but never actually does it. She always carries her Bible.

Most funerals provide food after the service, and when it's time to go through the chow line, Mable is there and she always goes back for "seconds." Sometimes, she's "too upset" to eat. In that case, she fills her huge purse and takes the food home to eat later. She admits she hasn't bought groceries in three years.

Who cares? Has she violated any law or breached any rules or customs? No. Etiquette? In California, everyone has his own.

93

Don't You Believe It

Mable the Mourner was only one example of the clever ways people devise to get by without much work.

After owning and managing apartments for thirty-two years, I've learned the hard way not to believe everything tenants tell me.

Most people shopping for an apartment are honest, and will pay their rent on time. Some won't. There are a few "deadbeats" who brag that they never pay any rent at all. They work through a kind of underground organization that looks out for its members. They know all the answers.

Most apartment owners have a rental and/or lease agreement approved by the Apartment Owners' Association (AOA). The applicant is required to fill out an official credit report and another form which includes three personal references.

A few years ago, one of my prospective tenants didn't want to fill out a questionnaire. He didn't want to put anything in writing.

I refused to rent to him until I learned what his income was, where he worked, and his last residence.

He told me he hadn't lived in this area recently, but had been away in the Islands.

He had. The Island of Alcatraz. He had just served ten years in the Federal Penitentiary for robbing a bank and shooting an F.B.I. Agent.

"Your last employer?" I asked.

"The federal government."

More recently, a lady came to my door looking for an apartment.

I asked her, "Why are you moving from your old place?"

"The landlord is a miser. The roof leaks and he won't fix it."

"How long have you lived there?"

"Almost four months now."

"Lady, it hasn't rained a drop here in the last six months. How can your roof leak?"

She walked away without answering my question.

She had already been evicted for not paying her rent. She had all her worldly possessions in her car, and was shopping for another apartment.

About one year ago, a lady called on the telephone answering my ad from the local newspaper.

My first question, "How many are in your family?"

"Three," she said.

"You, your husband, and one child?" I inquired.

"No, just me and my two babies," she said.

Being desperate for tenants, I told her to "come on down. I'm sure we can fill out the contract and get you moved in immediately."

When she arrived, her two "babies" were two pit bulls.

When I tried to explain our policy on pets, she interrupted, saying, "I've always called my dogs my 'babies', and if they can't move in, I don't want your old apartment! Furthermore, my dogs are nicer than some landlords I've met."

A tenant had just filled out the application to rent when I asked, "How many cars do you have?"

"None," he said.

The next day when the new tenant and his wife moved in, I discovered he was telling the truth about the cars. He had none, but he didn't mention anything about the two motorcycles they owned. When they unloaded their motorcycles, their possessions consisted of two bed rolls, and two duffel bags of clothes.

They invited all their friends, the Hell's Angels. It was a B.Y.O.P. party — Bring your own Pot.

The next day I heard from several of my other tenants. Each said, "The motorcycle gang must go," or they would move out.

If the rent is due and payable on the first of the month, and it is not paid by the fifth, I know its time to go looking for my money.

The tenant says, "I won't be able to pay the rent 'til the first."

"The first was five days ago."

"I mean the first of next month."

Some will lay a guilt trip on the landlord by saying: "I can't pay the rent, I have to buy milk for the baby."

After they get five or six months behind with the rent, the manager can start the eviction procedure. That will take another two or three months.

The tenant can sue me, the owner, for all kinds of imaginary problems with the apartment. That will give him another six weeks before he has to move.

When the landlord finally gets a court hearing, the judge will order the tenant to move and pay the back rent. Of course, you can't get blood out of a turnip.

The landlord can get a *writ of attachment*. But the tenant has nothing to attach. No job, no money, no car, and no wages. Nor does he have conscience or character. He doesn't have to worry about ruining his credit, or his reputation. He doesn't have either.

A tenant wouldn't think of going to the supermarket and loading up a cart of groceries and telling the clerk at the check-out counter, "I can pay the rest when I get the money." Nor would he think of going to the gas station to fill up his tank without first paying for the gas before pumping it. Why should he not pay his rent the first of the month when it is customary and legal to do so?

After I was elected president of the A.O.A., I was installed at a lavish inaugural ball, and handed the gavel from the outgoing president.

In my inaugural address, I told the apartment owners if they needed anything, just call me. I gave them my telephone number. That was my first and worst mistake.

My first call was from an irate tenant. She woke me up at one a.m., calling from Riverside, twelve miles away.

She said, "Dr. Holding, you better get over here quick."

"Why?" I asked.

"These damn tenants are fighting and tearing up furniture and disturbing everybody in the apartment house."

"Why don't you call the police?"

"I did, but they won't do anything."

"Well, what can I do?"

"Listen! You are the president of this organization, and if you can't do anything, who can? Now you get your butt over here!"

94

Formal vs. Informal

It is axiomatic. When it comes to a dress code here in California, anything goes. At weddings, funerals, or television talk shows, men often dress like hobos. Their tennis shoes are dirty and worn. The T-shirts must display some kind of commercial advertisement, or have obscene words on the front and back. Even their jeans are bleached to look faded and ready for the trash bag. They tear holes in the knees so their knee caps will show. These men aren't paupers. Some are well-known personalities and wealthy celebrities.

Why do they dress this way? Maybe they don't like rules or customs or conformity. Maybe they want to be iconoclasts. Their dress code has always been called reverse snobbism.

Mr. Blackwell has a one-man committee to judge the ten worst-dressed women every year. The men have had no such guidelines to follow until now.

We have just organized the California Association of Men's Dress Code (C.A.M.D.C.). This should clarify, once and for all, the difference between formal and informal dress. Most Californians have already been dressing in this fashion anyway.

Informal Dress: Sweat shirt and blue jeans.

Formal Dress: Sweat shirt, blue jeans and shoes.

95

You Know — I Mean — You Know

We had a weird English Professor at a University I attended one time. He almost lost his job because of his unique way of teaching English. He made the students spy on each other. During break, or anytime they overheard a conversation that included a split infinitive or dangling participle, the offending student would have to stand in front of the class and repeat bad grammar, then use the word or phrase correctly in several sentences.

Some of the students didn't like to speak in front of the class. At recess, they wouldn't speak to each other for fear of saying something wrong. They just stood around and gazed off into space.

One guy explained his reticence by joking, "You don't have to spy on me, I ain't gonna say nothing wrong."

Most of the student body liked the professor's method of teaching and stood behind him when the school board tried to "railroad" him. I'll bet most of the students still remember the mistakes they made in that class and their grammar has improved because of it.

Today I remember that class well because, for some reason, vocabularies have so deteriorated that too many words and phrases get overworked. A few years ago, the word "meaningful" was used in just about every sentence. Someone had a *meaningful* cup of coffee, or a *meaningful* dog, or a *meaningful* trip.

Several years ago, everything was *keen*; then *a-okay, hip, right on* became *cool, swell,* or *groovy,* then everything became *neat.* Now you have to be on the *"cutting edge"* or anything you own has to be *"state of the art."*

When I was in the third grade, a classmate named Vera got the words "come" and "came" mixed up. When she used the word "come," her teacher would make her stop, go back and repeat her statement and use the correct word "came." It happened several times each day.

One Monday morning in class, the teacher asked Vera why she hadn't attended the Halloween party last Friday night.

Vera replied, "Oh I know I should have came, and I would have came, but company came, and I couldn't came."

Today, if ten words are spoken, two will be "you know," four will be "I mean, you know," and the others will be trivia.

Perhaps a "neat" way to retire the national debt would be to exact a fine or a tax or a donation each time the following words are used:

You know — ten cents.

I mean, you know — twelve cents.

OK? — eight cents.

RIGHT?— eight cents.

Know what I mean?— nine cents.

Know what I'm saying — nine cents.

Every U.S. citizen should be armed with a tin cup bearing a sign that says, "Help balance the budget."

Start at home, at work, take your cup to the mall or anywhere you hear people talking. Walk right up and collect their fine whenever they over-utilize any of the listed words or phrases.

If everyone were honest and patriotic, we could have the national debt wiped out in twelve to eighteen months.

Know what I'm sayin'?

I plan to compose a song — a "you know" song. It will be to the tune of "Goodnight Irene."

Good Night Irene — Good Night Irene

You Know — You Know — I Mean, You Know.

If I can find someone with a guitar, we'll record it. It might become a gold record.

96

How'd He Do That?

I turned knobs, punched buttons, read the manual, went back and tried it again — nothing worked. I had bought the best VCR in the store, the most expensive with a book of simple instructions. The first button I punched, a red light flashed twelve o'clock. After working and reading the instructions for about thirty minutes, it was still flashing twelve o'clock. Must be something wrong with the clock I reasoned, I'll have to take the VCR back and get another one, or my money back.

Then I had another idea. I had a young teenage boy doing the yard work. He was trimming a hedge under my window. He had told me he couldn't read or write because he dropped out of school at an early age — he couldn't get along with the teachers. I called him and asked him if he could program a VCR. I first gave him a little lecture on how simple it was. I told him the reason I didn't do it myself, it was too hard for me to see those small black knobs. Actually, I have 20/20 vision, but I didn't want him to know how stupid I was. I showed him the manual, "It starts here on page twenty-four, and goes through page thirty, only six pages."

"Don't need no book," the kid said. He dropped his hedge clippers and genuflexed in front of the tube. In about thirty seconds he got up, picked up his hedge clippers and said, "O.K."

"What?" I asked.

"You are all set — your program will be recorded at ten p.m."

"Are you sure?" I asked.

He didn't answer, he just walked out slamming the door behind him, and went back to his yard work. I stood there dumbfounded, holding the book of simple instructions. I looked on the wall at all of my diplomas I had earned over the years, and remembered how many hours in school it took to earn them, and I didn't have sense enough to program my VCR — I had to ask a kindergarten drop-out to do it for me.

Then I remembered an article I had read in a magazine about VCRs. I retrieved it from the coffee table and read it again — this time very carefully. The author said, since VCRs went on the market, there had been about eighty million sold, but only about one half of the owners could program their own set. I felt much better. I further rationalized — maybe I'm not so stupid after all, maybe that kid out there is an electronic genius.

97

The Shut Up Club

There are excellent courses in college on public speaking. I have taken them. The Dale Carnegie course started in the Great Depression of the 1930s. I took that course, too. The Toastmasters, also, have a unique plan for anybody who wants to get up before an audience and speak. All of these programs have by-laws — rules and regulations — and they are fun to belong to.

Some of the students became so good they get carried away. They don't know when to be quiet — when to shut up.

For that reason, I'm organizing a SHUT UP CLUB. It will be a co-ed club. There is some concern about females. Can they be quiet for one hour? I believe they can. And politicians? Maybe.

We will have strict, but unwritten rules. Everyone will be on his honor. If he or she forgets and utters a word, without thinking, that person will put a dollar in the collection plate. The money will go into a fund for the Impaired Speaking and Hearing Institution (I.S.H.I.).

Shaking hands, back slapping, sleeping, snoring, reading, winking, are all strictly verboten. Nary a word will be spoken.

It is permissible to yawn, scratch, grin, cry, laugh — but don't talk. We can pray, meditate, cogitate or just think. We can look down at the floor, up at the ceiling, or stare at the walls. We can look at all the others when we want to. If any are crying, it may be because they are thinking about paying their income tax, if they are laughing — well you can guess what's on their minds.

If you have to go to the John or Johnette, just raise your hand. Two-thirds of the membership will have to vote by nodding for approval.

There will be no talking to yourselves in the restrooms.

Some people talk all the time, but never think. We think, but do not talk in the SHUT UP CLUB. There will be no speeches to rehearse, no committee reports, just one hour of peaceful silence.

The meetings will be held once a week from twelve to one o'clock. If anyone is late or has to leave early, a one dollar fine is exacted. Every member will bring his own lunch — preferably a peanut butter sandwich. You can't eat peanut butter and talk at the same time.

98

Travel for Seniors

Be careful, a salesman will sell you something you don't need, or can't afford. There are different names and different techniques for separating the buyer from his money.

In China, they set up shops at tourist bus stops. They can't speak English, but they get the attention of a potential customer by holding up a garment and saying: "Hello, hello, hello." If they can get you to stop, all the other sales people will converge with their wares offering a better deal than his competitor.

In Hong Kong, they are a little more sophisticated than in mainland China. Owners stand in front of their shops on the sidewalk and do everything but trip their customers to get them to come inside. They know if they can coax you in, they can cajole you into buying something. If you buy one suit, they will sell you another one at a reduced price. They will come to your hotel room for the first fitting.

They always give the customer a few extra buttons, just in case the originals fall off before they get on the plane.

In the Middle East, they are even more aggressive than in the Far East with their enterprising sales efforts, especially in Egypt. They will chase a potential customer down the sidewalk, into the middle of the street and even across the street with an armload of clothing. If you take a picture of them, they want to get paid for it. It can be frightening.

In the U.S.A., shopkeepers are a little more "laid back." Some of the huge department stores don't like to be bothered with customers. They make you feel that you are imposing on them, albeit, most of them are friendly and business like.

99

Ho! Ho! Ho! — Must Go!

Introduction: A few years ago when I was doing free lance writing, I wrote a tongue in cheek article about Santa Claus and Sonny Bono. At that time, Sonny had already served as mayor of Palm Springs, California, and had been elected a U.S. Representative.

When the new congressman got to Washington, D.C., everybody from both houses and both parties wanted to meet him. They felt that they knew him, because he had a top-rated television show, the "Sonny and Cher Comedy Hour," for several years. All the lawmakers thought he was a joke. A showman. They didn't take him seriously.

They soon found out that he was not only a politician with a sense of humor but a knowledgeable and conscientious lawmaker. He was so persuasive, he had some of the Democrats crossing over party lines to vote on his side.

Before Sonny met his tragic death on the ski slopes, I campaigned with him, not for Sonny, but for a candidate we were trying to get elected to Congress. Sonny was a terrific fundraiser.

At one of our meetings, I showed Sonny the magazine article that I wrote a year before. He read it, and said, "I like it. Put it in your book" and he flashed that big Sonny smile.

HO! HO! — MUST GO!

November 1, 2001:

Ho! Ho! Ho! Is now a matter of history, and this is to report on how it all came about.

By the year 2000, there was no more Santa Claus. He served us well for many years. Yes, he was late sometimes, and has not always delivered what he promised, but neither have most of our Presidents.

Nobody seems to know just how old Santa is. The long, cold rides in that antiquated sleigh from the North Pole every Christmas have been hard on him. That's why he told Mrs. Claus in the summer of 1999 that he wanted to move to a warmer climate.

At first, she wanted no part of it. "You can't break a tradition that has lasted all these years just because of the cold. What would the kids think? They expect you to live at the North Pole. Where would you move to?"

"We could buy a condo in Palm Springs," Santa explained.

"I don't want to move to California," Mrs. Claus protested. "You know all the trouble they have down there. Furthermore, you couldn't stand the climate. You'd get sunburned. You're used to six months of dark."

But this time, Santa got his way. "After all," he said, "its a new century and we've got to keep up with the times."

They moved to Palm Springs and bought a condo. That's when the trouble began.

While traveling east on the San Bernardino Freeway in his sleigh, he was stopped by a highway patrolman. "Where do you think you are going driving reindeer on a coast-to-coast freeway?"

"I'm Santa Claus, I'm on my way to my new home in Palm Springs."

"Oh, yeah, let me see your driver's license."

"I just rode into town from the North Pole, I don't have any driver's license yet."

"What's in the bag?"

"Toys for all the good little boys and girls."

"You are gonna have to empty that bag out here on the side of the road. What's this?"

"That's an inflatable doll, they're anatomically correct."

"Can I have one?"

"I have only two left, a boy and a girl doll. Which one do you want?"

"I want the boy doll." The patrolman gave Santa a ticket and told him to appear in court in two weeks.

Santa didn't want to go to court. Instead, he wrote to his new congressman, Sonny Bono.

Sonny answered with a cute letter, "I've got you, Babe."

He sent Santa a questionnaire to fill out and return: Were you traveling in the middle of the road or the far right?

Sonny also thanked Santa Claus for bringing him his first guitar when he was six years old. He asked Santa to do him a special favor: Don't bring Cher anything for Christmas.

Santa, not being familiar with politics in California, didn't know what the Congressman "was driving at." He took his case to traffic court. He had to appear at eight o'clock. The courtroom was full of traffic offenders. One man ahead of Santa told the judge he was in court to press charges against his neighbor.

"What did your neighbor do?" the judge asked.

"He let his dog run loose and he barked all night and kept me awake."

"You are in the wrong jurisdiction," the judge told him. "This is a traffic court. You will have to see Judge Wapner or Judge Judy. We don't do dogs here."

Next, a teenager stepped up in front of the court.

After reading the charges, the judge looked up and said, "According to this complaint, you went berserk and shot up a crowd of people down at the school house. How many did you kill, son?"

"I didn't count them your honor, but I'm not guilty."

"Why is that?"

"Because I came from a dysfunctional family."

"Oh, I didn't know that. Excuse me. Case dismissed. But you be careful with that gun, you hear?"

"O.K."

"You have a nice day."

Now it was time for Santa to face the Judge. He was scared and shaking in his boots.

The Judge looked down from the bench and asked: "What are you doing in my court wearing that ridiculous Santa Claus suit?"

"I am Santa Claus, your honor."

"Yeah, I know, we had a guy in here a few days ago who thought he was Julius Caesar."

"It says here, you and your reindeer were in a sleigh on the San Bernardino Freeway, speeding, without a license. How do you plead?"

"Not guilty, your honor. I know I wasn't speeding, because two cars and one motorcycle passed me."

The Judge thumbed through his traffic manual. "I can't find anything in this book about sleighs and reindeer. Could we have a side-bar?"

"Sure," Santa replied. "What do you want?"

"Well, I know this may sound silly, but when I was a kid, I never got my picture taken sitting on your knee. Would you mind if I sat on your knee and had my picture taken? My mother will never believe this."

When Santa got home from court, he found a registered letter. It was from the Society for the Prevention of Cruelty to Animals (SPCA) that complained about Santa's treatment of his reindeer. "They must be kept in a cool place, and you must not drive them across roof tops!" Then the Environmental Protection Agency (EPA) cited him because the condo property was not zoned for animals.

Claus was furious! He went to see Cal — Worthington — that is. He figured he could strike a deal, get rid of the reindeer, and buy a used car.

The "little woman," who was beginning to get used to the luxuries of the "Lower Forty-Eight," questioned the idea. "You've never driven anything but reindeer, and you don't have a driver's license."

Cal told Santa, "I've got a clean little car, just what you need to haul the kids' toys in." But first, I'll have to try out the reindeer." He rode Rudolph around the used car lot a couple of times, and said, "I like that red nose, it shines right through the smog." He put Rudolph in a pen with his dog Spot.

Cal put new vanity license plates on the car that said, "SANTA."

On the way home from Cal's place, Santa took the Slauson cut-off to the Santa Monica Freeway. As he was cruising in the number four lane, he was the victim of a drive-by shooting. Santa wasn't hurt, but he was all shook up.

He stopped at an Arco station in Cucamonga and was carjacked.

One morning they found graffiti on the condo reading, "Santa is a fake." The neighbors explained that this kind of freedom of expression was spreading throughout California and he'd better get used to it.

One dark night last season, when Santa was making his rounds, he was mugged. He lost his wallet and his bag of toys. When the police caught the thug, they explained all the jail cells were full, and they'd have to let another progeny of a dysfunctional family back on the street, and he might be worse.

When Mr. and Mrs. Claus couldn't pay the condo mortgage and their electric and gas bills, they filed for bankruptcy. That's the way it's done in California.

Even with all their troubles, they'd been able to get food stamps and so had eaten well. Last Christmas, Santa got trapped in the chimney with his huge bag and his big belly. When he finally got out, he went to his chiropractor who diagnosed a slipped sacroiliac and learned also that he had curvature of the spine from carrying that bag for so long. The doc couldn't persuade him to go on a diet, so he referred him to Jenny Craig.

Parents at the Palm Springs PTA voted to change Santa's image. They ordered him to donate his smelly Santa suit to the Salvation Army, and try to win over the younger generation by getting to know them and adopting more of their lifestyle.

He bought a pair of designer jeans, bleached them until they were spotted, and tore holes in the legs so his kneecaps showed. He found a pair of state-of-the-art sneakers, and removed the shoe laces. Then he cut a hole in the toe of one shoe so his big toe protruded. He finished off his "new look" with a T-shirt printed front and back with SANTA.

The school psychologist had him throw away his fake beard and grow his own. He had both arms tattooed and let his hair grow long enough for a pony tail.

Mrs. Claus gave him an earring, saying she couldn't afford two, and would buy him the other one later. She also bought him a chain for his neck. It dangled a medallion engraved with the face of Rudolph.

Santa had worn the same red suit for so long when he lived at the North Pole, that he didn't know anything about formal dress. From the printed high school dress code rule book, he learned that informal dress was a sweat shirt and blue jeans. For formal dress, sweat shirt, blue jeans, and shoes.

Sonny Bono explained that when greeting another person, Santa should no longer say "Ho, ho, ho." "Instead," he said, "you extend your hand with the palm up and say, 'give me five.' The other person extends his hand, and you slap your palms together."

Mrs. Claus was really getting into the Southern California swing. She played a CD to show Santa how the old, slow Christmas carols should be sung with a rap beat.

The old custom in which the kids left cookies and milk out for

Santa has also changed by the end of the century. They began switching from milk to eggnog and they laced it with rum. Santa really got to liking these midnight rounds too much. It worried him, so he had to take sleeping pills to get rest and wake-up pills to get going on the job.

It was not a surprise when he checked in at the Betty Ford Clinic for a few weeks. When he left the clinic, he needed to build up his immune system, so he went to a health food store and bought Nature's Sunshine Vitamins and Herbs. In a few weeks, he was able to tote the bag of toys without getting tired. The kids stopped putting out eggnog for him. Instead, they switched to navel orange juice. Straight.

Another job hazard Santa discovered as he worked the department stores the weeks before Christmas was lifting kids to his knee. One of them accused him of child molestation and Santa was arrested again.

Santa had no money. He applied for a job as a linebacker with the Rams, but they turned him down, because of his age. An attorney who remembered the old days took Santa's case pro bono. Just before the trial, the kid came forward and admitted he had made up the story because he was mad at Santa for bringing a bicycle instead of a Harley the year before.

As long as there are chocolate chip cookies and candy canes, there'll be a Christmas, but all of Santa's problems got him in trouble with Mrs. Claus. She filed for divorce, charging that her husband stayed out all night, especially on Christmas Eve, when he should be at home with his wife. She wanted him to join her on the Sally Jesse Raphael or Oprah show to get help patching things up. She had already bought a box of Kleenex to take on the show. But by now, there are 197 talk shows on TV, and all have long waiting lists.

California, being a community property state, the court divided their assets equally. He got the sleigh and she got the reindeer. They got joint custody of the Elves. Santa lucked out on Elf support payments, because they all left home and joined a gang.

Mrs. Claus applied for unemployment, and also got SSI for her broken heart. Its rumored that she is working as a stripper in a topless bar during the summer months.

Mrs. Claus kept her married name and took over the position as Santa Claus, swearing she could do a better job than her husband. But she couldn't keep up the pace and changed the gift delivery date from December 25th to March 1st. She made arrangements with K-Mart and Pick-n-Save to have the presents faxed to the kids. Palm Springs kids picketed the condo, then filed a class action suit against her. They wanted Mr. Santa Claus back and demanded a return to December 25th as Christmas.

When they appealed to Congressman Sonny Bono, the Honorable Sonny said he would look into it at the next congressional session. However, the project was tabled, and it may be four years before congress takes action. Bono warned his constituents that eventually, the Supreme Court would have to approve any change, and for a case as seasonal as this, it would be at least four years more before the case would be heard.

A 4.2 earthquake shook Palm Springs, but Santa was told that wasn't the "big one." It may be another thirty years before that would happen.

Just when Santa thought nothing else could happen to him, he got a letter from the IRS. Now he's really in trouble. He didn't know he had to file a return or pay income tax. He sent for Willie Nelson to put on a fund raising concert to help pay Uncle Sam.

Willy said he could sympathize with Santa, because he owed the IRS seventeen million dollars at one time. Willie put on his red headband, grabbed his guitar, and headed for California to do the concert.

With all the laws that California have to contend with, "Murphy's Law" is the worst. Anything that can go wrong — will go wrong.

There won't be another official report on Santa Claus for another ten years. In the meantime, have a Merry Christmas and a Happy twenty-first century. And the beat goes on.

100

If I Could Come Back
In One Hundred Years

I'm sure it could never happen, but if it could be arranged, I would like to come back for a three-day pass in one hundred years, just to see what's changed and what hasn't.

I can't imagine how big the national debt would be now. I would like to know who's President. Could it be one of my great, great grandchildren?

Is that senator still filibustering?

Are we in another shooting war, and what kind of weapons are being used?

I can't imagine what the new jet planes look like. Maybe they only fire rockets now. How many passengers can they carry? Will it take more than a couple of minutes to travel from New York to Paris?

Has there been a big earthquake in the last hundred years?

What does the new Cadillac look like?

What's happened to affirmative action?

Who is the minority race now?

I decided to look in on church. Everybody ran out the back door and some jumped out the windows. They treated me as if I were a ghost or ghoul.

Its hard to believe what changes have taken place in the last hundred years. Perhaps I'll find that some things haven't changed at all.

I go to see Paul, one of my best friends. He is still lying on the couch watching the ball game on television. Empty bottles and ash trays are stacked all the way to the ceiling.

"Drag up a chair," the affable Paul says. "How you been?"

"I've been dead for the last hundred years. That's how I've been."

"Well, I'll be damned!" he says, not taking his eyes off the television screen.

"Where's the kids?" I ask.

"They are still in the bedroom playing. I told them they could watch cartoons when the ball game is over."

How old are the kids now?"

"I have no idea."

"Where's Alice?"

"Who?"

"Alice, your wife?"

"Oh! Her. She's still waiting to watch the soaps as soon as the ball game is over. I don't know why anyone would want to watch that stuff. All she ever does is bitch, bitch, bitch!"

"Do you know where she is now?"

"No, I haven't seen her in several years. I suppose she's still talking on the telephone."

Since Paul didn't look up at me, I got the impression he wanted me to leave.

I remembered that I had left my car at Al's Garage before I died. I'll go by to check it out. It's still on the rack.

Al says, "We've been trying to get in touch with you, but your phone has been disconnected. Where have you been?"

"I've been dead for the last hundred years."

"Oh, maybe that's the reason we couldn't find you. Let me show you what's taking so long to repair your car. You've got an oil leak and we need another thirty five dollars to buy the parts. My mechanic is home watching the ball game. As soon as it's over, he'll be back."

"Do you think it will take much longer to fix it?" I ask.

"Oh no, why don't you go ahead and give us the thirty five dollars, and I'll order the parts. I'm sure we'll have it ready in another two or three years."

"Just keep the car. Where I'm staying now, we aren't allowed any."

I found a ticket in my shirt pocket from the shoe repair shop. It was for my dance shoes that had been left before I departed. I took the ticket to Little Joe's shop on Highland and Muscupiabe.

Joe looked at the ticket and asked, "When did you bring the shoes in?"

"Exactly a hundred years ago," I say.

He takes the ticket and goes to the back of the shop mumbling. After I wait a while, he returns. "They won't be ready 'til Tuesday," he says.

I have only three hours left down here. What can I do in three hours? Maybe there's a dance somewhere in town. Even without my dance shoes, I want to go. I rush over to Irene's place. Even after one hundred years, I knew she will want to go dancing. I find her at her make-up table.

She says, "I'm not quite ready yet, my hair is still damp. I have to make a telephone call and feed the cat. You will have to wait."

I guess I will, and I will know WHY.

EPILOGUE

You know what happened today, and maybe yesterday. But do you know what happened sixty-five or seventy-five years ago? Jim Holding takes you on a journey down memory lane, looking through the rear view mirror. He has written about the war, Depression, good times, and bad times. Some have been pathetic, some even funny. He writes only about the things he has seen or witnessed first hand through the twentieth century.

The book is:

96% Non-Fiction

2% Fiction

2% Other stuff.

With a trace of HYPERBOLE.